SUPERHEROES!

SUPERHEROES!

The History of a
Pop-Culture Phenomenon
from Ant-Man to Zorro

Brian R. Solomon

APPLAUSE
THEATRE & CINEMA BOOKS
ESSEX, CONNECTICUT

APPLAUSE
THEATRE & CINEMA BOOKS

An imprint of Globe Pequot, the trade division of
The Rowman & Littlefield Publishing Group, Inc.
4501 Forbes Blvd., Ste. 200
Lanham, MD 20706
www.rowman.com

Distributed by NATIONAL BOOK NETWORK

Library of Congress Cataloging-in-Publication Data

Names: Solomon, Brian, 1974– author.
Title: Superheroes! : the history of a pop-culture phenomenon from Ant-Man
    to Zorro / Brian Solomon.
Description: Essex, Connecticut : Applause Press, 2023. | Includes index.
Identifiers: LCCN 2022039980 (print) | LCCN 2022039981 (ebook) | ISBN
    9781493064519 (paperback) | ISBN 9781493064526 (epub)
Subjects: LCSH: Comic books, strips, etc.—History and criticism. |
    Superheroes in literature. | Heroes in literature. | Heroes—History. |
    Heroes—Mythology.
Classification: LCC PN6714 .S65 2023 (print) | LCC PN6714 (ebook) | DDC
    741.5/973—dc23
LC record available at https://lccn.loc.gov/2022039980
LC ebook record available at https://lccn.loc.gov/2022039981

∞™ The paper used in this publication meets the minimum requirements of American
National Standard for Information Sciences—Permanence of Paper for Printed Library
Materials, ANSI/NISO Z39.48-1992

For my son Peter,
whose wide-eyed wonder
is what this is all about.

Contents

CONTENTS

Foreword

In the mid-1960s, as a newbie comic book reader and burgeoning fan, I found few resources from which I could glean what had come before I had gotten caught up in the four-color fantasies of the superhero world. I was first and foremost a DC Comics fan. I started "reading" the then very juvenilely directed *Wonder Woman* in 1959 when I was four years old (actual literacy came a couple of years later) and *Superman* the following year, before the Marvel Comics we know today even existed.

But the rise of mighty Marvel aside, my discovery and growing consciousness of the DC superhero universe coincided with a pivotal time in comics history. After World War II, readers lost interest in superhero comics and the industry turned to genres like Westerns, war, mystery, romance, and humor to fill their pages. In 1956, the powers at DC decided to dip their toe back into the superhero pool and test the waters by reintroducing their largely forgotten 1940s "Golden Age" superheroes, beginning with the Flash in *Showcase* #4. But Julius Schwartz, the editor largely responsible for these revivals, didn't merely brush off the oldies and continue their stories. Instead, he and his small stable of writers and artists reinvented these characters from their secret identities and costumes on up. Their powers may have been similar, but the origins were updated and given a more science fiction-like edge, as with the Flash and Green Lantern, or rebuilt from the ground up, as in the case of the Atom, who went from a short guy who knew how to fight, to a scientist who could shrink from his normal six-foot height to the size of an atom.

In *The Flash* #123 (June 1961), police scientist Barry Allen, the secret identity of the modern-day (Silver Age) version of the Fastest Man Alive, used his superspeed to crash dimensional barriers to come face-to-face with his Golden Age counterpart, Jay Garrick (Golden Age), whose comic book exploits Barry had read about when he was a kid (a seed planted in Barry Allen's origin story five years earlier)! "The Flash of Two Worlds" not only set up the existence of the DC Multiverse, which was and continues to play an intricate part in the DCU across all media, but it did so, according to the date on a newspaper Barry consults, on June 14, 1961, which is also my birthday, albeit six years earlier. It was that moment, when I saw the story reprinted in a Flash annual several years later, that forever cemented my connection with DC Comics.

In retrospect, the Multiverse, and the various Golden Age character counterparts it reintroduced, was a straightforward idea, no matter how much writers and editors would later muddy the waters to appear sophisticated. But around 1965, readers were absorbing these concepts and characters in real time, most of us having to rely on character exposition and editor's footnotes to keep each character straight as well as know what was going on. There was no internet and printed reference books were few and far between. I was only vaguely aware of amateur-produced fan magazines, known as fanzines, that were being printed in small numbers on mimeograph and ditto spirit duplicators across the country. These fanzines contained an entire underground of published knowledge and information, however it took me a while to figure out how to access them.

A large piece of the puzzle would be filled by Jules Feiffer's 1965 classic *The Great Comic Book Heroes*. Playwright and political cartoonist for the *Village Voice*, Feiffer grew up during the Golden Age of comics before beginning his own cartooning career as assistant to the legendary Will Eisner on the weekly newspaper comic book insert feature *The Spirit*. At the time, reprints of Golden Age stories were few and far between because most publishers hadn't bothered to save the source material to reprint them (e.g., metal printing plates, photostats, black-and-white proofs, etc.), believing they were dealing in disposable junk. But somehow, Feiffer was able to get his hands on stories that hadn't been in print since the early 1940s and give readers the actual origins and/or early tales of such Golden Age luminaries as Superman, Captain Marvel, Batman, the Human Torch, the Flash, Green Lantern, the Spectre, Hawkman, Sub-Mariner, Captain America, Plastic Man, and The Spirit.

But even better were Feiffer's introduction and afterword to this hardcover collection of lost gems: he waxed nostalgic about his days as a reader and fan and his early hardscrabble experiences in the trenches of what was then a very low-rent business. It was the first time the curtain had been pulled aside and I could see what went on behind the scenes, or used to anyway, and it just made me love the medium all the more and deepened my desire to become a part of it someday, somehow.

I envy today's fans for their easy access to what is now, as I write this, the eighty-seven-year-long history of comic books, of which I have been a part for more than half its existence since I made my first professional sale to Charlton Comics in 1975. I've never lost my love for comic book history, even contributing what I can to the official record in essays, articles, and columns online, introductions and forewords for DC Comics' collections and other publishers, books like these, and in publications like *Back Issue*, as well as a pair of books of interviews with comic creators.

These days, there is a wealth of histories and biographies to choose from. Comic book scholarship has become a thing, but then, why not? Comic books and superheroes have come to dominate our popular culture and have inculcated themselves into the world's mythology. The number of books about comics and their creators is gratifying and, like all the current superhero movies and television programs, an embarrassment of riches compared to the trickle of such shows, which in 1967 consisted of the campy *Batman*, *Captain Nice*, *Mister Terrific* (none of which lasted more than two and a half seasons), and afternoon reruns of the 1950s *Adventures of Superman*.

There are books now on the history of Marvel Comics and DC Comics, and one book about the rivalry between them, and others about the Comics Code Authority or other specific aspects of the characters and their personalities, including a few "psycho-histories" of Superman and Batman. There are biographies and autobiographies, half of them, it seems, about or by Stan Lee, or books about the behind-the-scenes histories of the companies, as well as the writers and artists who created the stories. There are books that survey the "one hundred greatest" comic book covers, costumes, female heroes, lamest characters . . . you name it. The field has become large enough that it can support a wide range of titles focusing on specific companies, events, or creators.

When I wrote my first script for a Superman story, one of the comments from my editor, the aforementioned Julius Schwartz, pointed out that nowhere in the story did I tell the reader that Clark Kent is secretly Superman. "Well, everybody knows *that*," I scoffed. But Julie set me straight: *"Any story might be some reader's first story!"* Of course, the lesson hit home: I'd spent most of my early years as a reader searching my "first story" of so many characters for similar little hints and clues and footnotes to help me understand what had come before.

What I wouldn't have given to have a book like *Superheroes! The History of a Pop-Culture Phenomenon from Ant-Man to Zorro* available to me as that newbie fan of the mid-1960s. It asks—and answers—"What is a superhero?" and is an A to Z survey of comic book and superhero history that examines the roots of modern-day superheroes in ancient mythology and the more than century-long evolution of the masked hero with a dual identity, from the Scarlet Pimpernel and Zorro of literature to the Phantom of comic strips and into the world of comics as Superman, Batman, and the thousands that would follow.

Brian introduces readers to comics' predecessor publications, the pulp magazines of the 1930s and the heroes they spawned, such as The Shadow, Doc Savage, and the Spider, which served as vital links in the development of cheap ten-cent newsstand entertainment. He outlines the origins and complicated histories of the heroes themselves, from the archetypes to the endless variants of imitators who followed, and then takes a hard look at the medium's long slog to theatrical legitimacy, from the radio programs and cheapie movies serials produced by Hollywood's poverty row studios in the 1940s to the technological wizardry of today's latest blockbusters and TV hits.

He also pokes around some sore spots, like the legal ups and downs between Superman and Captain Marvel, those incidents reminding us that as much as we love our superheroes, there's a reason it's called the comic book *business*.

There's a phrase creators will sometimes use to describe the parts they want to skim past in a character's origin: "Who he is and how he came to be," as in, "And then we'll do the who he is and how he came to be before jumping into the battle scene." Consider *Superheroes! The History of a Pop-Culture Phenomenon from Ant-Man to Zorro* as one-stop shopping for all your "who he is and how he came to be" needs.

Paul Kupperberg

July 1, 2022

Acknowledgments

First and foremost, thanks must go to my very own Justice League, my very own Avengers, namely my wonderful wife Jaimee and my amazing children Layla, Jack, and Peter, for their love and support. In the case of my children, there's also been the joy of imparting to them my interest in and devotion to superheroes and comic books, a phenomenon that's been ongoing for the past two decades. Helping them to discover these magical, larger-than-life figures, just as I did in my own youth, has been one of parenthood's gratifying pleasures.

I also want to acknowledge from where my own love of superheroes came. Thanks must go to my late grandfather, Tony Salica, who one early September afternoon in 1985 bought me a copy of *Doctor Strange* #74 at the newsstand across the street from the Fortway Theater in Brooklyn, just before going in to see *Back to the Future*. That purchase kicked off my collection and sparked a lifelong obsession. And thank you also to some great friends over the years in whom I found kindred spirits, and whose own love for the genre rubbed off and nurtured mine, including Jon Costantino, Rich Thomas, Frank Cerillo, Erik Valko, and especially Chris Mari, my "Comic Madness" compadre.

In the pages of those comics I collected in childhood and adolescence, I was captivated by the work of writers and artists whose names became burned into my brain, seeing them so often in my favorite books: Jim Starlin and his enthralling cosmic storytelling; Ron Lim and his amazing work on *Silver Surfer* and *Captain America*; Norm Breyfogle and Jim Aparo, the two definitive Batman artists of my formative years, matching images to the compelling stories of Alan Grant; Peter David and Dale Keown, the innovative writer-artist team on *The Incredible Hulk*, the book I probably collected most; Erik Larsen, whose wild line work I always preferred to Todd McFarlane's; Alex Ross and his gorgeous, iconic paintings; John Byrne, genius of the word and the pencil; Frank Miller, whose innovative ideas helped redefine how I looked at superheroes; and the ubiquitous Tom DeFalco and Mark Gruenwald, well-springs of creativity on the Mighty Marvel bullpen.

And even outside the world of comic books, there were others whose work in film and TV sparked my fascination with superheroes from childhood, including Adam West, Tim Burton, William Katt, Lou Ferrigno, and of course, the one and only Christopher Reeve, a towering presence of my youth who made me believe a man could fly.

In putting *Superheroes!* together, I am deeply grateful to my friend and (brief) colleague from the weird world of WWE, Paul Kupperberg, a bona fide comic book industry legend who deigned to lend his memories and perspective in the form of this book's foreword. And to the incomparable team at Rowman & Littlefield, who helped me along through every step of the process, including Acquisitions Editor John Cerullo, for getting the ball rolling; Assistant Acquisitions Editor Laurel Myers, for helping everything run as smoothly as possible; Senior Editor Chris Chappell, who helped improve my title for the book and made sure the cover was per-fect; Editorial Assistant Barbara Claire for her expert assistance in sorting photography; and Production Editor Naomi Minkoff, who helped get me through the copyediting process. As corny as it sounds, these are the real superheroes, as far as I'm concerned.

Up, Up, and Away:
An Introduction

"With great power comes great responsibility . . ."

It may be hard to imagine today, but there was once a time when our culture was not completely dominated by superheroes. A time before multiple tentpole franchise blockbusters came out every year; before the words "Comic Con" became ubiquitous; before people proudly walked about in the daylight dressed as Moon Knight and Booster Gold. Back then, superheroes existed almost solely in the pulpy pages of comic books sold on corner newsstands and in the backs of drugstores, where kids would read with bated breath about the exploits of their favorite crusaders and carefully share that information only with the other members of that secret club. For the most part, they were far from mainstream consciousness. The average adult could probably name only the two or three most famous; and they were typically not seen in adapted form on the big or small screen, with the exception of the rare, patronizing attempt here or there, most of which refused to take the premise very seriously anyway, and instead chose to poke fun at it.

But times change. What started out as characters created by barely grown men during a time of world war, and printed on cheap paper for consumption by children, has grown into a popular culture whirlwind that has overtaken the world and crossed over into every form of media. From its earliest beginnings in the pages of those comic books, to the mega movie franchises of Marvel Studios and DC Films, *Superheroes!* chronicles the rise of a distinctly American invention, the modern-day evolution of the myths and legends of old. Superman, Batman, Spider-Man, Iron Man, Wonder Woman, the Flash, Captain America, X-Men, the Justice League, and the Avengers—they all represent our greatest hopes, and sometimes our darkest fantasies. In this book, you'll find a story that goes from the Golden, Silver, and Bronze Ages of comic book history right up to the Modern Age of multimillion-dollar Hollywood movies, and beyond. Perhaps no fictional genre has endured and blossomed over the past eighty-five years the way superheroes have. Learn here all about the visionary creators who have brought them to life: artists like Jack Kirby and Jim Lee, writers like Stan Lee and Alan Moore, actors like Christopher Reeve and Robert Downey Jr., and directors like Tim Burton and Joss Whedon. They're all here, in all their high-flying, eye-zapping, goon-punching glory.

Growing up on Marvel and DC comics of the 1980s and 1990s, I'll never forget the thrill of running to the newsstand for the latest titles and reading the adventures of my favorite men and women in costume. It's a love that grew as the heroes of my youth became mainstream cultural icons and movie megastars. When I was a kid, the very idea of a Spider-Man or X-Men movie was unthinkable—in part because the special effects industry hadn't yet caught up to comics, but also in part because the movie industry itself hadn't, which meant that most studios believed there wasn't enough popular interest for it to be worth the effort. Today, you'd be hard-pressed as a filmmaker to get a studio to greenlight your picture if it *wasn't* about superheroes. OK, I exaggerate . . . but you get my point. The niche "geek culture" of days gone by has become hip, pop culture.

Superheroes are big business. Superheroes are cool. Superheroes are everywhere. In this single-volume reference guide, I've tried my best to tackle all things related to them in our history and our culture—an in-depth look at the capes, the cowls, and the unforgettable characters who wear them. My aim was to create the ultimate reference book about the men and women in tights who fight for what's right as well as a resource discussing a comic book phenomenon that conquered the world.

1

LARGER THAN LIFE

The Mythological Role
of the Superhero in Society

What is a superhero? Though the answer to this question may seem self-explanatory, it really isn't. After all, many of the attributes we often associate with superheroes don't always apply to all of them, as the definition can be a bit broader than one would think. Coming up with defining criteria can be a bit challenging. Clearly, it's a whole lot more specific than just "superheroes are fictional good guys": So what about them makes them what they are, and what makes them stand out as a specific genre beyond just "characters who fight the bad guys"?

For instance, do we say that to be a superhero there must be a costume? While true of the lion's share of them, it's far from comprehensive. Charlton/DC Comics' the Question (inspiration for Watchmen's Rorschach) wears a business suit, as does Will Eisner's the Spirit, and John Constantine (is Constantine even a superhero?). The Hulk is barely wearing anything at all, let alone a costume. Swamp Thing and Groot are naked. And characters like Ghost Rider, Hellboy, and even the Mighty Thor aren't really wearing costumes so much as what they would consider to be their normal, everyday attire—insofar as such a concept can apply to such otherworldly beings. Do they require a fancy code name? Tell that to Constantine, as well as Zatanna, Jessica Jones, and both Jean Grey and Luke Cage, who long ago ditched their respective "Marvel Girl" and "Power Man" assignations. Some, like Rocket Racoon and Dr. Strange, are lucky enough to have "real" names that are cool enough just as they are.

Nevertheless, it is true that the *majority* of what we think of as modern superheroes wear an unusual costume or uniform and have some kind of catchy nickname. Another thing that many of them, though not all, have is an alter ego—a hidden, secret identity that allows them to move about in the everyday world in anonymity, that protects the people they love from reprisals, and in some cases protects them from the legal ramifications of their not entirely legal activities. But again, many, like Hellboy, do not have alter egos, and some, like Captain America and the Fantastic Four, while they have costumes and code names, do not hide their real identities from the public. Thor is a great example of a character who once had a secret identity—Dr. Donald Blake—but abandoned it long ago.

Generally speaking, superheroes possess some kind of superhuman and/or supernatural abilities, something that goes beyond the possible and puts them squarely in the realm of fantasy. But surely if we say that all superheroes must possess superpowers, we are eliminating the character who is arguably the most popular superhero of them all: Batman. Not to mention numerous others like Captain America, Iron Man, Doc Savage, the Punisher, Black Widow, and Green Arrow. These are characters who were not fortunate enough to have been born superhuman like Superman, Wonder Woman, and the X-Men; or to have experienced a freak accident that bestowed superhuman abilities upon them, like Spider-Man, Daredevil, the

Flash, or even the Teenage Mutant Ninja Turtles. These are characters who willed themselves to become heroes, who trained themselves to the very peak of human mental and physical abilities or used technology to artificially grant themselves abilities beyond their normal human ones (with Captain America being a great example of both).

What about their motivations? Certainly, what characters choose to do with their abilities helps distinguish them as superheroes. But even that requires qualification. We often think of superheroes as "costumed crime fighters." And while Batman is certainly the epitome of this, as are Spidey, Daredevil, Plastic Man, the Ninja Turtles, and even Kick-Ass, there are many superheroes whose calling places them far beyond what we'd consider "crime fighters." Is the Silver Surfer fighting crime? Is Captain Marvel? Is Aquaman? Perhaps it might be more apt to say that they are fighting evil, often of a much greater kind than falls within the parameters of terrestrial law. Even the way they take up the cause can vary. As "good guys," most superheroes adhere to a code of honor that distinguishes them from the criminals and villains they fight. And yet Batman is a vigilante who works outside the law and is sometimes at odds with it. And while he still has a strict code that prohibits him from taking life, as is the case with most superheroes, there are others like the Punisher, Wolverine, the Spectre, and Deadpool who have absolutely no qualms about killing, and in fact consider it their duty. In fact, many have made the argument that characters like the Punisher are no better than the criminals they oppose and stretch the definition of what can even be termed "hero" to its farthest limits.

So, having acknowledged that all these traits and attributes can be found in some superheroes, even in most superheroes, what can be found in *all* superheroes? If we're defining the term once and for all, what qualities come the closest to encompassing everything that makes a superhero a superhero—at least by the definition of this book? In 2013, Stan Lee, a man whom one would think had a greater leg up than most on defining the term, wrote in the book *What Is a Superhero?*, "A superhero is a person who does heroic deeds and has the ability to do them in a way that a normal person couldn't. So in order to be a superhero, you need a power that is more exceptional than any power a normal human being could possess, and you need to use that power to accomplish good deeds. Otherwise, a policeman or a fireman could be considered a superhero." This establishes our first two criteria:

- A superhero must have a greater-than-normal ability of some kind. This does not mean it has to be superhuman—it only means it must be something out of the ordinary, that the average person couldn't do. This might mean firing lasers out of one's eyes or being impervious to bullets or simply being the world's greatest detective, or an elite, perfect martial artist. The point is that they stand out from your typical well-meaning do-gooder. Tracing back to the original Latin root *super*, meaning above or beyond, and then applying that to the noun "hero," it's easy to get the idea.

- With their great ability or abilities, the superhero can do amazing and powerful things, in some cases pretty much anything they want. And yet, rather than be self-serving, or at the very worst, destructive, the superhero chooses to act for the greater good, to use their power to benefit others or to benefit society, usually by combating those who choose the opposite. Some superheroes may be less altruistic than others, and in some cases have some degree of self-interest in what they do, but the result is still the betterment of humanity.

In addition to these criteria from the mastermind of Marvel Comics, I will add my own third major criterion:

- Unlike "regular" heroes like firefighters, police officers, soldiers, etc. superheroes work outside society's established structures. They operate under their own agency, either completely solo, or in small autonomous groups. They may work in cooperation with law enforcement, the military, government, or other established entities, but they are independent of them, and typically operate under their own initiative. Thus, for example, the Jedi Knights of Star Wars could not properly be considered superheroes, as despite being superpowered and fighting for good, they are an official, quasi-military arm of government.

As we currently define them, for generations superheroes have filled an important role in popular culture, even before they came to exist in their modern form. There is something in our cultural DNA that has encouraged us to hope beyond our own abilities, and to look for those who can somehow save us from our various predicaments, both large and small. Superheroes represent this yearning and its fulfillment, and the contemporary comic-book variety are just the latest iteration of that. Despite how dark, and even hopeless, real life can sometimes be, there is a strong strain of optimism in human nature, and this has colored our cultural development. We are fascinated by those who can rise above the normal and the average, and who does that better than superheroes?

Bright colors. Awesome power. Clear-cut good and evil. The vanquishing of the darkness by the light. Happy endings. We innately crave these

Superhero Subtypes

In terms of categorization, many attempts have been made to determine the different types of superheroes that exist. If we accept the overall definition in this chapter, then a few reliable subdivisions emerge that might be helpful, and into which nearly all superheroes can be placed.

THE HUMAN AND/OR TECHNOLOGICALLY ENHANCED

As mentioned earlier, these are the heroes who do not possess inherent superhuman powers and are simply human beings, but they have either perfected one or more human abilities to their absolute maximum potential, or have augmented themselves through the use of mechanical, computer, or biotechnology.

Examples: Batman, Captain America, Hawkeye, Iron Man, Black Widow, Green Arrow, the Punisher, Deathlok, the Falcon, the Huntress

SUPERHEROES WITH SPECIFIC POWERS

These are heroes who have been imbued either by birth, through accident, or through purposeful design with a power or set of powers that fits into a very easily defined category. In other words, a superhero with a clear "gimmick," whose powers are themed. These heroes are usually ranked somewhere in the middle, power-wise.

Examples: Spider-Man, Daredevil, Wolverine, Iceman, the Flash, the Fantastic Four, Ant-Man, the Atom, Namor the Sub-Mariner, Black Panther

MAGICAL BEINGS

These heroes are mystical by nature and derive their powers through means that cannot be scientifically explained (not even with comic book science). In some cases, their very existence is supernatural in nature.

Examples: Ghost Rider, Dr. Fate, Dr. Strange, the Demon, Spawn, Zatanna, Deadman, Scarlet Witch, the Spectre, Man-Thing

THE GODLIKE

This is the very top tier of superheroes, the characters who approach omnipotence in their power, whether that is based purely on limitless strength alone or on a combination of other powers. In some cases, they may even literally *be* gods.

Examples: Superman, Thor, Silver Surfer, Hulk, Dr. Manhattan, Phoenix, Wonder Woman, Captain Marvel, Hercules, Shazam

As this is not a perfect science, naturally there is a great deal of overlap in these categories, and as with all fictional creations whose very nature derives from the narrative needs of their creators, their categorization can get a bit fuzzy. Shazam derives his powers from magic, but also possesses powers at a nearly godlike level—so, too, one could argue, does Dr. Strange. Even characters like the Flash and Martian Manhunter have powers that might put them into that category. Man-Thing was created through a combination of science and magic. Some heroes, like the Vision, Red Tornado, or Astro Boy, are products of technology, but are not human at all. To be sure, each of these four major categories could easily have several subcategories of their own. But for our purposes, they provide a helpful guide for the different types of characters who fit into our definition of the superhero.

things, which are rarely granted to us in real life. Superheroes have long been described as wish fulfillment, and they also appeal to certain fantasies of power that also seem to be inherent in who we are, particularly in our youth, when we are still relatively unspoiled by harsh realities and believe in limitless potential. Perhaps this is why superheroes hold a special appeal for children and teenagers; for the young, but also for the young at heart. The belief in superheroes, or at least in what they stand for, helps us preserve something of that innocence within us, and is a welcome catharsis that fends off the cares and burdens of the weary world. We can live vicariously through them and their exploits, confident in the knowledge that it will all work out in the end. And even though the concept of superheroes and what they represent has changed over time, just as our world has changed, at their very core, their appeal remains the same.

In this way, superheroes tap into something primal—they are just the latest incarnation of a trope that has existed as long as humans have populated the earth, playing an important mythological role in society. The infinite, godlike might of Superman; the dark avenging angel that is Batman; the mercurial trickster Spider-Man; the sense-defying and reality-bending speed of the Flash; the rampaging id of the Hulk, always at odds with the gentle undercurrent of Banner; the pure ideals of Captain America—these are character types that have existed for as long as people have existed, weaving their way into our history, into our stories, whether those stories were told around a blazing fire, in the four-color pages of a comic book, or on the giant multiplex screen.

Call it a desire for social order. Where there is evil, we hope for the good. Where there is wrong, we look for someone to make it right. Where there is injustice, we thirst for justice. It is something that even psychologists and other scientists believe is an intrinsic part of our psyche from a very early age. We seek out and admire those with the abilities to prevent harm. In fact, a 2017 psychological study in Japan involving infants demonstrated that when the babies were shown images of aggressive interactions involving a third party that either ignored or prevented the interactions, they overwhelmingly preferred the latter. Even as children, we admire those who protect others from bullies. Third-party intervention for good has thus been part of our mythology, of our literature, and most recently of our movies for as long as they've been around. Hero worship is quite a literal thing for us.

Thus, superheroes inspire us. We want to be them at the same time as we want them to be there for us, perhaps when no one else can be. They're people who not only possess the power for positive change, but who possess the will to stand up for what's right and do the right thing, time and again. It's no mystery that superheroes, like so many other mythic figures, are often born in the fiery crucible of pain and loss. Bruce Wayne witnesses the murder of his parents as a child and chooses to wage a never-ending war trying to prevent such things from happening to anyone else, or at least to punish those who do such things; Peter Parker learns the hard way that the responsibility of great power is something to be reckoned with, as his selfish hubris leads to the murder of his beloved Uncle Ben; Norrin Radd must sacrifice his own freedom in order to prevent the destruction of his home world and everyone he loves at the hands of Galactus. Their origins, their motivations, are very often informed by trauma, which is then linked to a sense of fate. They are destined for greatness in a very real way and convert the trauma that shaped them into something constructive rather than destructive—the latter, of course, being the path chosen by their archenemies, the supervillains.

Superheroes make the choice to be great, to overcome the forces that made them, or at the very least, to take advantage of the precious opportunity to improve the world, or even the universe. They are role models in the sense that they represent the very best in us. We like to think that maybe, if given the same opportunity, we would do the same things; that we could also rise above our own adversities, finding strength and meaning along the way. Superheroes aren't perfect, and this enables us to relate to them better. And if we never get the chance to leap tall buildings in a single bound, to change the course of mighty rivers, or strike terror in the cowardly and superstitious hearts of evildoers, at least we can revel in the adventures of those who do.

They make up our modern mythology. The archetypal "hero's journey" famously described by Joseph Campbell—linked from ancient times all the way to modern creations like *Star Wars*—can easily be found in the stories of modern-day superheroes. And just like any great, durable cultural mythos or archetype, they have survived through the generations and adapted to new forms, so that today they play their essential societal role primarily on the screen, both big and small, even more so than on the printed pages from which they originated. But whether we read about them or watch them, they remain a tangible part of the fabric of our culture—in fact, probably more now than ever. Their influence is keenly felt among all who dare to dream, who seek goodness in the world, and who believe in the inherent value of life and the importance of protecting it. Which is why that influence will always be with us.

ICONS #1

The Man of Steel

Creators: Jerry Siegel and Joe Shuster

First Appearance: *Action Comics* #1, June 1938

Alter Egos: Kal-El, Clark Kent

Powers: Superstrength, invulnerability, flight, superspeed, heat vision, X-ray vision, telescopic vision, microscopic vision, superbreath, freezing breath, superhearing

Archenemies: Lex Luthor, Ultra-Humanite, Metallo, Bizarro, the Toyman, Brainiac, Mr. Mxyzptlk, General Zod, Darkseid, Doomsday

More than just a superhero, more than just one of the great superheroes, **SUPERMAN** is *the* superhero. In fact, the very word "superhero" is a reflection of his name, and he is the ultimate template for absolutely everything that came after him, to this day. Although technically not the very first superhero, nor even the very first illustrated superhero, the success of Superman directly kicked off the superhero comics craze in America and later around the world, and the 1938 publication of *Action Comics* #1 is seen as the very beginning of the true superhero genre of fiction as we know it today. The importance of this strange visitor from another planet cannot be overstated.

THE ORIGIN

With the planet Krypton on the verge of destruction, scientist Jor-El and his wife, Lara, placed their infant son Kal-El in a tiny ship and rocketed him to safety on the planet Earth, where (according to some versions of the mythos, at least), the sun's radiation, combined with the reduced gravity in comparison to Krypton, would grant him near limitless powers. Discovered and raised by Jonathan and Martha Kent in the rural American town of Smallville, he is instilled with wholesome values, including the desire to use his powers to protect his adopted home and all who live on it. Disguised as mild-mannered reporter Clark Kent at Metropolis newspaper the *Daily Planet*, he wages a never-ending battle for truth, justice, and the American way.

THE CREATION

Jerry Siegel and Joe Shuster were seniors at Glenville High School in Cleveland, Ohio, in 1930, when they first formed their unique writer/illustrator partnership based on a common love for science fiction. After years of trying to sell their concepts to newspaper comic strip syndicates, they finally found a home for Superman at Detective Comics, Inc., one of the originators of the new medium known as the "comic book." Drawing inspiration from everything from silent film stars Douglas Fairbanks and Harold Lloyd, to Popeye cartoons, to literary prototypes like Zorro and the Scarlet Pimpernel, they also created a colorful costume for him that was inspired by circus strongmen and professional wrestlers of the day. In his Golden Age incarnation, the Siegel/Shuster Superman was not as all-powerful as he'd become later, choosing instead to fight for social justice and the plight of the poor, becoming a superpowered proponent of Franklin Roosevelt's New Deal.

THE EVOLUTION INTO A POP-CULTURE ICON

The explosive success of Superman's illustrated exploits, both in *Action Comics* and the self-titled *Superman* book, made him into a bona fide sensation, and the scope of his adventures was greatly expanded in the so-called Silver Age of the 1950s and 1960s. Under the supervision of editor in chief Mort Weisinger, in addition to established characters like Superman's love interest Lois Lane, his junior pal Jimmy Olsen, and boss Perry White, readers were introduced to his cousin Supergirl and his Kryptonian superdog Krypto, as well as concepts like the Fortress of Solitude and the Phantom Zone, expressed in the iconic artwork of Wayne Boring and especially Curt Swan, who created the definitive look for the Man of Steel for decades to come. This is also the era when his powers reached godlike proportions in both their extent and variety, so much so that his ultimate weakness, the radioactive kryptonite from his destroyed home world, became an integral—and much-repeated—story line device.

THE REINVENTION

After expanding his powers greatly and complicating his mythos for many years, first under Weisinger and later under editor Julius Schwartz, DC Comics made a concerted effort to simplify and relaunch the character in 1986 with its *Man of Steel* produced by writer and artist John Byrne. Byrne took the best aspects of the character and his many incarnations over the years, cut out a lot of the Silver Age silliness, and retold Superman's origins in a fresh way. He even rebooted his nemesis Lex Luthor from a raving mad scientist into a ruthless capitalist. Although further changes and rebooting have occurred in the decades since, including the 2003–2004 miniseries *Birthright*, the influence of Byrne's *Man of Steel* remains relevant to this day.

THE DEATH OF SUPERMAN

Superman made headlines with the January 1993 issue of the self-titled comic book, in which he was killed by the alien menace known as Doomsday. Although the death, as nearly all in comic books, was far from permanent, at the time it was promoted as such, and led to *Superman* #75 becoming the highest-selling comic book in history, selling twenty-three million copies. It became one of the most famous superhero story lines of all time, although in the years since, sales of his comic book, and of comic books in general, have flattened to the point of only being a small part of Superman's vast presence in our culture.

THE MANY VERSIONS OF THE LAST SON OF KRYPTON

Perhaps no other superhero has been adapted so many times and in as many ways in different forms of media, going back to the earliest radio serials of the 1940s. By doing so, it even helped create key elements of his mythos, including kryptonite, his ability to fly, and the catchphrase, "This looks like a job for Superman!" He's appeared on stage, in literary and animated form thanks to memorable cartoon series like the Fleischer Studios shorts of the 1940s and the Paul Dini/Bruce Timm series of the 1990s. TV viewers know him as memorably played by George Reeves in the classic 1950s series *The Adventures of Superman*, and his portrayal by Christopher Reeve in the 1970s/1980s film series is still the definitive portrayal to this day. In more recent years, Henry Cavill has taken up the cape for a whole new series of movies that have proven the durability of the character for all generations.

THE MAN OF TOMORROW

More than any other superhero, Superman represents the ideal of pure good, and has meant so many different things to so many different people. An allegory for the immigrant experience in America, a universal father-like figure, even a cipher for religious figures like Moses and Jesus Christ, he is a character that transcends his genre and has become one of the most well-known and iconic fictional creations of all time. Even as the world changes and other heroes challenge his top spot, he remains the unwavering symbol of justice and light, and a beacon of hope that still stands just as true as ever.

2

ORIGIN STORY

The Ancient History of Superheroes

It has often been said that superheroes do not really represent a new concept at all but are just a modern representation of something that's been buried deep in our cultural consciousness for as long as human culture has existed. From the very beginning of recorded history, and no doubt even earlier, we have been fascinated with stories of superpowered beings, of individuals who step out of the pack of normal humanity, or who were never part of it at all, and dare to do incredible things. Our earliest stories feature beings such as these, their exploits told and retold through the generations, moving from folklore to legend, reaching the level of myth and even religion.

When the great comic book creators of the twentieth century spun their original tales of men and women in outlandish outfits coming to the aid of humanity, of otherworldly beings dazzling humans with their unthinkable power, they were not operating in a vacuum—rather, they were drawing on concepts older than the written word itself. These stories began as a framework for people to explain the universe and the world around them—a bridge to understanding what in more primitive times could not be properly understood with the level of scientific knowledge available. More than simple entertainment, their significance took on religious nature, as many of these figures were worshipped and venerated. Fear was a common emotion for early man, and these stories and the characters who populated them helped to keep that existential fear at bay.

In the beginning, the sacred texts and literature that formed the foundation of Western civilization featured such supernormal characters, whether in divine or mortal form. The earliest known significant piece of literature, the *Epic of Gilgamesh*, traces its origins to ca. 2150–1400 BC in the region of Mesopotamia in the Middle East, often called "the cradle of civilization." Its story is similar to something we might very well expect from a comic book: Enkidu, a wild man with superhuman strength created by the Sumerian gods, faces off with the oppressive King Gilgamesh, eventually showing him the error of his ways and befriending him after a colossal test of strength between the two. Together, they embark on a mystical quest to slay the monstrous giant Humbaba the Terrible, only for Enkidu to be slain by the vengeful goddess Ishtar after he and Gilgamesh defeat her avatar, the Bull of Heaven. After Enkidu is put to death by the gods, Gilgamesh embarks on another journey to discover the secret of immortal life.

Setting the stage for many mythologies and religions, the Gilgamesh story also began a time-honored tradition of storytelling that many feel is continued today by tales of superheroes—almost a secular and commercialized version for a more secular and commercialized world. Some even point to the character of Enkidu as being one of the direct inspirations for the creation of the Incredible Hulk, for example. Gilgamesh himself is the original mythological hero-warrior, an archetype expressed creatively throughout history, and of which twentieth- and twenty-first-century comic books are only among the latest incarnations. In fact, in a great twist of irony, in the 1970s Gilgamesh would be incorporated as a character in the Marvel Universe by legendary creator Jack Kirby, and even spent some time as a member of the Avengers.

Undoubtedly, mythology and early religion were the catalysts of the earliest conceptions of superheroes, which can also be seen in the many cultures that followed. The Egyptian civilization, which flourished during much of the third and second millennia BC, developed a sophisticated and enduring mythology centered on concepts of immortality and the nature of death, which was the ultimate unknowable evil that humans sought to understand and even defeat. Egyptian gods like Osiris did exactly that, creating a template for the resurrected and metamorphosed deity that is still with us in the form of Jesus Christ. Much of this religion and its figures was preserved and glorified especially by Pharoah Nectanebo II, the last native ruler of ancient Egypt, whose efforts secured that figures like his beloved Isis would never be forgotten.

The Greeks, who followed the Egyptians as the Western world's next great civilization, left us with perhaps the best-known pantheon of gods and heroes in history, codified in the seventh century BC in the *Theogony*, a sacred text by the epic poet Hesiod. Other seminal texts of ancient Greek mythology included the epic poems *Iliad* and *Odyssey* by the blind scribe Homer, which give us tales of the Trojan War and the later twenty-year journey of Odysseus returning to his beloved Ithaca, which features many of the key gods and other mystical beings that populated Greek mythology. These supernatural characters existed in song long before their exploits were finally written down.

When the Romans eventually supplanted the Greeks in the centuries before and after the birth of Christ, they very handily adapted Greek folklore and religion into their culture, changing the names of the gods,

Lords of the Nile: The Egyptian Pantheon

OSIRIS

Not even murder and dismemberment at the hands of his son Seth could destroy the all-powerful Osiris, god of the underworld, who was resurrected by his wife Isis. He went on to become a god of fertility, controlling the ebb and flow of the mighty Nile that was so central to Egyptian life.

ISIS

Embodying the virtues of wife and mother, she was primary among Egyptian goddesses. Her worship persisted longer and farther than all other Egyptian deities, even spreading into Europe and influencing the Christian depiction of Mary, mother of Christ.

HORUS

Son of Osiris and Isis and often locked in combat with his evil brother Seth, he was depicted as a man with the head of a falcon, and was god of the sky, of war, and of the hunt. Some Egyptian kings were believed to be his physical manifestation.

SETH

The most feared and hated of Egyptian gods, he was a god of evil, chaos, violence, and the unforgiving desert that Egyptians knew all too well. A strange composite of human and dog form, his fury raged even against his own family.

RA

The brilliant god of the sun, he was said to ride across the heavens in a shining chariot and battle the snake god Apopis in the underworld each night in order to emerge again the next morning.

ANUBIS

Associated with funerary practices and the care of the dead, Anubis the jackal-god was the original lord of the underworld before the murder and resurrection of Osiris. The fabled mummy embalmers of Egypt looked to him as their master.

THOTH

The scribe of the gods, he was the deity of writing and wisdom and was said to have invented language and the hieroglyphics for which Egyptian culture was known. A master of magic, the ibis-god Thoth also stood in judgment of the dead.

AMON

The Hidden One, a god of the air, he was originally worshipped in the city of Thebes. He later merged with the sun-god Ra to become Amon-Ra, most powerful and revered of all Egyptian deities during the New Kingdom era.

but basically keeping their stories intact. No other mythology would have a greater impact on the imagination of European (and by extension European-American) cultures in later times than the Greek/Roman one, which was (and is) regularly taught in school long after it died out. But perhaps the most important original contribution the ancient Romans made to the folklore of superheroes was the literary concept of the *latrones*—noble bandits and vigilantes who revolted against the injustices of the regime in power and represented hope for the little man. This was a trope that existed in both Roman literature and history, with the most famous of the real-life latrones being the rebel slave leader Spartacus. The template of the latrone could be seen many centuries later in the birth of the vigilante-type of superhero best epitomized by the likes of Batman, Daredevil, Black Canary, Rorschach, Luke Cage, and the Punisher, among many others.

Olympian Gods: The Greek and Roman Pantheon

ZEUS/JUPITER
Lord of the Greek gods, endowed with the power of lightning, as well as the ability to control the weather and cause natural disasters. He hurled thunderbolts with a might feared by mortals and immortals alike.

POSEIDON/NEPTUNE
Brother of Zeus and god of the oceans, with ultimate dominion over the sea and everything in it. He was also responsible for earthquakes and was considered the god of horses.

HADES/PLUTO
Another brother of Zeus, this god of the underworld held sway over the land of the dead and was feared by all mortals who knew they would one day enter his domain.

HERA/JUNO
Queen of the Olympians, sister of Zeus but also his favorite wife. She was the goddess of marriage, which she knew a lot about, having to manage her husband's bold and multitudinous infidelities. Her wrath was legendary.

HEPHAESTUS/VULCAN
Although cursed with a misshapen form, his skills with the forge were unparalleled, and he even fashioned robotic servants to help him in the fiery lava pits where he built the armor and weapons for gods and heroes.

ATHENA/MINERVA
A formidable warrior, who sprung fully grown from the skull of her father Zeus, she was the goddess of wisdom and military strategy. In addition to an enchanted helmet and spear, she possessed a robotic owl made by her brother Hephaestus/Vulcan.

HERMES/MERCURY
Son of Zeus and the herald and messenger of the gods, he possessed immense speed and could even run across open water. Conniving when he needed to be, he was also the god of thieves.

ARES/MARS
Known for his trademark color red, the color of blood, the god of war was a ruthless and cruel tyrant who represented the fiercer, wilder side of

battle, as opposed to his more even-tempered and strategic sister Athena. No army fighting with him on their side could lose.

APHRODITE/VENUS

The mysterious and alluring goddess of love—or more appropriately, the goddess of sex. She had the power to make mortals and immortals fall in love/lust, as did her well-known arrow-slinging son, Eros/Cupid.

APOLLO

This son of Zeus was the god of many noble things, chief among them light, music, and poetry, but also medicine, truth, prophecy, and even the sun. He was also the only Olympian to be called the same name by both the Greeks and Romans.

ARTEMIS/DIANA

Twin sister of Apollo and goddess of the hunt, she was known for her proficiency with the bow, for her fleetness of foot, and for being worshipped by the elite tribe of warrior women known as the Amazons.

DEMETER/CERES

A sister of Zeus, she was the goddess of the harvest and as such, possessed control over the seasons that controlled the lives of so many Greek and Roman farmers who depended on her goodwill.

PERSEPHONE/PROSERPINA

The lovely daughter of Demeter/Ceres, she was the victim of the lust of her uncle Hades/Pluto. When he kidnapped her and brought her to the underworld with him, it sent her mother into a depression so strong it led to the advent of winter.

DIONYSUS/BACCHUS

The last of the major Olympians to ascend to a place in the hallowed hall, the god of wine and merriment was especially beloved by his followers, who worshipped him with orgies and drunken debauchery.

HESTIA/VESTA

Eldest sister of Zeus, and the goddess of hearth and home, her humility was her greatest virtue, and she famously gave up her throne on Olympus for the newcomer Dionysus/Bacchus. The opposite of him, her priestesses maintained a vow of celibacy.

Protosuperheroes: The Demigods and Heroes of Ancient Greece and Rome

HERACLES/HERCULES

Most famous of all ancient heroes, his legendary strength was the prototype for all superstrong heroes that came after him. Although he also committed some decidedly unheroic atrocities during his time, the completion of his twelve labors is one of mythology's greatest hero quests.

ACHILLES

Hero of the Trojan War, his invulnerability was another major prototype for the powers of later superheroes, as was his tragic weakness, his infamous heel, the only part of his body that could be harmed, and the cause of his eventual demise.

PERSEUS

Like Heracles a son of mighty Zeus, this demigod possessed a magic sword and shield, winged boots, and a helmet of invisibility, which enabled him to achieve his legendary feat of slaying the gorgon Medusa and turning the fearsome Kraken to stone.

ATALANTA

A fleet-footed huntress almost as formidable as the goddess Artemis herself, Atalanta reveled in her abilities, to the point that she dared any man who would wed her to first defeat her in a footrace. If he failed, he died.

JASON

Perhaps the leader of the first-ever superteam, the Argonauts, Jason commanded the enchanted vessel known as the *Argo*, on a quest to attain the magical Golden Fleece of Colchis and defeat the deadly many-headed Hydra.

ODYSSEUS/ULYSSES

The brave and cunning Odysseus, "the man of twists and turns," was characterized by his charismatic leadership, unmatched bravery, and the ability to talk his way out of nearly any situation. His skill with the bow and arrow was unparalleled in all of mythology.

THESEUS

Some stories name him as a son of the sea god Poseidon, while in others he is the son of Aegeus, king of Athens. Like Heracles, he completed a series of monumental tasks, the most well-known navigating Crete's impenetrable labyrinth and slaying the hideous man-bull known as the Minotaur.

BELLEREPHON

Rider of the fabled winged horse Pegasus, he defeated a host of mythological monsters, chief among them the fire-breathing Chimera. So drunk on power did he become that he even attempted to reach Olympus itself on his flying steed.

The most influential text of living religions in the world today, the Bible, contains many examples of superhuman beings in both its Old and New Testaments. It's easy to see Samson from the book of Judges, whose very name—much like that of Hercules—is synonymous with strength, his superstrength derived from his hair, and the loss of that hair being his great weakness, as an archetype for the multitude of superstrong heroes depicted in our culture. But even figures like Moses, who is depicted with the supernatural ability to manipulate the natural world around him, and David, whose keen fighting skills and courage belie his small stature and make him a natural leader of men, are arguably superheroic figures. Jesus Christ, the central figure of the New Testament and Christianity, the world's largest religion, is someone who demonstrates many attributes and abilities that would later be seen in superheroes. Even Christ's "origin story" as an omnipotent father figure sent to Earth to save its people, echoes in the stories of several popular superheroes, chief among them Superman.

One of the last of the world's great mythologies, the ancient Norse religion followed by the Vikings, dates back as far as the eighth century AD

Champions of Asgard: The Norse Pantheon

ODIN

The All-Father and lord of the Aesir, his was a story similar to many beings worshipped throughout human history, including a form of resurrection and sacrifice to attain a higher level of existence.

THOR

Most well-known today among Norse gods due to his reinvention by Marvel, this son of Odin was originally a hot-headed, crimson-haired fury, known for striking fear in the hearts of frost giants with his red-hot hammer, Mjolnir.

LOKI

The bane of the existence of the Aesir, this conniving trickster god of mischief and of fire would sometimes oppose the will of Asgard, while other times he would assist his adopted father Odin and brother Thor with his cunning ways.

BALDER

The purest and most beautiful of all Norse gods, he was a god of light who was adored and cherished by all—except for the jealous and spiteful Loki, who caused his cosmically tragic death with one of his cruel pranks.

FRIGG

Queen of the Aesir and wife of Odin, she was the goddess of the sky, as well as fertility, motherhood, and of family, and possessed the ability to see into the future.

TYR

The feared and respected god of war, justice, and heroism, Tyr was especially revered by the warrior Vikings and Germanic people. In some versions he is a son of Odin, while other legends consider him an even older and more powerful god than the All-Father himself.

BRAGI

The bard of Valhalla, the sacred hall of Asgard where the Aesir feast for all eternity with the souls of fallen warriors, Bragi was the god of poetry who preserved the feats of gods and heroes in song.

IDUN

The wife of Bragi, and goddess of youth and rejuvenation, she was said to be in possession of the mystical fruits that the Aesir consumed to preserve their immortality, making her a crucial member of the pantheon.

HEL

The daughter of Loki, the fearsome Hel was ruler of the underworld, which for the Norse and Germanic peoples was the place to which anyone who died by any other method except combat was consigned.

HEIMDALL

The guardian of Asgard, who stands at the rainbow bridge with his mighty horn Gjallarhorn to sound the alarm during any attempted invasion. In some versions of the mythology, he is also considered the father of mankind.

FREY

Although not a member of the Aesir but rather the lesser tribe of gods known as the Vanir, Frey was worshipped far and wide due to both his powers over the harvest and masculine virility.

FREYA

Sister of Frey, Freya was the formidable goddess of destiny, also seen as the embodiment of beauty, love, and of pleasure. Along with her brother, she was accepted into the Aesir after the conclusion of their war with the Vanir.

but was preserved in the Prose Edda and the Poetic Edda of the thirteenth century. It has taken on a new life in recent decades due to its successful adaptation by Marvel Comics, and centuries-old characters like Thor, Odin, and Loki are today probably the most popular they have been since the Middle Ages. With its emphasis on individual heroism and its origins in the inherent powers of the natural world, the Norse mythology of Scandinavia is especially pertinent to the development of the concept of superheroes. The Aesir of Asgard, seated on their thrones in Valhalla, much like the Greek gods in the halls of mighty Olympus, aren't all that different from the Justice League in their orbiting satellite headquarters, or the Avengers in their majestic New York mansion.

The Middle Ages, with its many tales of brave warriors, magical creatures, codes of chivalry, and men and women of honor, was fertile ground for the continuing development of hero worship and the refinement of the superheroic template. Early Irish and Scottish folklore from as far back as the third century gives us the legendary hunter and warrior Fionn mac Cumhaill (aka Finn MacCool) and his battles with the strange, otherworldly tribe of monsters known as the Tuatha de Danann. As Christianity spread across Europe, Christian saints such as England's Saint George, Ireland's Saint Patrick, and Italy's Saint Francis were revered for their supposed divine abilities, and stories of George vanquishing the dragon, Patrick driving snakes out of Ireland, and Francis's ability to communicate with animals are well-known to this day.

Of all the legends of the Middle Ages, the mythos of King Arthur and his noble knights of Camelot has resonated the most through the centuries. Beginning in the sixth century and gaining momentum and detail over the entire medieval period, the legendary ruler of the Britons, with his magical sword Excalibur, messianic origin story, and mystical adviser Merlin by his side, was a superhuman figure around which much of Anglo-Saxon identity was built—not to mention the derring-do of his brave cohorts like Sir Lancelot, Sir Galahad, and Sir Gawain, whose exploits facing the Green Knight were recounted in an anonymous fourteenth-century chivalric romance. But Britain wasn't the only source of medieval heroes—there was also Roland of France, Germanic warrior Sigurd/Seigfried, and of course, the mighty Beowulf, whose own anonymous tenth-century epic poem recounts his battles with sea monsters, the demon Grendel and his sinister mother, and the dragon who eventually fells him.

One of the more human heroes to emerge in the Middle Ages, and yet the one with some of the clearest connections to modern superheroes, is Robin of Locksley, better known as Robin Hood. Seen as early as the thirteenth century in the tales of troubadours and balladeers, he leads his band of "merry men" from their headquarters in Sherwood Forest, on a mission to aid the poor of England by stealing from the gluttonous and oppressive wealthy class. The original socially progressive vigilante, Robin as a figure of legend inspired the downtrodden of Britain and served as a rallying figure. It's not hard to see how his spirit lives on in so many modern-day superheroes, especially those who don't let the absence of superpowers prevent them from fighting for the greater good.

Long before the concept of popular fiction, or even before the printing press itself, in the cultures mentioned here, and in many others, the earliest seeds of the superhero genre were being planted and cultivated over time. From the beginnings of civilization itself, storytelling was a central part of human life—a way of passing on knowledge and memories, and imparting wisdom. Mythology and folklore helped us to understand and explain our

The Hero's Journey

Perhaps no other critic or scholar in modern times has contributed more to our understanding of the ancient heroes of our distant past than acclaimed literature and comparative mythology professor Joseph Campbell. Beginning with his seminal 1949 book *The Hero with a Thousand Faces*, Campbell worked to distill the many myths and legends of the world, to find their common threads and archetypes, and link them to what he called the "monomyth"—the theory that all myths are variations on a central, great, common story, or set of stories. In the case of the heroes of old, Campbell identified important Jungian aspects that intersect with countless heroic tales of yore, including the supernatural nature of the hero's origin, his obscured upbringing and call to action, the older mentor that sets him on the righteous path, the archenemy or feat he must overcome, the magical abilities or tools he is endowed with in his task, the manner in which he is transformed by his experiences, and so on.

The so-called hero's journey archetype that Campbell outlined has been linked not only to ancient and medieval legends the world over, but also to the many modern interpretations that rely on the same structures and cultural touchstones, including *Star Wars*, *Lord of the Rings*, *Harry Potter*, and of course, the modern superheroes of comic books and films. We can easily see classic elements of Campbell's hero's journey in characters like Superman, Batman, Spider-Man, Wonder Woman, Daredevil, Captain America, Aquaman, Blade, Shazam, and countless others. Since superheroes merely represent the latest incarnation of a cultural phenomenon that dates back millennia, it should be no surprise that the same theories that explain Gilgamesh, Hercules, and King Arthur would also apply to Green Lantern, the Silver Surfer, and Spawn.

world. Each fulfilled the need, from the very start, for saviors and beings whose abilities stood out from the rest of us, and who would use those abilities to help us. As it turns out, one of the world's most popular fictional genres was always this way, only in different forms.

ICONS #2

The Dark Knight

Creators: Bob Kane and Bill Finger

First Appearance: *Dectective Comics* #27, May 1939

Alter Ego: Bruce Wayne

Abilities: world's greatest detective; master of hand-to-hand combat; genius intellect; wide array of weapons and gadgets, including batarangs, flame and bullet-resistant cape and cowl, pocket explosives, grappling hooks, and much more

Archenemies: The Joker, Two-Face, Catwoman, Bane, the Riddler, the Penguin, Poison Ivy, the Scarecrow, Mr. Freeze, Ra's al Ghul

Although he was the second major superhero to emerge during the Golden Age of comics, in many ways **BATMAN** has grown to be a huge cultural presence who has almost eclipsed his immediate predecessor, Superman. Certainly, in the past thirty years or so, a case can be made that he has become the world's most popular costumed character. Possessing no superpowers but fighting crime with the sheer force of his will (and all the technological wizardry a billionaire can afford), Batman tirelessly battles evildoers in Gotham City, and his embrace of the dark side of the hero dynamic has made him an especially relatable figure in a darker and grittier age.

THE ORIGIN

When young Bruce Wayne's parents are murdered right before his eyes in a senseless act of violence on the streets of Gotham, he vows to combat the forces of crime that threaten to overtake his city. As he matures to manhood, he hatches a plan to become the ideal crimefighter, training his body to be a fighting machine, using his family's untold riches to equip himself with all manner of high-tech vehicles and weaponry, while taking a vow never to take human life as his parents' murderer had done. From his secret underground Batcave, with the assistance of his beleaguered butler Alfred and the complicity of Gotham's Commissioner Gordon, he becomes a vigilante whose very image strikes terror in the hearts of criminals.

THE CREATION

When National Comics Publications, the company that would eventually become DC, was looking for an exciting follow-up to the smash hit they had with Superman, they turned to writer and illustrator Bob Kane, whose initial sketches and ideas were augmented by his collaborator, artist Bill Finger. Taking inspiration from pulp heroes like The Shadow, Johnston McCulley's Zorro, and comic strips' first costumed hero the Phantom, they created a bold vigilante who couldn't have been more different from the Man of Steel. With a black-on-gray costume (later changed to blue-on-gray for greater detail), a voluminous cape that billowed like bat wings, and a sinister cowl obscuring his face, they envisioned him as a crime-fighting detective working outside the law. His secret origins among the wealthy class were also there from the beginning to account for his access to all manner of crime-fighting tools.

CAMP ICON

Although Kane and Finger introduced Batman as a rather dark character, this didn't last. Over the course of the 1940s–1960s, the Caped Crusader was somewhat softened and watered down, his adventures made more palatable for young readers. The gun he toted in early issues was taken away, and a plucky, juvenile sidekick, Robin, was added. A colorful rogue's gallery developed, headed up by the Clown Prince of Crime, the nefarious Joker, and rounded out by other wild adversaries worthy of Chester Gould's Dick Tracy. As epitomized in the work of artists like Dick Sprang and Carmine Infantino, the Silver Age brought things like the Bat-Hound, the Bat-Mite, and of course, the very parodic and lighthearted, yet highly successful *Batman* TV series of the 1960s.

REBORN IN DARKNESS

Although cherished by millions, the campy television antics of Adam West had turned the character of Batman into something of a goof, and by the 1970s DC decided to try and return him to his darker, more serious origins. Writer Denny O'Neil and artist Neal Adams helped breathe new life into the Batman as a kind of costumed James Bond, which in the late 1980s led to the work of Frank Miller in *The Dark Knight Returns* and *Batman: Year One* (1986), Alan Moore in *The Killing Joke* (1988), and others, which firmly established Batman as the gritty avenger Kane and Finger originally envisioned, adding even more layered psychological issues than even those creators intended. Since that time, Batman has remained true to his vigilante roots.

THE BOY WONDER

Batman had several faithful sidekicks over the years. Dick Grayson, the original Robin, suffered a similar fate as Bruce Wayne—his parents were killed when their high-wire circus act was sabotaged, leading him to become Wayne's young ward. Later incarnations of Robin have included Jason Todd, who was killed by the Joker in the memorable 1980s *Death in the Family* story line; Tim Drake, whose 1989 introduction also led to a revamp of the iconic yellow, red, and green costume; and even Damian Wayne, the son of Bruce Wayne and Talia al Ghul (R'as al Ghul's daughter). After moving out of Wayne Manor, the adult Dick Grayson would later take on the solo vigilante identity of Nightwing.

THE CAPED CRUSADER HITS THE SCREEN

Along with Superman, Batman might be the character most often adapted into other forms. He was first brought to the screen with a pair of successful movie serials in the 1940s. Following the campiness of the 1960s William Dozier-created TV show, Tim Burton's hugely popular 1989 movie starring Michael Keaton returned more of the dark feel, while keeping some of the fun as well. Burton's approach continued with three sequels that became progressively less serious. The success of that franchise also inspired the fan-favorite *Batman: The Animated Series* (1992–1995), the most beloved

34

of the Caped Crusader's cartoon exploits. Later versions, such as Christopher Nolan's *Dark Knight* trilogy (*Batman Begins*, 2005; *The Dark Knight*, 2008; and *The Dark Knight Rises*, 2012) starring Christian Bale and the most recent appearances by Ben Affleck and Robert Pattinson under the cowl, have kept things decidedly on the dark side.

THE SHADOW OF THE BAT

Much like one of his own archrivals, Two-Face, Batman himself represents something dark and damaged, as compared to the light and purity of Superman. Presenting an alternative that is based more on reality and that is grounded in the human world of politics and crime, Batman has found an audience of loyal followers that is about as passionate as any in the realm of superheroes. His iconography is woven into the fabric of popular culture, and his darkness has inspired much of what we now recognize in superhero fiction.

3

ON THE PRINTED PAGE

The Earliest Superheroes in Popular Culture

The twentieth century gave birth to superheroes as we know them today, but it didn't happen overnight. The seminal characters of the late 1930s and 1940s—Superman, Batman, Wonder Woman, Captain Marvel, Captain America, Namor, the original Flash and Green Lantern, etc.—were not created in a vacuum. They were the products of superhero fiction, an emerging genre that had already begun taking root in the previous decades. Even before the term "superhero" was being used, tropes and trappings were taking shape: The idea of telling these stories in illustrated form, and publishing them in four-color booklets, came a little later, but the notion of costumed crimefighters, themed vigilantes, and superhuman adventurers fomented for decades before these themes emerged.

As the world moved from antiquity and into modern times, new technologies and social evolution brought with them new concepts, particularly in the way stories were told, and the reasons they were told. Whereas stories proliferated in earlier centuries in the form of legends and folklore, events like the invention of the printing press and the emergence of capitalism made it easier to create and disseminate stories, and also introduced a new reason to create stories and invent characters: money. This led to an explosion of prose and illustrated fiction writing and publishing, and with that came a multitude of specific targeted genres aimed at different and, sometimes, overlapping audiences and demographics. Adventure stories and supernatural tales had always been popular, and it was easy to understand why they would become more popular than ever in the age of the printed word.

It's believed that the word "superhero" dates to at least 1917, although at that time it was coined merely to describe high-profile and highly accomplished public figures like Teddy Roosevelt, Thomas Edison, or Booker T. Washington. But even before its formation, or its relevant application, what would become the genre of superhero fiction was already being established. Like the hard-boiled detective, the mustache-twirling robber baron, the noble cowboy, or the mad scientist, the superhero was becoming a fictional archetype for consumption by the masses of eager readers, listeners, and theatergoers. Baroness Orczy's Scarlet Pimpernel is often noted as being of particular importance in establishing this archetype, including the costumed and masked disguise, the secret identity, the code name and iconic symbol, the sense of vigilante justice, and other ideas. Her 1903 London play, *The Scarlet Pimpernel*, was a smash international hit, as was the series of novels that followed.

In the early twentieth century, many different ideas and concepts were gaining steam and contributed to the evolution of exactly what a superhero was. There was the growing popularity of science fiction, birthed in the nineteenth century by authors like Mary Shelley, Jules Verne, and H. G. Wells, and further fueled by the scientific and technological innovations that followed, as well as stirring interest in the concept of space exploration

Extraordinary Gentlemen: Superhero Prototypes

SHERLOCK HOLMES

Sir Arthur Conan Doyle's supersleuth Sherlock Holmes first appeared in the 1887 novel *A Study in Scarlet*. Over the next forty years it was followed with three additional novels and fifty-six short stories. Although more important to the detective and mystery genres, Holmes's borderline supernatural detecting skills and analytical mind put him in a category with such cerebral superheroes as Batman, Mr. Fantastic, Hank Pym, and the Atom.

THE SCARLET PIMPERNEL

Often viewed as the beginning of the definable superhero fiction genre, Baroness Emma Orczy's wildly popular 1903 London stage play and ensuing novels, set during the French Revolution, gave us the world's first costumed crusader, Sir Percy Blakeney (aka the Scarlet Pimpernel), whose foppish façade is a front for the exploits of a swashbuckling master of disguise, symbolized by the flower that gives him his name.

JOHN CARTER OF MARS

The mysterious immortal created by Edgar Rice Burroughs first appeared in the pages of *All-Story* magazine in 1912 and in the serialized novel *Under the Moons of Mars*, which was later published as *A Princess of Mars*. After serving in the Confederate Army during the Civil War, Carter finds himself transported to the red planet, where the decreased gravity gives him superhuman strength and the ability to leap great distances. His adventures continued in a series of *Mars* novels.

TARZAN

Immediately following the success of John Carter, Burroughs brought forth his greatest creation in *All-Story* later in 1912. Raised by apes after losing his parents to the dangers of the African jungle, Tarzan (aka John Clayton, Earl of Greystoke) develops remarkable strength and agility as well as the ability to communicate with animals. Although of noble birth, he remains as protector of the jungle and its wildlife.

ZORRO

A major forerunner to so many masked vigilantes and avengers, Johnston McCulley's Zorro first appeared in *All-Story Weekly* in 1919 in the serialized novel *The Curse of Capistrano*. Set in eighteenth-century Spanish California, the adventures of Zorro follow the Gay Blade (so-called for his lighthearted demeanor while vanquishing his foes) defending the poor from tyrannical officials and robber barons, all the while protecting his true identity—Don Diego de la Vega.

THE SHADOW

"Who knows what evil lurks in the hearts of men? The Shadow knows!" So went the famous introduction to the 1930s radio serial that gave rise to the most popular 1930s superhero of the pre-Superman era. Shortly after his radio debut, the character was adapted in a beloved series of pulp novels by Walter Gibson. With his trademark wide-brimmed hat, scarf, and cloak, The Shadow possesses powers of telepathy and invisibility, and is an expert marksman.

CONAN THE BARBARIAN

Debuting in the seminal genre pulp *Weird Tales* in 1932, the grim Cimmerian warrior of the ancient Hyborean Age belongs more to the world of fantasy than superheroes, but as envisioned by Robert E. Howard, his matchless physical and combat prowess and code of honor, nihilistic though it may be, helped establish him as an influential antihero-type. Famously played on screen by Arnold Schwarzenegger, his adventures have also been told in comic books for decades.

DOC SAVAGE

Credited by Stan Lee himself as one of the major antecedents of modern-day superheroes, the Man of Bronze first appeared in 1933 in pulp magazines released by revolutionary publishers Street & Smith. As envisioned by writer Lester Dent and publishers Henry W. Ralston and John L. Nanovic, he is a brilliant polymath who uses his vast knowledge of science, medicine, and detection to battle evildoers everywhere from his New York City headquarters.

THE LONE RANGER

"Who was that masked man?" The answer is Texas Ranger John Reid. His brother is killed in an ambush, leading Reid to fake his own death. He is joined by the trusty Native American scout Tonto, who saves his life, and

Reid's famous steed Silver. Reid dons an iconic domino mask to hide his identity and embarks on a crusade against outlaws throughout the Old West frontier. First appearing on radio in 1933, The Lone Ranger was also featured in a highly successful 1950s TV series.

THE GREEN HORNET

Although the intellectual properties are now owned by different entities, when he debuted on WXYZ radio out of Detroit in 1936, Green Hornet was originally envisioned as the great-nephew of John Reid, The Lone Ranger. A heavy influence on Batman, newspaper publisher Britt Reid wears the green coat, fedora, and mask of the Hornet by night, a vigilante infiltrating the urban underworld in his high-tech car Black Beauty, his martial artist sidekick Kato by his side.

as fictionalized in early adventure comic strips like *Buck Rogers* and *Flash Gordon*. There was a cultural openness to the supernatural and the paranormal, as typified in the magician/mentalist/illusionist entertainer craze of the late nineteenth and early twentieth century that gave rise to performers like Herrmann the Great, Harry Houdini, Harry Blackstone, J. N. Maskelyne, and others, as well as the accompanying interest in seances, exorcisms, and the idea of communing with other worlds. And there was also a growing awareness of urban crime and decay, and frustration with the ineffectiveness of politicians and law enforcement to properly address them—thanks in part to the explosion of urban populations and the unprecedented work of crusading journalists who brought such issues before the eyes of average Americans daily.

The public was ready for characters that would combine these elements and address these problems in satisfying, fantastical ways. Fiction was seen as wish fulfillment.

BEFORE THERE WERE COMICS:
THE LEGACY OF THE PULPS

In the 1910–1930s, before comic books arrived on the scene, what we would now call superheroes were being portrayed in popular pulp magazines. These magazines published novellas and short stories in cheaply printed, bound editions sold on newsstands. They were consumed voraciously. Chief among the early pulp heroes were The Shadow and Doc Savage, who represented two major subarchetypes that would later become commonplace: the dark and gritty avenger and the brilliant polymath adventurer, respectively. The pulps were the true antecedent of comic books, and to a lesser degree there was the ever-popular medium of comic strips, beloved in daily and weekly newspapers ever since the introduction of *The Yellow Kid* in the 1890s. In fact, the first superhero/costumed crimefighter stories to be told in illustrated form were found in the strips and included characters like Mandrake the Magician and the Phantom, both created by Lee Falk.

Today, it's hard to grasp exactly how much of a cultural impact pulp magazines had, how ubiquitous and important they were to the development of the modern superhero. At one time, they were one of the most popular forms of entertainment, competing directly with radio and the movies during the Golden Age of both those mediums. Prior to the comic book explosion of World War II, and even during it, they introduced daring heroics and wild adventure stories in a cheaply printed, mass market format to a generation of Americans and anyone else who consumed American media exports. They were literature for the masses, read religiously by millions, in hundreds of titles published each month.

Printed on low-quality, ragged pages that gave them their name, the pulps were a phenomenon of the early twentieth century, reigning from the 1890s all the way to the 1950s, enjoying a peak period during the 1920s–1940s. Frank Munsey's *Argosy* kicked off the trend in 1896, followed by the rise of pulp powerhouse Street & Smith at the turn of century, with their *Popular Magazine* and countless others. Soon, subgenres emerged, including science fiction, western, romance, crime, adventure, and horror. There were titles such as *Amazing Stories, Black Mask, Weird Tales, Blue Book, Startling Stories*, and scores of others that competed on newsstands for the attention of readers with a dime or quarter in their pocket. In addition to creations like The Shadow, Conan, Tarzan, Doc Savage, and Zorro, there were early protosuperheroes like the Black Bat; Ka-Zar, who was later absorbed into the Marvel Universe as a comic book character; The Phantom Detective; Robert E. Howard's Kull the Conqueror, Solomon Kane, and Bran Mak Morn; Domino Lady; and the Spider, who all populated the pages of the pulps with their breathless tales of conquest, crimefighting, and derring-do.

The fiction printed in the pulps was usually not of the highest quality, but it didn't matter. Like the penny dreadfuls and other mass-market fiction before them, they were the literary equivalent of comfort food, and their no-nonsense, bare-knuckles style had wide appeal. There were certainly gems to be found among the vast output, as the pulp phenomenon included the first published works of authors like Tennessee Wiliams, Robert Bloch, H. P. Lovecraft, Philip K. Dick, Raymond Chandler, William S. Burroughs, Upton Sinclair, Ray Bradbury, F. Scott Fitzgerald, and many others.

The decline of the pulps started to take place by the mid-1940s, thanks to several factors, including the rise of the simpler and more visual medium of comic books, rising prices due to World War II paper shortages, and most crucially of all, the rise of that most passive and monolithic of all media, television. Many heroes of the pulps continued into film, TV, comics, radio, and other formats, and their influence on those early

The Ghost Who Walks

In the early days of the modern superhero, Lee Falk's the Phantom holds a very special place. Generally regarded as the first true costumed crime-fighter to appear in illustrated form, the Phantom predates Superman and Batman by a few years, and even precedes the comic book medium itself, having been featured in the newspaper comic strip format, which was much more popular and prestigious at the time. Many of the tropes associated with the Phantom would inspire what came after him, including the visual appeal of his colorful adventures and how they leant themselves to a pictorial medium.

The Phantom first appeared in February 1936 with the acclaimed "The Singh Brotherhood" story line. He was a dark and mysterious avenger, striking from his secret headquarters, the ancient Skull Cave, somewhere in the fictional Asian (later African) nation of Bangalla. Clad in his trademark skin-tight purple bodysuit and black domino mask, he used his skull signet ring to scar those he faced in combat. He was really Kit Walker, the twenty-first in his family's line to take on the family mantle that began in the sixteenth century when the original Phantom, Christopher Walker Jr., vowed to fight for justice after his father was murdered in a pirate ambush. Thus, the Phantom became a mythic figure to the locals, who believed he had been the same man all those centuries, and thus called him "The Man Who Cannot Die."

Falk's creation has been drawn by numerous artists over the years, and his strip continues in hundreds of newspapers worldwide, even after Falk's passing in 1999. Although the character's popularity in America has waned in the past fifty years, he has attained cult followings in international markets like Scandinavia, Australia, and Papua New Guinea, where the indigenous people were so enamored with him they used his iconography on their war shields. He's been licensed in comic book form by both Marvel and DC, was featured in a 1940s movie serial in which he was played by Tom Tyler (the same actor who also starred in the Captain Marvel serial), and was the subject of a poorly received1996 film adaptation starring Billy Zane.

Although now a relatively obscure figure, the shadow of "The Ghost Who Walks" is long indeed, and looms over all the costumed and masked heroes whose adventures have been told in illustrated form in the ninety years since he first emerged from his cave.

generations of comics creators, who digested them on a regular basis along with the rest of America, was incalculable.

INVENTING THE SUPERHERO

In the early iterations of the superhero, many of the devices and elements we have come to associate so strongly with them were already coming into focus. In addition to the Pimpernel and Phantom, characters like Zorro and Green Hornet wore distinctive costumes. They also hid their identities with masks in order to either escape the law or protect the people they were close to, as was also seen with characters like The Lone Ranger and Domino Lady—the pulp heroine who was the earliest known masked female vigilante in fiction. There were sometimes sidekicks, such as Lone Ranger's Tonto, Green Hornet's Kato, and Mandrake's Lothar, who served as crime-fighting companions. The secret lair was another early trope, as seen with Doc Savage's skyscraper headquarters, or the Phantom's Skull Cave. These lairs were sometimes mysterious and primitive, and sometimes high-tech and state-of-the-art, but all served as a haven or nerve center—a base of operation for these unusual characters and their crusades.

What's interesting is that many of the early superheroes didn't really have anything in the way of superhuman powers, but rather fought crime and injustice with just their wits, ingenuity, and natural human abilities—not to mention a handy array of weaponry. Still, we do see the concept of superhuman abilities being explored with characters like Popeye and his spinach-enhanced superstrength, The Shadow and his psychic powers, and Mandrake with his magic. The necessity for superheroes to have actual superpowers didn't really crystallize until the comic book era—and even then, it never really became a requirement.

See You in the Funny Papers: Comic Strip Crusaders

BUCK ROGERS

Helping to launch the genre of space/science-fiction adventure, Buck Rogers first appeared in the pages of *Amazing Stories* in 1928, but it was the syndicated newspaper comic strip that immediately followed and ran for nearly forty years that launched him into the popular consciousness. The exploits of a twentieth-century war veteran in the twenty-fifth century were later recounted in an iconic 1939 movie serial starring Buster Crabbe, and a 1970s TV series starring Gil Gerard.

POPEYE

Although it may seem surprising, the one-eyed sailor man was a major influence on early superheroes of the 1930s and 1940s, with recurring archenemies like Bluto and the Sea Hag, beleaguered love interest Olive Oyl, and the superstrength derived from his precious spinach. Created in 1929 by E. C. Segar for the King Features syndicated comic strip *Thimble Theatre*, he also achieved major fame thanks to the 1930s–1950s animated Fleischer/Paramount cartoons.

DICK TRACY

Perhaps the most popular newspaper comic strip of the Depression and World War II era featured Chester Gould's lantern-jawed police detective, busting up an outrageously colorful rogue's gallery in his trademark yellow fedora and trench coat. So many aspects of Tracy's adventures would resonate later, like his famous radio wristwatch and villains like Flattop, Prune Face, the Brow, Itchy, Mumbles, and numerous others.

FLASH GORDON

The greatest of all the Buck Rogers imitators, Alex Raymond's vibrant and memorable strip carved out an identity all its own, following the efforts of polo player (later football player) Gordon, his love interest Dale Arden, and the scientist Dr. Hans Zarkov to thwart the evil plots of Ming the Merciless, ruler of planet Mongo. Filled with colorful characters and warring tribes, it was later played for camp effect in a decadent 1980s film adaptation.

MANDRAKE THE MAGICIAN

The forefather of all mystical-themed superheroes, including Dr. Strange, Dr. Fate, and Zatanna, Mandrake was the creation of Lee Falk and illustrator Phil Davis. He first appeared in newspaper strips in 1934. Although a stage magician by trade, Mandrake possessed real magical abilities including invisibility, mind control, shapeshifting, teleportation, and levitation, and battled all forms of mad scientists, aliens, and interdimensional beings. His strip ran for almost eighty years.

SHEENA

Though heavily influenced by Tarzan, Sheena, the Queen of the Jungle, spawned a slew of her own imitators and is the first female character to get her own titled comic book. Created by legendary comic creator Will Eisner and his partner Jerry Iger in 1938, Sheena first appeared in Britain, but was soon a hit in the United States as well. Her battles with slave traders, wildlife hunters, evil cults, savage natives, and fearsome beasts later found their way to multiple TV series and a 1984 feature film.

The word "superhero" was not utilized to actually describe these kinds of characters until August 1937, when it was used in the Letters column of the pulp magazine *Thrilling Wonder Stories*. The term referred to Max Plaisted's Zarnak, a somewhat obscure pulp hero who had been appearing in its pages. Obviously, quite a few people who would later become important to the development of the superhero were faithful readers of the pulps, and very well could've been reading that exact issue. Or maybe it was just a case of the inevitable, as some ideas just slip into the zeitgeist in ways that are hard to explain. Although no one could have known it at the time, that term as it appeared in *Thrilling Wonder Stories* would catch on in a big way. A brand-new medium was coming, even cheaper and more accessible than anything that had come before it, that would turn "superhero" into a household word and turn its first characters labeled as such into cultural icons of the highest order.

ICONS #3

The Scarlet Speedster

Creators: Gardner Fox and Harry Lampert (Golden Age); Robert Kanigher and Carmine Infantino (Silver Age); John Broome and Carmine Infantino (Modern Age)

First Appearance: *Flash Comics* #1, January 1940; *Showcase* #4, October 1956; *Crisis on Infinite Earths* #12, March 1986

Alter Egos: Jay Garrick, Barry Allen, Wally West

Powers: superhuman speed and endurance; enhanced healing abilities; phasing through matter; time travel

Archenemies: Reverse-Flash (aka Professor Zoom), Captain Cold, Gorilla Grodd, Mirror Master, Weather Wizard, Heat Wave, Captain Boomerang, The Thinker, Cicada, The Trickster

One of the oldest, most popular, and most important of all DC heroes, **THE FLASH** was the third major crimefighter DC Comics created after Superman and Batman, and has been around in one form or another since before World War II. Although several different people have taken on the mantle of Flash over the decades, they are all united in their powers of incredible physics-defying speed—a true fantasy-fulfillment ability that has fascinated readers and viewers for generations. The character has been reinvented several times, and in this way has reflected the change and development of the comics industry itself, while also being integral to several dimension-spanning story lines at the heart of DC Universe continuity.

THE ORIGIN

The original Flash was Jay Garrick, a college student who develops powers of superspeed after accidentally inhaling dangerous vapors produced by hard water in a lab accident. In a later revision of the character in the 1960s, a time when the world was fixated on the dangers of radiation, the hard water origin was changed to irradiated water. Garrick dons a red suit with a thunderbolt, similar to his college football uniform, adding the flat doughboy helmet worn by his father in World War I. As the Flash, Garrick was a founding member of the Justice Society of America, comics' first superteam.

THE CREATION

Brooklyn-born Gardner Fox, whose fertile mind also played a role in the creation of Hawkman, Doctor Fate, Zatanna, the Sandman, and others, as well as both the Justice Society and the Justice League, was responsible for co-creating the original Flash. Although Fox remained with the character for decades, even helping develop the concept of the multiverse in the 1960s, his creative partner, former Fleischer Animation Studios cartoonist Harry Lampert, only remained with him for a handful of issues before abandoning superhero comics to return to the world of humor illustration. Their original Flash creation was depicted in the pages of *Flash Comics*,

All-Star Comics, and *All-Flash* from 1940 through 1951, when the character vanished amid the decline of superhero popularity.

THE REINVENTION

When DC decided to reboot some classic Golden Age characters, it started with the Scarlet Speedster. But this was a different speedster, namely police scientist Barry Allen, who gains superspeed when doused with electrified chemicals in a freak lab accident (later revealed to have tapped into an energy field known as the Speed Force). Having grown up reading original Flash comics, Allen adopts the persona with a whole new red and gold bodysuit. The most well-known version of the character, Allen was first introduced by writer Robert Kanigher and prolific DC artist Carmine Infantino in 1956 and became a charter member of the new Justice League. In the 1960s, he first met Jay Garrick, who was revealed to exist on an "alternate Earth"— both men having the power to cross the dimensional barrier due to their light-speed abilities.

THE CRISIS

When the DC's multiverse concept became too unwieldy, it was decided to eliminate all alternate Earths in a major mid-1980s comics event called *Crisis on Infinite Earths*. By combining the timelines of several alternate realities, Jay Garrick officially became part of DC's "Earth-1" main continuity as an elder statesman hero, while Barry Allen sacrificed his life to save the universe during the reality-altering conflagration. Assuming the mantle of the new Flash was Allen's nephew Wally West, who had first appeared in the late 1950s as Kid Flash, Barry's junior crime-fighting counterpart. West served as DC's main Flash for nearly a quarter-century, until Barry Allen was resurrected, as comics characters often are, to retake his spot in 2009.

SPEEDSTERS GALORE

True to his reality-bending nature, Flash's many incarnations can be quite complex at times. Allen and West have returned to the role several different times in recent years, with West most recently, once again, becoming DC's main Flash in 2020. Plus, there have been a number of other Flashes over the years, including Bart Allen (Barry's grandson from the future), Chinese American Avery Ho (member of the Justice League of China and Justice League Incarnate), Jesse Chambers (daughter of Golden Age speedster Johnny Quick), and assorted Flashes from the future such as John Fox (named for Wally West creator John Broome and Jay Garrick creator Gardner Fox).

SPEEDING FROM PAGE TO SCREEN

The most beloved adaptation of the Fastest Man Alive would have to be the one played by Grant Gustin on the enormously popular *Flash* TV series that ran from 2014 to 2023 and has become one of the longest running live-action superhero TV shows of all time. Gustin plays Barry Allen, and ironically, Jay Garrick has been portrayed by John Wesley Shipp, the actor who originally played Allen on the short-lived *Flash* TV series of the early 1990s. Audiences have also recently witnessed the first cinematic Flash, played by Ezra Miller in Zack Snyder's 2017 *Justice League* film, as well as his first standalone feature set for release in June 2023. In animated form, the Flash has appeared in Filmation's 1960s *Superman/Aquaman Hour of Adventure*, *Challenge of the Superfriends* in the 1970s, and the *Justice League* series of the early 2000s.

THE FASTEST MAN ALIVE

Along with the ability to fly and superstrength, the ability to move at limitless speed is something many of us have secretly wished for, and it's not hard to understand why the Flash has been so popular over the years, especially with youngsters. Just as Flash himself can tap into the Speed Force, he also taps into something inside the human psyche, as all enduring superheroes should. Through his many incarnations and reboots, from *Showcase,* to *Crisis on Infinite Earths*, to *Final Crisis*, to *The Flash: Rebirth*, to *Flashpoint*, to *DC Rebirth*, the names and origins may change, but the streak of red and gold remains the same.

4

GOLDEN AGE

The Comic Book Explosion

In terms of the rise of superheroes in our cultural consciousness, everything that came before was just a dress rehearsal for what happened at the end of the 1930s and continued throughout the ensuing decade. Around the time of World War II and its postwar boom, thanks to the birth of a new, illustrated print medium, the superhero genre as we know it today appeared, as did many other important concepts in American culture. That medium was the comic book, a product of the Great Depression that would single-handedly propel the superhero directly into the pop culture firmament. In later years, this era would become known as the Golden Age of Comics. And although superheroes would initially seem to be just another fad that almost died out before being dramatically resurrected, the seeds planted during the 1940s grew roots that would never die. It was the moment when the superhero arrived.

The Golden Age would be the time when all the familiar trappings of the superhero would fall into place, when the word "superhero" and its meaning would become common knowledge, and when the first major pantheon of beloved heroes—the most popular of which are still relevant today—would come into being. They leapt off the pages of comic books and into the minds and hearts of millions and began to take on a life beyond the four-color wood-pulp pages. It was the era of Superman, Captain Marvel, Batman, Captain America, Wonder Woman, Plastic Man, and many other iconic creations. And it all began with that first issue of *Action Comics* in the fall of 1938, and the red-and-blue suited Last Son of Krypton whose popularity would transcend the genre itself and make him a cultural touchstone.

Although superheroes would eventually become what comic books were most associated with, the birth of comics had occurred a few years before the Man of Steel foiled his first bad guy. In fact, they were initially created as an extension of the extremely popular medium of newspaper comic strips. Although there was a handful of prototypes that predate it, Eastern Color Printing's *Famous Funnies*, which began publication in July 1934, is considered the first true regularly published comic book. Its contents, like most of the early comic books, consisted of reprints of the most beloved newspaper strips of the day, including *Mutt and Jeff*, *Hairbreadth Harry*, *Tailspin Tommy*, *Dixie Dugan*, *Joe Palooka*, and others. In fact, in those early years, and for some time after, comic strips were considered the more respectable and higher quality art form, attracting greater mainstream interest and superior artists, while comic books were considered strictly for undiscriminating kids.

Although National (DC) was the first to publish a comic book with wholly original content in 1935, for the most part the industry remained geared toward piggybacking on the popularity of the newspaper strips that were daily reading for most Americans in those days. That all changed when DC took a chance on two young men and their idea, inspired by their mutual love of science fiction, for a superpowered alien visitor, raised

First Wave: Heroes of the 1940s

AQUAMAN

First appearing in DC's *More Fun Comics* in 1941 before switching over to *Adventure Comics* in 1946, this creation of future Superman editor Mort Weisinger and artist Paul Norris was originally a normal human who had been taught by his oceanographer father the secrets of living undersea. With his ability to breathe underwater and communicate with ocean life, he regularly battled Nazi U-boats, pirates, and other maritime menaces.

THE ATOM

Although later reinvented, DC's original Golden Age Atom was created by Bill O'Connor and Ben Flinton in 1940 was Al Pratt, a small-yet-scrappy physicist who possessed superstrength and the ability to throw energy-charged "atomic punches." A product of the World War II-era fascination with atomic energy, the Atom was a founding member of DC's original supergroup, the Justice Society of America.

DR. FATE

DC Comics' most powerful sorcerer, the original Dr. Fate was Kent Nelson, discoverer of the tomb of the ancient wizard Nabu, who became his mentor in the magical arts. The creation of science fiction author and comics creator Gardner Fox and artist Howard Sherman, he first appeared in *More Fun Comics* in 1940 and later served as a member of the Justice Society.

DR. MID-NITE

The first physically impaired superhero, Dr. Mid-Nite was Charles McNider, a surgeon blinded by a gangster's bomb. Gaining the ability to see in the dark, he donned a mysterious mask and cape and added special goggles to help him see in daylight, fighting crime while still posing as a helpless blind man when out of costume. Created by Charles Reizenstein and Stanley Aschmeier, he appeared in the pages of DC's *All-American Comics* beginning in 1941.

GREEN ARROW

Bearing similarities to Batman, Oliver Queen first appeared with his popular sidekick, Speedy, in the pages of *More Fun Comics* in late 1941, eventually becoming the monthly featured cover story of the comic book. Mort Weisinger and artist George Papp were inspired partly by Robin Hood as well as the 1940 movie serial *The Green Archer*. Using his limitless capital and endless arsenal of trick arrows, Green Arrow served as Star City's defender all through the Golden Age.

HAWKMAN

The original version of Hawkman, as created by Gardner Fox and Dennis Neville, first appeared in *Flash Comics* #1 in 1940 as archaeologist Carter Hall, the reincarnation of ancient Egyptian Prince Khufu. After regaining his past life memories, Hall uses "Nth metal" to craft an antigravity belt and wings that enable him to fly. A fierce warrior, Hawkman eventually becomes chairman of the Justice Society.

THE HUMAN TORCH

One of the first two superheroes introduced by Marvel Comics' predecessor Timely Comics, and not to be confused with the Fantastic Four member who came along twenty years later, the original Human Torch, created by writer-artist Carl Burgos, was the android Jim Hammond. Built by scientist Phineas Horton, Hammond possessed the ability to control fire while engulfing his body in it. As first depicted in *Marvel Comics* #1 in 1939 he was a villain, but that soon changed.

JOHNNY THUNDER

Debuting in *Flash Comics* #1, the same issue that saw the first appearance of Hawkman, Johnny Thunder was the creation of John Wentworth and Stanley Aschmeier. Thanks to a magical spell during his youth, Johnny possesses the ability to summon the electrified genie-like "Thunderbolt," or Yz, with the magic words "Cei-U." Although usually a figure of comedy without even a costume, Thunder was invited to join the Justice Society.

PLASTIC MAN

One of the first characters to directly embrace humor and camp, the stretchy, shape-shifting Plastic Man was the creation of cartoonist Jack Cole, and first appeared in 1941 in the pages of *Police Comics* #1 from publisher Quality Comics (the character would be acquired by DC in the 1960s). Once a criminal, Patrick "Eel" O'Brian abandons his life of crime after a heist-gone-wrong sees him doused in the chemicals that grant him his elastic powers.

THE SANDMAN

A cross between a pulp detective and a superhero, the original Sandman was Wesley Dodds, who donned a fedora, green business suit, and World War I gas mask, and wielded a gas gun that put victims to sleep as well as compelled them to tell the truth. First appearing in 1939 in *New York World's Fair Comics* but featured in *Adventure Comics*, this creation of Gardner Fox and Bert Christman later loosely inspired Neil Gaiman's more cerebral DC/Vertigo 1990s *Sandman* comic.

THE SPECTRE

A grim supernatural avenger, the original Spectre was the brainchild of Superman co-creator Jerry Siegel and Bernard Bailey, first appearing in DC's *More Fun Comics* in 1940. After police officer Jim Corrigan is murdered by criminals just before his engagement party, his spirit is sent back to Earth to exact often-brutal vengeance against all the forces of crime and evil. Although the dark character was phased out early in the Golden Age, he was brought back in later years.

THE SPIRIT

Of all Golden Age characters, Will Eisner's The Spirit is often pointed out as the one having the highest quality writing and artwork. First appearing in a special insert in the *Register and Tribune* syndicated newspapers, he would find a regular home in his own book published by Quality Comics. With a strong nod to the pulp heroes of old, The Spirit was a more cerebral alternative for discerning Golden Age readers.

THE SUB-MARINER

One of the first antiheroes of superhero comics, Bill Everett's Sub-Mariner was Prince Namor, son of a human sea captain and an undersea princess of Atlantis. Possessing mutant powers of superstrength and flight, he also has a notoriously hot temper and arrogant demeanor. He first appeared in *Marvel Comics* #1 and shortly thereafter as an aggrieved prince of Atlantis defending his realm against surface dwellers. He has walked the line between hero and villain ever since.

on Earth by human parents, who would use his great abilities to protect the citizens of his adopted home world and battle injustice wherever he saw it. The publication of *Action Comics* #1 in June 1938 was the ultimate watershed moment, not only establishing comic books as a viable source of original content but ushering in the era of the superhero. The concept, based on tropes that had been cultural archetypes for eons, and gradually codified in the adventure fiction of previous generations, had now resulted in a character we would all recognize as a true superhero, complete with costume, secret identity, origin story, specific powers, a rogue's gallery, a love interest, and a memorable name. With Superman, the pieces had all finally fallen into place.

The comic book and the character were overnight sensations. DC responded by not only eventually giving Superman his own self-titled comic book, but also introducing a series of new supercharacters, the first of which was Batman, a crime-fighting vigilante who immediately became the flipside of Superman, and would be his closest rival in popularity forever after. They were followed by the likes of Green Lantern, the Flash, Wonder Woman, Aquaman, Green Arrow, and others, eventually giving rise to the first superteam ever created: the Justice Society of America, the conception of editor Sheldon Mayer and writer Gardner Fox. It was a no-brainer joining these immensely popular heroes. The concept would remain a permanent staple of superhero fiction.

Naturally, all the other major comics publishers wanted in on the new craze, with some even opening shop specifically in DC's wake. Chief among these rivals was Fawcett Comics, founded by William Fawcett in 1919 and originally bursting onto the scene with the ubiquitous magazine *Captain Billy's Whiz Bang*. Fawcett's *Whiz Comics* series, introduced in 1940, gave the world the wizard Shazam and his champion Captain Marvel, sometimes

DC: A National Concern

DC Comics was the first of the two giants of comic book publishing that would emerge during the Golden Age, the other being Marvel. It had a rather byzantine beginning back in the 1930s and 1940s and went through several name changes. Founded in the fall of 1934 by pulp magazine writer and publisher Malcolm Wheeler-Nicholson as National Allied Publications, the company was initially located at 423 4th Avenue (present-day Park Avenue South) in lower midtown Manhattan. It immediately made waves in the nascent comic book industry by becoming the first company to publish original material with *New Fun* #1 in February 1935, as opposed to reprints of newspaper comic strips.

But sales didn't immediately set the world on fire, and to settle his debts, Wheeler-Nicholson was forced to go into business with his distributor Harry Donenfeld to form a second company, Detective Comics Inc., which hit the ground running with the first issue of that same-titled comic in 1937. Just as the company began experiencing success with its new superhero concept, beginning with *Action Comics* #1 (Superman) and *Detective Comics* #27 (Batman), Wheeler-Nicholson found himself forced out in a political power struggle. By the mid-1940s, Detective Comics merged with National Allied, as well as a third affiliated company, Max Gaines's All-American Comics, to form National Periodical Publications in 1946. That would remain the company's corporate name for decades—nevertheless, it was already being casually referred to as "DC Comics" as a nod to its flagship title. But the name change didn't become official until the 1970s.

Although followed almost immediately by a myriad of competitors looking for the next hot trend, DC Comics deserves credit for innovating the concept of superheroes in comic book form. Although it might not have been fully appreciated at the time, it had just invented a new form of printed entertainment, and the superheroes that would initially lead that charge—including Superman, Batman, Wonder Woman, Aquaman, the Flash, Green Lantern, Green Arrow, Hawkman, the Atom, Black Canary, and others—would not only still be with us, but would live on stronger than their creators could have ever imagined.

seen as a Superman copycat, but whose adventures would begin to out-sell Superman's as the Golden Age wore on. Fawcett also created Ibis the Invincible, Spy Smasher, Bulletman and Bulletgirl, and other early superhe-roes. But everyone was getting into the act: Harvey Comics produced Black Cat; Gleason Publications featured the original Daredevil; Quality Comics had the extremely popular Plastic Man, and Will Eisner's highly influential character, The Spirit. There wasn't a major comics publisher of the era that wasn't trying their hand at men and women in tights.

Among the National/DC competitors that emerged during this era, the one with the most staying power would turn out to be Timely Comics, which eventually reinvented itself as Marvel Comics. Although characters like Miss America, the Human Torch, Whizzer, the Sub-Mariner, and the Blonde Phantom didn't quite have the same cultural impact in those days as Superman, Batman, and Wonder Woman, one Timely character from the World War II era, Captain America, struck a special chord with patri-otic readers, and was undoubtedly Timely's most beloved character of the Golden Age.

Superheroes, in general, were striking a chord with American readers. From the beginning, there can be no doubt that the target readership was young boys—and that target was decidedly reached. By the legions, boys across the country became enthralled with the exploits of their favorite char-acters, with early comic books becoming arguably the most popular reading material for boys under the age of eighteen. Adventure stories had always had a unique appeal with youngsters, but the superhero was something spe-cial—a figure that young kids could aspire to be, could live through vicar-iously as they socked it to bad guys of every stripe. For kids growing up in a time of war and uncertainty, their families struggling to emerge from the perils of the Depression, superheroes were a shining source of inspiration

Marvel: A Timely Arrival

Five years after the foundation of National/DC, on the other side of town at 330 West 42nd Street, another pulp publisher, Martin Goodman, also decided to get into the comic book business. His company would be called Timely Publications, soon incorporated as Timely Comics Inc. However, from the beginning, Goodman developed several subdivision imprints of Timely through which to publish his many titles, and one of these would eventually lend its name to the entire company when they rebranded a generation later: Marvel Comics.

Marvel Comics had also been the title of the very first comic book published by Timely in October 1939. Although like most comics publishers of the era, Timely put out a wide array of genres; from the beginning they were also trying to mimic the success National was having with its early superhero line. In addition to well-known creations like Captain America, the Sub-Mariner, and the original Human Torch, this also included characters like the Destroyer, the Whizzer, Miss America, and Golden Age versions of the Vision and the Angel. Goodman served as editor, managing editor, and business manager. At the end of 1939, he hired his wife's sixteen-year-old cousin Stanley Lieber as an office assistant. Before long, Lieber was writing comics under the pen name Stan Lee, and by 1941 Goodman had named him editor of Timely's entire comics line—a position he'd hold for decades to come, shaping the company's destiny in the process.

During the Golden Age of Comics, Timely was not really the cultural powerhouse that National/DC was, and realistically was a second-tier publisher in terms of popularity, behind companies like DC, Fawcett, Quality, and Dell Comics during that early era. By the start of the 1950s, with superheroes falling out of fashion, Goodman rebranded Timely as Atlas Comics, attempting to diversify into even more genres. It wasn't until the 1960s, with the superhero renaissance and the kick-off of the so-called Marvel Age, that the company became not just a contender, but an industry leader.

and excitement; powerful figures who weren't bound by social norms or the dreariness of everyday life. They were modern-day demigods.

Catering to children as it was, the style of these early superhero comics of the Golden Age were admittedly crude compared to what would come after. Stories were simplistic, artwork was dashed off in a hurry by artists who were often extremely young and inexperienced—and who would eventually discover that they had been taken advantage of by unscrupulous profiteering companies looking to exploit that inexperience. But it wasn't refined art and nuanced storytelling that led comic books to fly off shelves by the millions; readers wanted action, wonder, bright colors, and moralistic tales of good versus evil that were relatively easy to digest. And they got that in spades, with the popularity of comic book superheroes being sustained throughout the 1940s, even in the years beyond the war.

But unlike Superman, that popularity would not prove to be bulletproof. It did indeed wane as the 1940s drew to a close, and by the start of the 1950s, it seemed like the superhero craze would be just another entertainment fad, to enjoy its time and then move aside for the next big thing. Most of the major publishers began to phase out their superhero titles. DC retained only the most popular characters like Superman and Batman; Fawcett was completely swallowed up by DC due to a copyright infringement suit over Captain Marvel; Timely changed its name to Atlas Comics and shifted, as many publishers did, to other comic book subgenres like war, romance, science fiction, westerns, crime, and perhaps the most popular comic book genre of the 1950s, horror.

It appeared that the superhero had had his moment, and that moment was largely over. But the craze wasn't really over; it had just gone dormant for a little while. The concept of the superhero, and its ultimate distillation of social and cultural urgings, had touched on something primal and undeniable.

Keep 'Em Flying: Superheroes and World War II

It's worth noting that the famous *Captain America Comics* #1 featuring Cap on the cover punching out Hitler was published almost a year before the United States even got into World War II. Brewing for years as Americans looked on anxiously, that defining conflict of the twentieth century also provided a unifying force in American life. And that unifying force also applied to the comic book industry and its exploding superhero subgenre. In fact, one could even argue that the urgency of World War II, the terror of its Axis Power threats, and the patriotic fervor that was its inevitable by-product, helped sustain and amplify the very popularity of superheroes.

The popularity of superheroes derived from wish fulfillment, especially that of the disenfranchised. So it made sense that for Americans, especially American children, it would provide a needed catharsis in the face of the uncertainty of war. Superman was depicted bringing both Hitler and Stalin to justice in a special comic produced for *Look* magazine in 1940. Characters including Batman, Captain Marvel, the Sub-Mariner, Wonder Woman, and others all took time out from whatever bad guys they were battling to take on the Nazis, the Japanese, and even fifth-column saboteurs in America's midst. In addition to Captain America, other superpatriotic characters emerged, including Archie Comics' the Shield and Captain Flag; DC's Star-Spangled Kid, Liberty Belle, and Uncle Sam; and Fawcett's Spy Smasher. They often battled supervillain personifications of Axis evil, including the likes of Captain Nazi and the Red Skull.

Whether seen as simple patriotism or outright propaganda, superhero fiction helped galvanize the United States at a time when the country needed it most. Tapping into the zeitgeist as it always did, the comic book industry identified the threat overseas even before it became a direct threat and responded with a zeal that only increased when that threat became official. In the age of war bonds, victory gardens, and Rosie the Riveter, superheroes helped simultaneously allay American fears and unite citizens during trying times. Like they would do many other times over the years, they entertained and comforted the masses when they needed it most.

Collector's Items: Landmark Issues of the Golden Age

ACTION COMICS #1, JUNE 1938

Featuring the first appearance of Superman and credited with kicking off the Golden Age of superheroes, this issue is also considered the most valuable comic book ever published, with a near-mint copy going for $3.25 million in 2021.

DETECTIVE COMICS #27, MAY 1939

A detective-story comic anthology that had already been around for a couple of years by 1939, *Detective Comics* eventually put Batman on the map by debuting him with the story "The Case of the Chemical Syndicate."

SUPERMAN #1, SUMMER 1939

Rightfully, Superman, the first comic book superhero, was also the first hero to get his own self-titled comic book. It contained several stories featuring the Man of Steel, including his origin.

MARVEL COMICS #1, OCTOBER 1939

The very first comic book ever published by Timely Comics, the company that would later take its name from the title of this issue. Included were the first appearances of both the Golden Age Human Torch and Namor the Sub-Mariner.

FLASH COMICS #1, JANUARY 1940

Built around DC's next major superhero, this issue featured the debut of Jay Garrick, the Golden Age version of the Flash. As if that weren't enough, it also featured the first appearances of Hawkman and Johnny Thunder.

WHIZ COMICS #2, FEBRUARY 1940

Starting with this issue, Fawcett Comics brought forth the original Captain Marvel, a character that would at one point become the best-selling superhero of the Golden Age. It also featured the debut of his archenemy, Dr. Sivana.

BATMAN #1, MARCH 1940

After less than a year, Batman (now with Robin) was deemed popular enough to get his own self-titled comic book—the only superhero other than Superman to do so. This debut issue told his origin, plus featured the debuts of the Joker and Catwoman.

ALL-AMERICAN COMICS #16, JULY 1940

This issue featured the debut of DC's fourth major superhero, Green Lantern. This Golden Age version of the character, Alan Scott, differed from the more well-known Hal Jordan version that would emerge in the following decade.

CAPTAIN AMERICA COMICS #1, MARCH 1941

With its famous cover depicting its titular hero slugging Adolf Hitler, this comic gave us the debut of the most iconic hero of the Golden Age of the future Marvel Comics, as well as his faithful sidekick Bucky Barnes.

ALL STAR COMICS #8, DECEMBER 1941

The last of the major Golden Age superheroes to emerge, and the third member of DC's most famous trio, was Wonder Woman, who made her debut in this comic book.

It would go low profile for a few years, only to come back stronger, more innovative, more polished, and more profitable than ever before. The Golden Age may have ended by the early 1950s, but the Silver Age was about to dawn.

ICONS #4

The World's Mightiest Mortal

Creators: C. C. Beck, Bill Parker, and Pete Costanza

First Appearance: *Whiz Comics* #2, February 1940

Alter Ego: Billy Batson

Abilities: The wisdom of Solomon, the strength of Hercules, the stamina of Atlas, the power of Zeus, the invulnerability/courage of Achilles, the speed of Mercury

Archenemies: Dr. Thaddeus Sivana, Beautia Sivana, Black Adam, The Monster Society of Evil, Mr. Mind, the Crocodile Men, Captain Nazi, The Seven Deadly Enemies of Man, The Dummy, Mr. Who

Of all the great heroes of the Golden Age of Comics, the one who consistently doesn't get enough credit for his importance, influence, and popularity is the original **CAPTAIN MARVEL**, better known these days as Shazam. One of the most beloved characters of the 1940s, his name ranks right alongside that of Superman and Batman as far as the creations that helped establish the superhero genre and its conventions. In fact, for decades his very name was almost synonymous with the word "superhero," and his adventures have charmed generations of fans who look to him as the embodiment of a more innocent time. His name was even dropped in a Beatles song—as impressive a pop culture achievement as there is.

THE ORIGIN

Young orphan Billy Batson follows a mysterious stranger onto a supernatural subway train, which takes him to the magical Rock of Eternity, where the ancient wizard Shazam selects him as his champion, bestowing upon him the abilities of six legendary figures: Solomon, Hercules, Atlas, Zeus, Achilles, and Mercury, the first letters of whose names make up his own name. By saying the wizard's name aloud, Billy is transformed from a child into the fully grown Captain Marvel, the World's Mightiest Mortal. Dressed in his iconic red and gold uniform and flowing cape, he battles the mad scientist Dr. Sivana, the megalomaniacal, interdimensional worm Mr. Mind, the sinister Egyptian prince Black Adam (previous champion of Shazam turned to evil), and other outrageous villains.

THE CREATION

Seeing the success that National Comics was having with the brand-new Superman and Batman, publishing company Fawcett Publications decided to start up Fawcett Comics as direct competition and charged writer Bill Parker and artist C. C. Beck with creating a competing character. Initially conceptualizing a team of heroes each embodying a different mythological figure, they combined them all into one instead. Beck's assistant Pete Costanza offered his own contributions, including changing the character's name from Captain Thunder to Captain Marvelous (soon shortened).

Drawing more inspiration from comic strips than the crude comic books of the time, Beck's art was vibrant and colorful, and embraced a cartoonishness that made Captain Marvel comics a fun alternative right from the start.

SUPERMAN COPYCAT?

In an era when the concept of superheroes was new and there weren't many of them, some found Captain Marvel to be a Superman rip-off, with his union suit and cape, chest insignia, superstrength, and flying ability. National Comics (the future DC) thought so and was also troubled by Fawcett's Captain Marvel titles often outselling their Superman comic books. They took Fawcett to court over copyright infringement, and the legal battle raged from the early 1940s to the early 1950s. It looked like DC was going to win, and by that point, sales of superhero comics were on the decline anyway, so in 1953 Fawcett settled out of court with DC, paying $400,000 in damages, agreeing to cease all publication of Captain Marvel comics, and shuttering its comics division altogether.

CAPTAIN MARVEL VERSUS SHAZAM

There has long been confusion over the names Captain Marvel and Shazam. After Fawcett ceased publication, the copyright lapsed. In 1967, Marvel Comics introduced their own completely different Captain Marvel, establishing ownership of the name for marketing purposes. By the time DC Comics bought the rights to the original character in 1973 from Fawcett to revive him, they found they had lost the rights to use "Captain Marvel" as an official title. They could continue to use the name for the character, but any product titles would be named "Shazam!" Captain Marvel was absorbed into the DC Universe, but after decades of fans' mistakenly calling him "Shazam," plus the success of Marvel Comics' own Captain Marvel, DC finally gave up in 2012 and changed the character's name to Shazam.

THE MARVEL FAMILY

The original Captain Marvel was known for his colorful cast of supporting characters. There was disabled newsboy Freddie Freeman, who gains the power of Shazam and becomes the blue-suited Captain Marvel Jr.; and Billy Batson's older sister Mary, who becomes Mary Marvel. Fawcett even introduced the whimsical Hoppy the Marvel Bunny, a cartoon animal take on the mythos. A mischievous old man who originally passed himself off as Billy's Uncle Dudley became adopted as Uncle Marvel, an unofficial member of the team who only pretends to have powers and is humored by everyone else. And who can forget Tawky Tawny, the genteel talking anthropomorphic Bengal tiger known to make memorable appearances from time to time?

THE BIG RED CHEESE ON THE BIG SCREEN

Captain Marvel was the first comic book superhero to be adapted into other media, starring in *The Adventures of Captain Marvel*, a 1941 Republic Pictures serial featuring Tom Tyler, who would also later play the Phantom in a 1943 serial. Due to DC Comics' legal scuffle, Captain Marvel remained dormant on screen until the mid-1970s, when a live-action Saturday morning *Shazam!* TV series was produced by Filmation. In the early 1980s, the same company produced the animated Captain Marvel series, *The Kid Super Power Hour with Shazam!* He would later make several memorable appearances in other DC animated projects of the 2000s and 2010s. In 2019, a feature-length *Shazam!* motion picture finally came to fruition, memorably starring Zachary Levi. Its success led to the sequel *Shazam! Fury of the Gods*, released in March 2023.

CHAMPION OF THE ROCK OF ETERNITY

A warm and fuzzy Golden Age anachronism, Captain Marvel/Shazam has long retained a more fun, lighthearted, and magical tone that has helped the character and his world stand out in sharp relief to the often ultra-grim and sober superhero landscape of the modern era. He is in many ways the ultimate superhero in the traditional sense, always there with a wink and a smile to make sure we never take all this stuff too seriously. His 2019 movie continued this tradition by upholding the whimsical and childlike wonder and innocence of what Beck, Parker, and Costanza first envisioned all those years ago.

5

IN THE AIR AND ON THE AIR

Superheroes in Radio and Movie Serials

The test of the endurance and relevance of any major movement or concept in popular culture is its ability to transcend its original form; to leap from whatever medium birthed it and branch out into different media and forms of presentation. Does it have the staying power and appeal to move beyond its origins and take on a life of its own? This was most definitely the case with the new superhero genre that emerged in comic books during the Golden Age of the late 1930s and 1940s. Although it was in four-color format in the pages of those early comics that the iconic superheroes were first introduced to us, it didn't take long for them to be adapted into other configurations. Rather than dilute their power, it only added to their mythos, and made them more of a household name than ever.

In the case of superheroes, there were two specific forms of media, both of which were arguably at their very peak at the time, that benefited from these characters and gave them their first non-comics platform. One was radio, which was ubiquitous in the homes of most Americans by the 1930s.

The other was a unique cinematic form that was highly popular in pre-television days: the movie serial, which featured an ongoing story told in short chapters each week in theaters nationwide. Radio and the movie serials made characters like Superman, Batman, Captain Marvel, and Captain America, not to mention original characters like the Spider and The Shadow, known even to those who had never picked up a comic book in their lives. It was the beginning of the mass media superhero takeover.

TUNE IN NEXT TIME: ADVENTURE ON THE AIRWAVES

Unlike today, when the main reason people might turn on a radio is to listen to music, or perhaps the news, in its earliest years, radio was most known as a medium for telling stories. Television would eventually make the radio obsolete as a storytelling tool by adding a visual element to the mix and forcing radio programmers to focus on music instead. However, from the 1920s through the 1940s, radio was a way for stories to be broadcast directly into people's homes for the very first time. Just like sitting around a hearth, families would gather around that giant wood-encased frame of dials and vacuum tubes to listen to their favorite programs: dramas, situation comedies, crime sagas, horror, adventure, tales of science fiction, and romance. Just as comic books were having their Golden Age, so was radio.

Imagination was key when it came to radio shows. And being a genre that was already built around a healthy suspension of disbelief to begin with, the new superhero craze seemed a perfect fit for radio. Fantastical and colorful stories could be brought to life with a minimal budget. With a decent script, some voice actors, and a clever sound effects team, suddenly these characters lived and breathed like never before. They were already becoming enormously popular in illustrated form, and for radio networks and sponsors looking to attract an audience, they appealed due to their built-in following and name recognition. And besides, as with all adventure tales or stories of the fantastic, they seemed especially fit for exciting dramatization.

Even before comic book superheroes made their way to radio, listeners were first enthralled by the on-air adventures of two protosuperheroes who were created specifically *for* radio: the Green Hornet and The Shadow. In fact, the voice of "The Shadow" was heard as early as 1930 as the anonymous narrator of *Detective Story Hour*, a show produced in part by pulp publisher Street & Smith in support of its *Detective Story Magazine*. Listeners immediately took to the narrator, so much so that Street & Smith had one of its stable of writers, Walter Gibson, develop The Shadow as his own character for its line of pulp magazines the following year. In an ironic roundabout turn of events, *Detective Story Hour* eventually gave way to *The Shadow* radio program, produced by Street & Smith and its sponsor, Blue Coal, for the brand-new Mutual Broadcasting System, a radio network that would become known for its adventure series.

On September 26, 1937, the fleshed-out Shadow character took to the airwaves for the first time, voiced by noted radio producer and actor Orson Welles. Welles would continue to lend his distinctive tones to the character for the first year of the show before leaving to embark on a historic career in Hollywood. Margo Lane, the love interest of The Shadow's alter ego Lamont Cranston, would be voiced by actress Agnes Moorhead, at the time one of Welles's famed Mercury Players radio drama troupe. The show was hugely popular and ran for seventeen years, well into the heyday of 1950s television.

Although the Green Hornet character was introduced six years after the debut of *Detective Story Hour*, *The Green Hornet* debuted one year before The Shadow got his own show. Beginning on January 31, 1936, on local Detroit station WXYZ, *The Green Hornet* was soon being carried on Mutual as well, right alongside *The Shadow*. Another big hit, it ran until 1950 on a series of radio networks, jumping from Mutual to NBC and then ABC, and was briefly revived in 1952. *The Green Hornet* and *The Shadow* laid the groundwork for the popularity of superheroes on the radio, and ironically ran longer than any radio program featuring heroes drawn from comic books.

But when it came to superheroes crossing over from comic books to radio, it was quite fitting that the one who would be the originator, and become the most iconic, would be the first and most iconic comic book superhero of them all. Less than two years into his run in *Action Comics*, Superman received his first official adaptation when National Comics made a deal with New York City radio station WOR to adapt its star character into a syndicated radio series based on the success not only of the comic books but also the newspaper comic strip that had kicked off the previous year. The show debuted on February 12, 1940, and within two years was picked up by the Mutual network, which carried it for most of its incredible eleven-year run. Several times a week listeners across the country tuned into Superman's fifteen-minute adventures (expanding to thirty minutes in its final years), sponsored for most of that time by Kellogg's Pep cereal.

Accomplished radio actor Bud Collyer gained the distinction of being the first person to portray Superman in any form, his performance helping establish many of the accepted elements of the Man of Steel's character, including catchphrases like, "This looks like a job . . . for Superman!" and "Up, up, and away!" Collyer was also the first to change his intonation between mild-mannered Clark Kent and his superpowered alter ego—an approach that would become standard not just in portrayals of Superman, but of many other superheroes. Tremendously influential, *The Adventures of Superman* radio show contributed other original ideas that would later become canonical to the Superman mythos, including kryptonite and characters like *Daily Planet* editor-in-chief Perry White and photographer Jimmy Olsen. Both Collyer and Joan Alexander, the voices of Superman and Lois Lane, respectively, became so identified with their characters that they would eventually lend their voices when the property was first adapted into an animated series.

The opening of the show, which eventually included the immortal lines, "Faster than a speeding bullet, more powerful than a locomotive, able to leap tall buildings in a single bound—Look! Up in the sky! It's a bird! It's a plane! It's Superman!" would live on long after the show had run its course, becoming part of the very fabric of American pop culture. And in an episode from 1945, Superman would even be introduced—for the very first time anywhere—to Batman and Robin, National Comics' other superstar characters. (The Dynamic Duo would make several appearances on Superman's radio program but would ironically never receive a radio show of their own.) Usually airing in the late afternoon, *The Adventures of Superman* was a popular after-school listen for kids everywhere, contributing to the show's impressive longevity. In fact, the only reason it was canceled in 1951 was that plans had been put in place to turn it into a television series.

By the end of the 1940s, television was taking the country by storm. It was clear that the days of the radio drama were numbered. Nevertheless, superheroes remained highly successful with audiences and their shows stuck it out on the air until the bitter end. In fact, one of the last, *Planet Man*, combining superhero adventure with science fiction to tell the story of intergalactic alien law enforcement agent Dantro and his faithful band of Earthling astronauts, didn't appear until 1950. However, *Planet Man* didn't

More Memorable Crusaders of Radio

CAPTAIN MIDNIGHT

Extremely popular during the World War II era, with tales of aviation adventure and spy-busting, the show's titular hero was the leader of the Suicide Squadron, foiling espionage wherever they found it. Carried for most of its run on the Mutual network and sponsored by Ovaltine, the show ran from 1938 to 1949 and was adapted into comic books, movie serials, and even a 1950s TV show.

THE BLUE BEETLE

Fox Comics' leading superhero of the Golden Age was Dan Garret, son of a murdered police officer who wore a bulletproof costume and gained superstrength via a special vitamin. Debuting shortly after Superman, *Blue Beetle* was an early hit, and Fox sold the radio rights to CBS, where it was developed for radio in 1940. Despite the popularity of the character, the show only ran for five months.

MANDRAKE THE MAGICIAN

Airing from the same WOR studios as *The Adventures of Superman*, *Mandrake the Magician* brought to life Lee Falk and Phil Davis's mysterious comic strip sorcerer with thrice-weekly fifteen-minute broadcasts. The show ran from 1940 to 1942 and featured future legend of stage and screen Jessica Tandy in an early role as Princess Narda.

THE AVENGER

While not as popular as pulp icons like The Shadow and Doc Savage, the Avenger was a character who ran in Street & Smith publications from 1939 to 1943. He was first brought to radio on New York City station WHN (now the city's ESPN Radio affiliate) in 1941 for a series that lasted a year and a half, then brought back in 1945 for an even shorter run in national syndication.

even make it to 1951. The writing was on the wall—the 1950s was to be the era of TV. Nevertheless, the popularity of superheroes would ensure that they would eventually make the transition to that medium as well.

CAPERS AND CLIFFHANGERS: THE SUPERHERO SERIALS

While radio kept people entertained at home, the movies entertained people when they went out. And go out they did—before the advent of television, most Americans went to the movies at least once a week, and often more frequently than that. For this reason, the movies served much of the purpose that TV would later serve in that it provided a variety of entertainment options in one. Not only did you go to the movies at that time to see an actual feature film (or sometimes more than one in a single sitting), but most shows also included a newsreel, comedy and animated short subjects, contests, sing-alongs, and that precursor to the TV series, the serial drama. In short, going to the movies back then was something people made a day of, and they expected all the different options we've come to expect from our home viewing experience today.

Like many TV series today, the serial was produced as a series of chapters with a continuing story. They were usually made with a cheaper budget than most feature films, were shorter in length, and were distributed by studios to accompany the feature. Each week, a new episode would be released, and moviegoers would have to return to the theater over and over to see what would happen next. Known for their suspense, the format of the serial was usually best suited to adventure stories, and in fact the very word "cliffhanger" originated with the serials and their typical suspenseful ending (which would, on occasion, feature characters literally hanging from the edge of a cliff at the end of an episode).

Before they would ever appear in feature-length films, superheroes made their first on-screen appearances in movie serials. In a time when most escapist-themed entertainment like adventure, science fiction, and fantasy was deemed somewhat juvenile and not worth the big-budget feature treatment, swashbuckling costumed crimefighters were perfect material for the B-movie serial mill. Although often crude and silly, and sometimes woefully unfaithful to their source material compared to the screen adaptations that would come in later decades, the superhero serials provided hours of breathless entertainment for fans and allowed comic book readers to see their favorite heroes in action for the first time.

Although not a superhero in the strictest sense, no discussion of superhero serials would be complete without mention of *Flash Gordon*, the groundbreaking and smashingly successful series produced by Universal Pictures in 1936, which first brought space adventure to the silver screen and helped put fantasy/adventure serials on the map in a big way. Starring action icon Buster Crabbe as Gordon, the serial proved there was a big audience for this kind of hero-driven spectacle and provided a blueprint for how visually depicted adventures (in this case a newspaper comic strip) could lend themselves quite well to film adaptation. The original thirteen-episode *Flash Gordon* serial ran through the spring of 1936 and was a smash hit. Its massive popularity led to it being cut into feature film form later in the year, which was followed by two sequel series, *Flash Gordon's Trip to Mars* (1938) and *Flash Gordon Conquers the Universe* (1940). The success also led to the *Buck Rogers* serial, also starring Crabbe.

Studios had been flirting with science fiction material for their serials as far back as Universal's *The Vanishing Shadow* in 1934, but it was the hysteria

More Adventures on the Serial Screen

THE SPIDER'S WEB
This fifteen-part adaptation of the popular pulp magazine was the most successful serial of 1938, and even spawned a 1941 sequel, *The Spider Returns*, both from Columbia Pictures. The Spider's adventures were partly directed by James Horne, best known for his work with the likes of Buster Keaton and Laurel & Hardy.

MANDRAKE THE MAGICIAN
From comic strips to radio and finally to serials, Lee Falk and Phil Davis's creation was adapted into a twelve-part story for Columbia in 1939, as Mandrake and his assistant Lothar lock horns with the Wasp for possession of a dangerous radium energy weapon.

SPY SMASHER
After achieving success with Captain Marvel, Republic took on a second Fawcett Comics character for a twelve-part series in 1942. Spy Smasher's battles with secret Nazi agents were perfect material for World War II-era audiences, and the footage was even reedited into a TV movie some twenty-four years later with *Spy Smasher Returns*.

THE PHANTOM
The Ghost Who Walks made his way to the screen with this fifteen-part cliffhanger from Columbia, which ran from late 1943 into early 1944. With Tom Tyler trading in his Captain Marvel duds for the Phantom's bodysuit and mask, and the Hollywood hills standing in for the jungles of Africa, the serial came to be regarded as one of Columbia's best.

CAPTAIN AMERICA
Timely Comics, the future Marvel, landed its first-ever screen adaptation with this fifteen-parter from Republic in 1944. Decades before Chris Evans, Dick Purcell (who died suddenly several weeks after filming) donned the patriotic uniform, although he never got a chance to wield the iconic shield. In fact, few elements of Cap's comics mythos are to be seen here at all—no Nazis, no serum, no Bucky, and a totally different secret identity.

KING OF THE ROCKET MEN
One of the last of the major superhero serials, this 1949 inclusion from Republic featured Tristram Coffin as Jeff King, alias Rocket Man, who wears a jet pack, leather jacket, and bullet-shaped helmet to battle the forces of the evil Dr. Vulcan. This serial was a direct inspiration for the retro-themed *Rocketeer* comic of the 1980s and its 1991 film adaptation.

around the character of Flash Gordon that really opened the floodgates. In 1940, the same year as the final *Flash Gordon* serial, the Green Hornet and The Shadow, two heroes from radio and pulp novels, made their way into chapter movie form with Universal and Columbia Pictures, respectively. *The Green Hornet* even saw legendary actor Keye Luke in one of his first screen appearances as the Hornet's sidekick Kato—a role that would later be played on television by a young Bruce Lee.

As the 1940s began, the stage was set for the new wave of comic book superheroes to leap to the serial screen. And it just goes to show the enormous popularity of Fawcett Comics' red-and-gold suited dynamo that the first comic book superhero to be portrayed on the silver screen was the original Captain Marvel (aka Shazam), not Superman or Batman. The World's Mightiest Mortal was played by popular stuntman/actor Tom Tyler (also known for playing the immortal Kharis in several of Universal's *Mummy* films) in the twelve-part series *The Adventures of Captain Marvel*, released by B-movie powerhouse Republic Pictures in the spring of 1941. Republic's serial tinkered a bit with the Shazam mythos, but with a decent budget, the result was what is often considered the best of all the superhero serials, as Captain Marvel matches wits with an original villain, the Scorpion.

Although Captain Marvel was indeed beloved by comic book readers of the 1940s, the fact is that Republic would've jumped at the chance to do a Superman serial but were prevented from doing so because Paramount Pictures then owned the exclusive license for screen adaptations of the Man of Steel, stemming from their beloved series of animated shorts then in production. Perhaps this is also why it was the Caped Crusader who preceded Superman to the silver screen as National/DC's first character to be adapted. Before Robert Pattinson, Ben Affleck, Christian Bale, George Clooney, Val Kilmer, Michael Keaton, and even Adam West, *The Batman* introduced Lewis Wilson as the first actor to take on the cape and cowl. Produced in 1943 by Columbia during the depths of World War II, the fifteen-chapter serial sees Batman and Robin (played by Douglas Croft), acting as secret US government agents, taking on Japanese saboteurs, led by the sinister Dr. Daka.

Despite the baggy batsuit, floppy ears, and Robin's dime-store domino mask, the low-budget serial was a hit, and even introduced permanent pieces of Batman lore, including the Batcave, and remade Bruce's butler Alfred Pennyworth from short and chubby to tall and thin, to better resemble the actor who played him, William Austin. It was followed in 1949 with a sequel series, *Batman and Robin*, with new actors Robert Lowery and Johnny Duncan replacing Wilson and Croft as the Dynamic Duo. The first comic book superhero film adaptation to get a sequel, *The Batman* even received a rerelease in 1965, and its unintentional camp is credited with partially inspiring the parodic *Batman* TV series, which followed in 1966.

But just before the second Batman serial was released, legal rights issues were finally sorted out regarding the most coveted comic book superhero property of all. Once Paramount ceased production on its acclaimed animated Superman short films, veteran serial and B-movie producer Sam Katzman was able to finally land the screen rights to the Man of Steel and brokered a deal with Columbia Pictures, his usual studio partner, to produce *Superman*, a fifteen-part serial that marked the first live-action appearance of the Last Son of Krypton. Unknown actor Kirk Alyn would star in the enviable position as the first on-screen Superman, which would make his career. Noel Neill, who played Lois Lane, was so memorable in her part that she would return to the role when Superman was adapted for TV in the 1950s. Former *Our Gang* child star Tommy Bond served as Superman's pal Jimmy Olsen.

Superman kicks off with a dramatization of the character's origins on the doomed planet Krypton and as Clark Kent, adopted son of human foster parents. Once he makes his way to Metropolis and goes to work for the *Daily Planet*, he crosses paths with another villain cooked up especially for the movies, the diabolical Spider Lady. Although highly popular, the series is also marked by Katzman's notorious cheapness, with all flying Superman sequences being achieved through animation that is often shoddily blended with live action. This trend continued in the 1950 sequel serial, *Atom Man vs. Superman*, in which audiences learned that the so-called Atom Man was Superman's archnemesis Lex Luthor, portrayed on screen for the first time by actor Lyle Talbot (who had also played Commissioner Gordon in the Batman serials). Despite their low budgets, the Superman serials were fondly remembered—so much so that both Alyn and Neill received a clever cameo appearance thirty years later as the parents of a young Lois Lane in Richard Donner's *Superman: The Movie* (1978).

But it was very telling that by the time the rights to adapt Superman became available in the late 1940s, it had become more difficult to get studios interested in taking on the project, with Republic and Universal among the companies that passed on it. This was largely because by then, most studios were getting out of the serial business. Television had arrived in a big way, bringing daily and weekly episodic video programming directly into people's homes, and the very concept of the movie theater serial was fast becoming obsolete. The serials had introduced large audiences to the magic of superheroes, but in the decades immediately following, it would be on the small screen that they would find their new home. And when they finally returned to the big screen many years later, it would be in a more ambitious and impressive way than anything that had been attempted before.

The Fleischer Superman: An Animation Landmark

Although it was neither a radio drama nor a live-action serial, no discussion of multimedia superhero adaptations of this era would be complete without remembering the incredible series of seventeen animated theatrical short subjects distributed by Paramount Pictures between the fall of 1941 and the summer of 1943. With their amazingly high standard of quality, these shorts were among the finest products of the Golden Age of American movie studio animation, and a strong influence on later animated superhero projects like Bruce Timm and Paul Dini's *Batman: The Animated Series* of the 1990s, and other related series that followed. The first animated superhero adaptation of any kind, the series is still often cited as the best.

Initially produced for Paramount by the Fleischer animation studio headed by brothers Max and Dave Fleischer, also celebrated for their Betty Boop and Popeye shorts of the 1930s, from their first episode, the films stand out due to their large budget—reported as $50,000 per seven-minute film. The early installments often feature the Man of Steel—voiced by Bud Collyer of the popular and concurrent *Superman* radio series—battling monsters, giant robots, mad scientists, and other wild science-fiction elements that further emphasize the impressive draftsmanship and animation style. After ousting the Fleischers in late 1942, Paramount took over production, and these later entries tend to focus more on Superman's struggles with Nazis, saboteurs, and other wartime adversaries. Budgets also began to shrink, and the plug was eventually pulled by the middle of the following year as a cost-cutting measure.

This revolutionary animated series, originally seen on the big screen in all its full-color glory, marked the first time Superman was ever depicted as flying (the character originally leapt long distances instead), which would remain a permanent part of his powers. Its opening sequence and bombastic musical theme would set a standard that influenced other incarnations of the character on screen in both live action and animation. A high watermark of superhero adaptation and animation to this day, the Fleischer Superman shorts stand as one of the most remarkable translations of comic book characters to appear on the big screen.

ICONS #5

In Brightest Day, in Blackest Night

Creators: Martin Nodell and Bill Finger (Golden Age); John Broome and Gil Kane (Silver Age); Dennis O'Neil and Neal Adams (Bronze Age); Ron Marz and Darryl Banks (Modern Age)

First Appearance: *All-American Comics* #16, July 1940; *Showcase* #22, October 1959; *Green Lantern* #87, December 1971; *Green Lantern* (vol. 3) #48, January 1994

Alter Egos: Alan Scott, Hal Jordan, John Stewart, Kyle Rayner

Powers: derived from a green power ring that allows the wearer to fly, and to transform green energy into physical objects and constructs through force of will. Alan Scott's original ring also gave him power to shrink objects and turn them invisible. Later Green Lantern Corps members can travel at immense speeds through space and survive in almost any environment.

Archenemies: Sinestro, Hector Hammond, Vandal Savage, Solomon Grundy, Parallax, Atrocitus, Krona, the Manhunters, Mongul, Volthoom

From a mystical protector to an interstellar enforcer, **GREEN LANTERN** has changed quite a bit over the years, but one thing has remained constant, and that is his mission to defend the innocent and defeat wrongdoers through the power of his will, aided by a very special ring. Like several characters in the DC Universe, most notably the Flash, there have been a few important versions through different eras, with the most well-known and longest running being Hal Jordan, the Silver Age champion who perhaps best embodies his heroic characteristics. But no matter the person who wears the ring, as his unforgettable oath goes, no evil shall escape his sight.

A RING OF MAGIC

Using the pen name Mart Dellon, illustrator Martin Nodell joined with Batman co-creator Bill Finger to develop the next in All-American/National/DC's line of successful superheroes of the 1940s. In the origin story, railroad engineer Alan Scott discovers a magic green lantern from which he constructs a ring that gives him magical powers that can affect anything not made of wood. The ring must be charged every twenty-four hours. After his first appearance in 1940, Green Lantern appeared in comic books throughout the Golden Age, until, like other characters, he went dormant in 1951. Although the Alan Scott Green Lantern was later returned to action, he remained a secondary character after the total revamping of the Green Lantern concept in the 1950s.

ENTER THE GREEN LANTERN CORPS

Entrusted with reinventing Green Lantern for DC's second wave of superheroes in 1959, it was writer John Broome and artist Gil Kane—whose artwork came to be closely associated with the Silver Age incarnation of the character—that reimagined him not as a being of magic, but rather of science fiction. Fighter pilot Hal Jordan discovers the downed spaceship of Abin Sur, a member of an intergalactic police force who, with his dying breath, recruits Jordan to replace him and become the official Green Lantern Corps member assigned to Earth. With a totally new costume and an appearance inspired by actor Paul Newman, he became the most enduring iteration of the character, and a central member of the Justice League.

AN EXPANDING ROLE

Because the Green Lantern Corps was envisioned as a sprawling team of beings from various planets, commanded by the all-knowing Guardians of the Universe on Planet Oa, the Green Lantern mantle became more of a symbol, and not just assigned to one character. New Lanterns would eventually be introduced, including Guy Gardner, who was selected as Jordan's backup and first appeared in the late 1960s. And when Jordan stepped away from the role for a time during the 1970s Bronze Age period, it was John Stewart, the first African American Green Lantern and a creation of revolutionary comics creators Denny O'Neil and Neal Adams, who filled his spot. Stewart would continue to play an important role in the Green Lantern mythos over the years.

POST-PARALLAX

Like Barry Allen, who was killed off as the Flash in the 1980s, Hal Jordan also met his end in the 1990s when he seemingly lost his mind after the destruction of his hometown of Coast City and merged with the maniacal entity known as Parallax. After Jordan sacrificed himself to save the earth in an act of redemption, it was a new human, Kyle Rayner, who assumed the role for several years of Earth's Green Lantern. Jordan would eventually escape the influence of Parallax and return to his Green Lantern role, but several other human Lanterns have emerged in recent years, including Simon Baz, Jessica Cruz, and Sojourner Mullein.

RINGS OF MANY COLORS

The Green Lantern concept evolved and came to include other kinds of Lanterns. While the green rings were determined to draw their power from the will of their users, it was determined that the yellow power ring of Sinestro, a disgraced former Green Lantern, drew its power from fear. After the acclaimed *Sinestro Corps War* of 2007, in which Sinestro forms a team of evil Yellow Lanterns, many other colors were introduced, mainly by writer Geoff Johns and artists Ethan Van Sciver and Ivan Reis during another crossover event, *Blackest Night*. Each team member was powered by different emotions or properties, such as the Red Lantern (rage), Blue Lantern (hope), Orange Lantern (greed), Indigo Lantern (compassion), White Lantern (life), and even Black Lantern, consisting of reanimated dead superheroes.

THE LANTERN'S FLICKERS

Green Lantern hasn't been represented in other media quite as often as his fellow major DC characters. He's mainly been seen in animated form, beginning in the 1960s with *The Superman/Aquaman Adventure Hour* and in the 1970s with the *Super Friends* (both of which featured Hal Jordan), and later in the 2000s *Justice League* series (featuring John Stewart). A feature film was produced in 2011 starring Ryan Reynolds as Jordan but was a commercial and critical disappointment. Zack Snyder planned to include Green Lantern in his 2017 *Justice League* film, but creative differences with the studio prevented it. As of this writing, the first live-action Green Lantern TV series is in the works for HBO Max for 2024.

THE GREEN GUARDIAN

"Let those who worship evil's might, beware my power—Green Lantern's light!" So concludes the oath that has united the Green Lantern mythos going all the way back to Alan Scott in the 1940s. The nature and look of the character may change, as may the wearers of the ring, but what remains is a hero of epic proportions, whose abilities are limited only by his own imagination. What a perfect metaphor for the very idea of superheroes and the work of those many creative individuals who have been responsible for bringing them to life.

6

SILVER AGE

The Marvel Renaissance and Beyond

As universally appealing as superheroes seem today, it was not always so. The first half of the 1950s was an all-time low point in the popularity of caped and cowled crimefighters and do-gooders. The glory days of the 1940s Golden Age were long gone, and it appeared that the appeal of superheroes had all been a fad, like the jitterbug, zoot suits, and pea shooters. There were a few exceptions, like DC icons Superman, Batman, and Wonder Woman, whose comic books continued to be printed—not to mention the successful *Adventures of Superman* early TV series starring George Reeves—but except for those transcendent characters, superheroes had simply fallen out of fashion, as dwindling sales of their comic books attest. Readers had tired of the concept and moved on to other stuff.

Thankfully, this turned out not to be the death of superheroes—just their dormancy, which didn't last long. In just a handful of years, a whole new era, a second explosion of interest in costumed crusaders would take hold, and this time it would stick. With a combination of reinvention of the old, as in the case of stalwart National/DC Comics, and the creation of entirely fresh and new ideas, in the case of the newly rebranded Marvel Comics, it was a time that revitalized the industry and came to be known as the "Silver Age of Comics." In many ways more exciting, more vibrant, and more creative than what had come before, the heroes of this era really struck a chord with the public, and its effects continue to be felt to this day. Perhaps never before was there such a productive age in the history of superheroes.

In the wake of the decline of superhero comics, comic book publishers had turned to other genres to spark readers' interests. Among them were war comics, romance comics, western comics, science fiction comics, and perhaps the most popular genre of all—horror comics, as epitomized by *Tales from the Crypt*, *The Vault of Horror*, and other titles put out by EC Comics, the company spearheaded by former DC honcho William Gaines. The industry's reputation was also taking a hit, having long been linked to juvenile delinquency. This link was further strengthened by the landmark 1954 book *Seduction of the Innocent* by German psychiatrist Fredric Wertham, in which the author made his case for how comic books warped the minds of the young. Wertham condemned the popular horror comics of the day, and even took aim at superheroes, pointing out what he saw as sexual deviancy in characters like Wonder Woman, as well as Batman and Robin, whom he identified as implied homosexuals.

Wertham's findings led to Senate investigations opened by Estes Kefauver, the same Tennessee senator who had famously gone after organized crime, to explore comic books' connection to the corruption of children. The industry went into damage control mode. Much like the motion picture business had done twenty years earlier, in 1954 the comics business decided to self-regulate with the establishment of the Comics Code Authority, which would clamp down on supposedly objectionable content.

Second Wave: DC Heroes of the 1950s and 1960s

THE ATOM

A complete reinvention of his original Golden Age incarnation, the new Atom was the creation of editor Julius Schwartz, writer Gardner Fox, and artist Gil Kane. First appearing in October 1961 in the pages of *Showcase* comics, Ray Palmer is a physicist who learns how to shrink himself to any size, even to a subatomic level. This allows him to travel on air currents and along electrical wiring while also retaining the ability to strike objects with the force of a normal-sized man.

AQUAMAN

One of the very few characters to remain in publication from the Golden Age into the Silver Age, Aquaman retained some elements of his 1940s version. Beginning in *Adventure Comics* #260 in May 1959, he was established as Arthur Curry, the son of a human lighthouse keeper and an exile from the undersea kingdom of Atlantis. His new powers included superstrength, the ability to breathe underwater, and the expansion of his aquatic telepathy.

BATGIRL

Although there were a few attempts to create a female counterpart to Batman and/or Robin in the 1950s and early 1960s, the one that stuck was Barbara Gordon, the daughter of Gotham City police commissioner Jim Gordon. She takes on a similar bat-inspired persona to fight crime, her secret identity unknown even to her father and the Dynamic Duo. Conceptualized by Julius Schwartz and artist Carmine Infantino, she was partly created at the request of the runners of the 1960s *Batman* TV series.

ELONGATED MAN

Unaware that DC had acquired the rights to Quality Comics' Plastic Man in 1956, in 1960 Julius Schwartz greenlit the creation of a new elastic superhero by Carmine Infantino and writer John Broome. Originally a supporting character for the Flash, he first appeared in *The Flash* #112. A private detective by trade, Ralph Dibney uses his stretching powers to solve mysteries along with his faithful wife, Sue. He'd later become a member of the Justice League of America.

KID FLASH

Introduced in *The Flash* #110 in December 1959 by Infantino and Broome, Wally West was one of the many sidekicks created in the Silver Age, such as Speedy (Green Arrow), Aqualad (Aquaman), and Wonder Girl (Wonder Woman), to try to replicate the chemistry of Batman and Robin. Of particular significance is that after the Silver Age's Flash Barry Allen was killed off in 1985, West graduated from Kid Flash to the new Flash, a role he filled for twenty-five years until Allen returned.

HAWKMAN

Totally revamped for a new readership, the new Hawkman was no longer human archaeologist Carter Hall, but rather alien police officer Katar Hol from the planet Thanagar. First appearing in *The Brave and the Bold* #34 in 1961, Hol and his wife, Shayera (aka Hawkgirl), the creations of Gardner Fox and artist Joe Kubert, come to Earth in pursuit of a criminal and decide to stay, using their flight suits and antigravity belts to fight crime alongside US authorities.

LEGION OF SUPER HEROES

Intended originally as a one-shot Superboy story in *Adventure Comics* #247 (April 1958), this group of aspiring young superheroes from the thirtieth century proved so popular they became a regular fixture of Silver Age DC and beyond. Comprising Lightning Lad, Saturn Girl, Cosmic Boy, Brainiac 5, and a host of other futuristic members, the team was the creation of Otto Binder and Al Plastino.

MARTIAN MANHUNTER

Stranded on Earth by an experimental teleportation beam, green-skinned Martian detective J'onn Jonzz disguises himself as John Jones. Able to shapeshift into human form, he possesses a wide range of powers that make him one of DC's most powerful characters. He was also a founding member of the Justice League along with DC's heavy hitters like Superman and Batman, and it was in fact in the pages of *Detective Comics* that he first appeared in 1955, the creation of Joseph Samachson and Joe Certa.

METAMORPHO

Originally created by Bob Haney and Ramona Fradon as a parody of fanciful 1960s superheroes, shortly after his first appearance in *The Brave and the Bold* #57 (1965) he became a legitimate part of the DC pantheon, at times a member of the Outsiders and the Justice League. Exposed to a radioactive meteorite, professional adventurer Rex Mason gains the ability to metamorphosize into any element found in the human body.

SUPERGIRL

Born in Argo City, a Kryptonian enclave that had survived the explosion of the planet Krypton, Kara Zor-El was sent to Earth by her parents when the city's survival in space became untenable. She was specifically sent there due to the presence of her cousin Kal-El, aka Superman. First appearing in *Action Comics* #252 in 1959, she was the creation of Al Plastino and Otto Binder, who had also created Captain Marvel's female counterpart, Mary Marvel, back in the 1940s.

TEEN TITANS

In 1964, Bob Haney and Bruno Premiani developed a junior group of heroes for the pages of *The Brave and the Bold* as a nod to the growing youth culture. They were envisioned as a teaming of the various young sidekicks of DC Comics, including Robin, Kid Flash, Aqualad, and Wonder Girl. They soon got their own comic book, and later included members such as Speedy, Lilith Clay, Mal Duncan, Beast Boy, and super duo Hawk & Dove.

ZATANNA

The daughter of Golden Age character Zatara, who had appeared as a side story back in *Action Comics* #1, like her father she is a stage magician who also happens to possess actual magic powers. Created by Gardner Fox and Murphy Anderson and first appearing in *Hawkman* #4 in November 1964, she is known for her magical incantations consisting of speaking backward in English.

A shift away from horror, westerns, war, and other edgy material began to take place, and ironically, the genre that was reevaluated was superheroes, which was deemed more wholesome, kid-friendly, and relatively harmless.

Leading the way, as they had done in a previous generation, was National Periodicals, colloquially known as DC Comics. Under the guidance of chief editor Julius Schwartz, it was decided that some of the company's classic characters from the 1940s could be reinvented for a new generation of readers. This began in 1956 with the Flash, who was given an entirely new identity, origin, costume, and amped up powers. In fact, the first appearance of the new Flash, Barry Allen, in *Showcase* #4, is regarded as the official start of the Silver Age. Others soon followed, like Green Lantern, Hawkman, and Atom. Unlike their more mystical predecessors, these new versions were inspired by the science fiction craze then sweeping popular culture. Joining the still-present Superman, Batman, Wonder Woman, and Aquaman, they even combined forces in a new reinvention of the Justice Society of America, rechristened the Justice League of America.

Eventually, it would be explained that the earlier versions of the characters—along with the 1940s versions of Superman, Batman, Wonder Woman, etc.—existed in an alternate reality that came to be known as "Earth-2." These realities would even come into contact with one another, and several other "Earths" would be introduced with other pantheons of superheroes. This would start rather innocently, but over time grow into a complex and somewhat confusing web of continuity—a situation DC would one day have to address and simplify.

As the 1950s closed, superheroes were back front and center in the reading habits of kids across America. And yet, they still seemed very much the domain of children only, as evidenced by DC's emphasis on whimsical, often goofy story lines and characters who, for all their color, were more two-dimensional

A New Breed: Marvel Heroes of the 1960s

The "Marvel Age" helped redefine superheroes. Along with heroes like Spider-Man, Hulk, Thor, Iron Man, Black Panther, and the X-Men, other landmark Silver Age creations included:

ANT-MAN

Scientist Hank Pym uses the newly discovered "Pym particles" to shrink himself to ant size while retaining normal human strength. His special helmet also grants him the power to control ants while in his shrunken state. A founding member of Marvel's Avengers, Ant-Man was one of the many creations of Stan Lee and Jack Kirby (in this case with Lee's brother Larry Lieber), first appearing in *Tales to Astonish* #35 in 1962. Pym later took on other superpersonas like Giant-Man, Goliath, and Yellowjacket.

BLACK WIDOW

When she first appeared in *Tales of Suspense* #52 in April 1964, Natasha Romanova was a Soviet spy working against Iron Man. However, she soon defected to the United States and became a member of the secret American spy agency known as SHIELD. Stan Lee and regular Iron Man artist Don Heck created her, along with scripter Don Rico. She would go on to become a member of the Avengers.

CAPTAIN MARVEL

Due to complicated copyright issues, Marvel Comics was able to create its own Captain Marvel, copyrighting the name originally given to Fawcett Comics' Golden Age superhero in the 1940s. This version, introduced in 1967 by Roy Thomas and Gene Colan, was alien military officer Mar-Vell of the Kree Empire. The character died of cancer in 1982's *The Death of Captain Marvel*, generally considered the first graphic novel. Later Captain Marvels followed, including current captain Carol Danvers.

DAREDEVIL

Doused by radioactive waste in a childhood accident that took away his sight but enhanced his remaining senses to superhuman levels, Matt Murdock adopts the mantle of Daredevil, the Man Without Fear, protecting the rough streets of New York's Hell's Kitchen by night while working as a crusading lawyer by day. Marvel introduced him in his own self-titled comic book in April 1964, the brainchild of Stan Lee along with Sub-Mariner creator Bill Everett.

DOCTOR STRANGE

Marvel's Sorcerer Supreme battles supernatural threats from his Sanctum Sanctorum in New York's Greenwich Village. The creation of Stan Lee and Steve Ditko—the same duo responsible for Spider-Man—Stephen Strange is a former surgeon who loses his abilities due to a car crash and reinvents himself as Master of the Mystic Arts. Inspired by 1930s radio drama *Chandu the Magician*, he first appeared in *Strange Tales* #110 in July 1963.

THE FALCON

One of the first African American superheroes, Falcon was created by Stan Lee and Gene Colan as a supporting character for Captain America, and first appeared in *Captain America* #117 in September 1969. Originally trained by Cap to help free the enslaved natives of Exile Island, social worker Sam Wilson becomes an expert fighter, and with the help of Black Panther, builds a winged harness that allows him to fly. Cap's longtime crime-fighting partner Wilson eventually took over the Captain America mantle himself.

HAWKEYE

The orphaned Clint Barton became a master archer while training as a circus performer but was later inspired by Iron Man to use his skills to fight crime and took on the persona of Hawkeye. Although first introduced by Stan Lee and Don Heck in *Tales of Suspense* #57 (September 1964) as an enemy of Iron Man's, Hawkeye soon became one of the good guys, and an early member of the Avengers in good standing.

QUICKSILVER

The son of mutant archvillain Magneto and twin brother of the Scarlet Witch, Pietro Maximoff was born with the ability to move at superhuman speeds. He first appeared in *X-Men* #4 in March 1964 as an evil mutant and supervillain, but eventually changed his ways and has frequently teamed with both the X-Men and the Avengers. Stan Lee and Jack Kirby created the character, as they did all the early X-Men characters.

THE SCARLET WITCH

First appearing alongside her brother, Pietro, in *X-Men* #4, Wanda Maximoff possesses powers that have increased over time. At first, her mutant abilities allowed her to "alter probability," thereby generating "bad luck" for her enemies, but this later grew to an ability to alter reality itself, making her one of the Marvel Universe's most powerful mutants. She has long been a cornerstone of the Avengers, both alongside her brother and her great love, the Vision.

THE SILVER SURFER

In an effort to save his home world from the planet-eating titan Galactus, astronomer Norrin Radd agrees to become the herald of the world eater, soaring the cosmos on the silver board crafted for him by Galactus, coated in an impenetrable silver skin. After aiding the Fantastic Four in protecting Earth from Galactus's hunger in *Fantastic Four* #48 (March 1966), the Surfer is banished from Galactus's service and confined to Earth for many years. The Surfer was the creation of original *Fantastic Four* artist Jack Kirby.

THE VISION

Loosely based on a 1940s Timely Comics character of the same name, the new Vision was created by Roy Thomas and John Buscema. He was an android built by the evil robot Ultron to help him destroy the Avengers but eventually turns on his maker and winds up becoming a regular member of the team. First appearing in *Avengers* #57 in October 1968, the Vision is a completely synthetic human with the ability to phase through matter as one of his several powers.

THE WASP

The longtime partner of Hank Pym, Janet van Dyne uses his "Pym particles" to also shrink herself to tiny size, initially enlisting him to help avenge the murder of her father. In addition to shrinking, she also gains insectoid wings that allow her to fly, and the ability to zap enemies with bioenergy blasts. Created by Stan Lee, Jack Kirby, and Ernie Hart in 1963, she first appeared in *Tales to Astonish* #44, and was a founding member (and eventual leader) of the Avengers.

archetypes than actual people. This was the era of Krypto the Superdog, the Justice League fighting a giant alien starfish, Batman turning into a baby, and other silly shenanigans. The comic books were vibrant, imaginative, fun, and popular, but there was certainly room for innovation, new ideas, and a fresh approach to superheroes, not to mention their audience.

This innovation would come from a company across town that had been a somewhat lesser competitor of National back in the 1940s, when it was known as Timely Comics. By the start of the Silver Age, it was called Atlas Comics, but at the beginning of the 1960s, publisher Martin Goodman changed the name to Marvel Comics, in a nod to the name of the first issue published back in 1940. With the name change came a shift in strategy, as the company hurled itself headlong into the superhero space in an attempt to outdo DC. Stanley Lieber, aka Stan Lee, who had already been in charge of editorial for years, was tasked with creating a whole slew of costumed heroes for Marvel Comics, and he would be joined in that endeavor by such talented stable artists as Don Heck, Steve Ditko, but most importantly, a fellow streetwise New Yorker and a World War II vet by the name of Jack Kirby, who had had some experience with the company working on Captain America in the 1940s.

Kirby's bold, expressive style of illustration, with its explosive kinetic energy, came to epitomize the Silver Age of Comics, and was the perfect vehicle for this new breed of superhero. It started in 1961 with a team he and Lee created as a response to the Justice League. But their creation, the Fantastic Four, couldn't have been more different. For one thing, their powers were often more of a curse than a blessing, particularly in the case of Ben Grimm, mutated into the fearsome Thing. They also bickered constantly and lived not in some imagined metropolis but in New York City. This was the beginning of the Marvel approach to superheroics: characters who dealt with real problems, who acted more like real people, and who seemed to live in the real world. The trend continued with other Lee/Kirby creations like the X-Men, Black Panther, the Hulk, Iron Man, and most notably the Lee/Ditko character named Spider-Man, whose daily banal life struggles as unpopular high school science nerd Peter Parker were more grounded than anything before seen in the pages of superhero comics. These characters couldn't have been more different than their more staid, conservative counterparts at DC. In short, the Marvel Age had arrived.

It was a period of breathtaking creativity, which gave rise to characters that remain the backbone of the superhero pantheon to this day. DC, forced to respond to the hot new competition, worked to make their characters more relatable as well, and to tackle reality-based social and cultural issues the way Marvel was doing. In fact, the comics of the 1960s became very popular with the burgeoning counterculture of the era. For the first time, superheroes gained popularity not just among children, but young adults as well. In so many ways, even as superheroes have migrated from the printed page to the silver screen, their exploits and cast of characters remain rooted in the accomplishments of the Silver Age. That migration really began in earnest in the 1960s, as superheroes started to infiltrate the small screen with the first real boom in live action and animated superhero TV series.

In the end, the true legacy of the Silver Age was in those young readers whose imaginations were being ignited by what they were reading. A whole generation of young baby boomers grew up with those comics, and some of them wanted to do more than just read them. They would go on to become the next generation of comics creators, who would take the medium and its icons in directions previously unimagined. The maturity and sophistication of the art form was at hand, and it was in this crucial period that comic book superheroes became permanently burned into the very fiber of our culture.

Collector's Items: Landmark Issues of the Silver Age

SHOWCASE #4, OCTOBER 1956

The comic book that kicked off the Silver Age, this issue introduced a new version of the Flash. This was the start of DC reinventing several of its Golden Age characters and sparking a new superhero craze in comics.

SHOWCASE #22, SEPTEMBER 1959

Just as they'd done with the Flash three years earlier, DC reimagined another Golden Age character, Green Lantern. This time he was Hal Jordan, who gains a power ring and joins an interstellar police force.

BRAVE AND THE BOLD #28, MARCH 1960

DC introduces the Justice League of America, a team then composed of Superman, Batman, Wonder Woman, Aquaman, the Flash, Green Lantern, and Martian Manhunter, who join forces to battle the evil menace of Starro the Conqueror.

FANTASTIC FOUR #1, NOVEMBER 1961

Although the company had been around for years, the "Marvel Age of Comics" begins here with the introduction of the company's new team of superheroes and a new focus on superhero comics.

THE INCREDIBLE HULK #1, MAY 1962

Taking inspiration from Mary Shelley's Frankenstein, Stan Lee and Jack Kirby give us Dr. Bruce Banner, a weak and insecure nuclear scientist who becomes a mighty mass of rage and muscle when doused with gamma radiation.

AMAZING FANTASY #15, AUGUST 1962

A holdover series from Marvel's earlier specialty in science fiction and horror comics, this issue introduced the Amazing Spider-Man, who soon became their most popular character. In 2021, a copy sold for a record-setting $3.6 million.

JOURNEY INTO MYSTERY #83, AUGUST 1962

"Thor the Mighty and the Stone Men from Saturn" was intended as just another fantasy story in an anthology series dating back to the mid-1950s. But Marvel's interpretation of the Norse god was so popular he became an ongoing character.

TALES OF SUSPENSE #39, MARCH 1963

This comic book of mystery and adventure stories produced the memorable tale of Tony Stark, the wealthy industrialist who becomes the Invincible Iron Man, another in Marvel's ongoing parade of iconic characters during this period.

X-MEN #1, SEPTEMBER 1963

Professor Xavier's team of mutant teenagers represented a ground-breaking concept in superheroes, and its original grouping of Cyclops, Marvel Girl, Iceman, Beast, and Angel made its first appearance in this issue.

AVENGERS #4, MARCH 1964

Marvel's greatest Golden Age hero, Captain America, is thawed from years of icy hibernation to join the superteam of the Avengers in their struggle against vengeful Atlantean Namor, the Sub-Mariner. Cap soon becomes team leader.

ICONS #6

The Sentinel of Liberty

Creators: Joe Simon and Jack Kirby

First Appearance: *Captain America Comics* #1, March 1941

Alter Ego: Steve Rogers

Powers: enhanced strength, speed, stamina, endurance, agility, reflexes, senses, and cognitive abilities; master of hand-to-hand combat; accelerated healing; slowed aging; master of field strategy; impenetrable vibranium/adamantium shield that can be used for defense and as a throwing weapon

Archenemies: the Red Skull, Baron Zemo, Baron Strucker, Batroc the Leaper, Crossbones, the Hate-Monger, MODOK, the Serpent Society, Mister Hyde, the Winter Soldier

A living, breathing embodiment not just of a nation, but more importantly, of the ideals and strengths of that nation, **CAPTAIN AMERICA** has been inspiring fans worldwide for more than eighty years. Forged in a time of world war, his image rallied Americans in the real world just as much as it did in the pages of early Marvel Comics. Defying eras as well as changing tastes and values, he has led the charge against the forces of evil and is the spiritual leader of all the Marvel Universe and its mighty heroes. Whether a supersoldier or an Avenger, his brand of justice has never been out of style.

THE ORIGIN

Back in the 1940s, Steve Rogers was a scrawny kid from New York City—a proverbial ninety-eight-pound weakling who nevertheless wanted desperately to serve his country and fight the growing menace of Nazi Germany. Although he failed the military's physical due to his sickly nature, his grit and resolve led him to be accepted as an experimental test subject for Project Rebirth, in which he received the US government's supersoldier serum. The serum worked, pushing Rogers's physical attributes to the very limits of human capability, transforming him from weak and skinny to massive and powerful. However, plans to create a supersoldier army were foiled when a Nazi spy killed the serum's inventor.

THE CREATION

Appalled, as Americans and as Jews, at the growing power of Hitler and the Third Reich, writer Joe Simon and artist Jack Kirby, two young employees of Timely Comics, the predecessor to Marvel, set about designing a character that would represent American ideals of freedom and equality, and stand up to the Nazis—even before the United States actually went to war. Simon originally considered "Super American" for his name—an indication of Superman's inescapable influence on early superheroes. It was

Kirby, brilliant even then in his novice years, who designed the character's iconic look. Timely publisher Martin Goodman was so impressed he immediately greenlit a self-titled Captain America comic book—a rarity in those days of anthology comics.

PATRIOTIC ICON

The assassination of the supersoldier serum's creator left Steve Rogers as the only beneficiary of its effects. The United States responded by making him a figurehead, dressing him in red, white, and blue armor, and granting him a weapon that was as much a symbol as he was—an unbreakable shield to hurl at his enemies and to defend the targets of Nazi aggression. As Captain America, he entered the field of battle alongside his young sidekick, Bucky Barnes, going toe-to-toe with the Axis Powers just as many of his readers were doing in real life. Although not the first, he most certainly was the most popular and enduring of all the patriotic-themed superheroes to emerge from that era.

REBORN FROM THE ICE

In the years after the war, the popularity of Captain America and superheroes in general waned. The character was retired and became virtually nonexistent for a dozen years, before being brought back with the newly renamed Marvel Comics' commitment to reviving the superhero genre. In the story line, it was explained that Cap had gone missing after the war, frozen in ice that preserved him in suspended animation, until in 1964 he was discovered by the Avengers superteam in *Avengers* #4 and made a member of the group. Before long he was the leader, adapting his 1940s sensibilities to 1960s America, and confronting a whole new set of threats. He has remained the leader of the Avengers for most of the past sixty years.

OTHERS TO WIELD THE SHIELD

Over the years, there were moments when Steve Rogers stepped away and others took hold of his mantle. Disillusioned by Watergate-era America in the 1970s, Rogers gave up his shield and renamed himself the Nomad. During this time a short-lived series of would-be Caps attempted to fill his boots. When Rogers walked away again a decade later, he was replaced by "Super Patriot" John Walker, who proved so unstable that Rogers felt compelled to return. As of 2014, perhaps the most well-known replacement is Sam Wilson, also known as the Falcon, whose contribution as Captain America has played out in both the comics and in the Marvel Cinematic Universe.

MARVEL'S LONGEST-RUNNING MULTIMEDIA SUPERSTAR

No other Marvel Comics character has been adapted into different forms for as long as Captain America. Today, he is best known as the character faithfully portrayed by Chris Evans in a series of highly successful Marvel Cinematic Universe blockbuster movies, highlighted by the trilogy of *Captain America: The First Avenger* (2011), *Captain America: The Winter Soldier* (2014), and *Captain America: Civil War* (2016). But Cap could be seen as early as 1944, when he first appeared on screen in his own self-titled movie serial. There were also two made-for-TV movies in 1979 which, like the 1940s serial, took major liberties with the character. A 1990 motion picture adaptation starring Matt Salinger attempted to be more faithful to the character but was a critical disaster.

THE STAR-SPANGLED AVENGER

Always true to the ideals first imbued in him by Simon and Kirby, Captain America has been a tried-and-true symbol of hope, admired by fans of all political and social stripes. Although it would've been easy to turn such a character into a corny, or phony, façade for shameless propaganda, those entrusted with his legacy have resisted this move at every turn. In fact, at various points in his history, the character has even been at odds with his country whenever it may stray from the ideals on which it was founded. An incarnation of the best that his nation can be, on what it represents, Captain America is Marvel's most enduring creation and contribution to popular culture.

7

A MODERN CRISIS

The Superhero Deconstructed

The Silver Age had seen a massive explosion of creativity and vibrancy in the superhero genre, and what followed was a further development, and in many ways a reaction, both to and against that era. Marvel might have helped to modernize superheroes in the 1960s, but in later decades these superheroes would be taken in even bolder directions and modernized in further ways intended to maintain their relevance in a changing world and a changing America. Sometimes this included breaking down, analyzing, and questioning their very nature and what defined them in the first place. An entire generation that had grown up reading about them now had its chance to make its mark. Along the way, the superhero was growing up.

Looking back, the period immediately following the Silver Age, specifically the 1970s and into the 1980s, would come to be known as the Bronze Age of Comics. Although this might seem a downgrade to some, it should not detract from the output of that period—a time of turbulent change and material whose maturity was at an all-time high. The direct result of those stormy times came to be known as the Modern Age of Comic

Books, beginning in the final years of the twentieth century and continuing beyond. Although these labels are pliable as time moves forward, it can be argued that the late twentieth century represented the final era in which the comic book could be considered the primary home of the superhero.

The 1960s had been a turbulent time for Americans, and that trend both continued and heightened heading into the 1970s, with the seemingly endless Vietnam War and then Watergate taking center stage and causing people to question authority and the character of their nation like never before. Just as they always had, superheroes, too, had to change with the times, as this questioning of traditional roles and fascination with moral ambiguity would extend into the realm of escapist fantasy fiction. What did it mean to be a superhero? What was the difference between a hero and a villain? What were the potential consequences of their actions?

The Bronze Age is often denoted as beginning with the start of the 1970s, but there are also many who claim that the official beginning came in 1973, with *Amazing Spider-Man* #121, the comic book that depicted Spider-Man's failure to save the life of his girlfriend, Gwen Stacy. Seeing the Green Goblin emerge victorious, and not foiled by the hero as villains always had been, was a shocking moment for readers, and the all-too-real stakes took superheroes into a whole new realm of reality. The masks were on, but the gloves were off.

"Reality" was definitely the word of the moment, as both major comic companies attempted to build on what had come before and take superheroes in a grittier direction. DC teamed up two unlikely characters united only by a color: the cosmic guardian Green Lantern and the cynical vigilante Green Arrow. No longer quite literally above the problems of common people on Earth, GL (aka Hal Jordan) was forced to confront the harsh realities of street crime and drug addiction—as did Green Arrow himself when his

Rise of the Antihero: Superheroes of the Bronze Age

CYBORG

The brainchild of revolutionary 1970s/1980s creators Marv Wolfman and George Perez, Victor Stone was the son of scientists, accidentally mutilated in one of their experiments, who can only be saved by the implantation of extensive cybernetic attachments that make up most of his body. First appearing in *DC Comics Presents* #26 in October 1980, and hailed as a groundbreaking Black, disabled superhero, he started as a member of the Teen Titans before becoming an integral member of the Justice League.

FIRESTORM

Possessing a unique dual identity, the original Firestorm, first appearing in *Firestorm: The Nuclear Man* #1 in March 1978, was a combination of high school student Ronnie Raymond and nuclear physicist Martin Stein, both caught in a freak accident that allows them to merge into one. Developed for DC by writer Gerry Conway and artist Al Milgrom, he became a member of the Justice League (as well as TV's *Super Friends*). A second version of the superhero, Jason Rusch, the creation of Dan Jolley and ChrisCross, appeared in 2004.

GHOST RIDER

The 1970s was a time of horror-themed heroes at Marvel, epitomized by the motorcycle-riding spirit of vengeance. Inspired by a phantom gunslinger of the same name in a 1960s western comic, the most prominent Ghost Rider was Johnny Blaze, an Evel Knievel-esque stunt rider who unwittingly sells his soul to the devil in *Marvel Spotlight* #5 (August 1972), in a story developed by Marvel editor-in-chief Roy Thomas, writer Gary Friedrich, and artist Mike Ploog. Other versions followed with Danny Ketch (1990) and Robbie Reyes (2014).

GUARDIANS OF THE GALAXY

What started as a minor creation of the tail end of the Silver Age has become one of Marvel's most successful creations. The original team was conceived by Stan Lee, Roy Thomas, and Arnold Drake as space heroes of the thirty-first century in an alternative timeline, first appearing in *Marvel*

Super-Heroes #18 (January 1969). Keeping their lighthearted tone, the team was reinvented in 2008 by Dan Abnett and Andy Lanning as a present-day space force containing preexisting Marvel characters. It's this version that was adapted into cinematic form to such great acclaim.

IRON FIST

Marvel in the 1970s was also influenced by the kung-fu and martial arts movie craze, as epitomized by Danny Rand, master of Eastern fighting techniques and wielder of the "Iron Fist" force that allows him to focus his energy force, or chi. Created by Roy Thomas and Gil Kane (creator of the Silver Age Green Lantern in the 1950s), he first appeared in *Marvel Premiere* #15 in May 1974. Teamed up for years with Luke "Power Man" Cage as Heroes for Hire, he now operates on his own.

LUKE CAGE

A product of the blaxploitation boom of the 1970s, Luke Cage was wrongly imprisoned and then subjected to an experimental procedure that gave him great strength and invulnerability. Calling himself "Power Man," he put his services up for hire, eventually joining Iron Fist as a mercenary crimefighting duo. Created by Archie Goodwin, Greg Tuska, Roy Thomas, and John Romita, and first appearing in his own self-titled book in June 1972, he was the first Black superhero to get his own Marvel comic.

THE PUNISHER

Inspired by the growing awareness of crime and urban decay in America, in addition to grim crime dramas like *Dirty Harry* and *Death Wish*, the Punisher was Frank Castle, a Vietnam vet who loses his family to a senseless mob killing and embarks on an ultraviolent one-man war against crime. First appearing in *Amazing Spider-Man* #129 in February 1974, as conceived by Gerry Conway, John Romita, and Ross Andru, he was an edgy and remorseless killer who attracted a cult following despite thoroughly stretching the definition of "hero."

SHE-HULK

Lawyer Jennifer Walters finds herself seriously injured and in need of a blood transfusion, which she receives from her cousin. However, her cousin turns out to be Bruce Banner, who also passes along his gamma-irradiated cells, thus transforming Walters into the She-Hulk. Unlike her cousin, She-Hulk retains her normal personality while in "hulk" state, and usually remains permanently in green form. Introduced in *The Savage She-Hulk* #1 in February 1980, she was created by Hulk creator Stan Lee and artist John Buscema.

SWAMP THING

A truly unique character, Swamp Thing is an elemental creature of plant and humanoid matter, a pro-environment hero who fights to protect his swamp and the world at large from terroristic and supernatural threats. Developed by Len Wein and revolutionary artist Bernie Wrightson, he first appeared in DC's *House of Secrets* #92 in July 1971 but was also developed and retooled to great effect by visionary creator Alan Moore in the 1980s. Marvel developed its own version, Man-Thing, at almost the exact same time.

WOLVERINE

Of all the new characters created during the Bronze Age, the most enduring and popular would have to be the cigar-chomping Logan, introduced by Roy Thomas, Len Wein, and John Romita in *Incredible Hulk* #181 (November 1974) and soon becoming the most beloved of all X-Men members. The product of a secret government experiment, his natural mutant healing abilities were enhanced with an unbreakable adamantium skeleton and the trademark claws that extend from his hands at will.

sidekick Roy "Speedy" Ward was revealed to be addicted to heroin. Jilted by Mary Jane Watson, Peter Parker's best friend Harry Osborn became dependent on LSD in an *Amazing Spider-Man* story line considered so edgy the Comics Code Authority refused to give its approval (Marvel ran it anyway). A few years later, rich playboy Tony Stark's casual drinking developed into full-blown alcoholism. This was territory previously unheard of in the pages of superhero comics.

Thanks to its innovations of the 1960s, Marvel had become the hottest company in the business, and new creative forces like editors Roy Thomas and Jim Shooter, under the watchful eye of Stan Lee, were exploring new themes and ideas. Horror was a major influence, with characters like Man-Thing, Ghost Rider, Werewolf by Night, and Morbius the Living Vampire, as were other popular 1970s movie genres like kung-fu (Iron Fist, Shang-Chi) and blaxploitation (Luke Cage, Blade). Writers like Jim Starlin, Steve Gerber, and others were experimenting with creative ideas (among other things), and the results were obvious, with cosmic characters like the Defenders, Guardians of the Galaxy, Captain Marvel, Adam Warlock, and the evil Thanos being taken in decidedly weird directions, as well as the introduction of utterly bizarre "heroes" like Howard the Duck.

Not to be outdone, DC also took its characters in darker directions than they would've dared during the Silver Age, typified by the legendary run of writer Denny O'Neil and artist Neal Adams with Batman. Under O'Neil and Adams's stewardship in the 1970s, the Dark Knight became darker than he'd been since the earliest Bob Kane/Bill Finger issues of 1939, shedding his campiness and embracing a more serious, brooding persona that came to define him for the modern era.

The 1980s saw even further deconstruction. The format of the graphic novel, first used in 1982 with *The Death of Captain Marvel*, allowed more mature themes to be explored thanks to a loophole in the Comics Code, which technically only governed comic books in traditional magazine form. The stakes were rising, and all traces of silliness were being rooted out, as perpetually grinning superheroes were replaced with perpetually grimacing ones. DC literally wiped out its forty-plus years of continuity with the *Crisis on Infinite Earths*, streamlining its fictional universe and its iconic characters. This led to the modern reboot of Superman in John Byrne's 1986 *Man of Steel* miniseries, as well as Batman in Frank Miller's *Batman: Year One*. It was Miller who took what O'Neil and Adams had started and sent

Grim and Gritty: Superheroes of the Modern Age

BATWOMAN
Different versions of Batwoman have appeared over the decades, but the one that stuck was Kate Kane, wealthy cousin of Bruce Wayne who, inspired by his mission, takes on a similar one. Influenced by Silver Age Batwoman Kathy Kane, the new version was the product of DC creators Geoff Johns, Grant Morrison, Greg Rucka, Mark Waid, and Keith Giffen, first appearing in the company's reboot series *52* in 2006, where she takes the place of the missing Caped Crusader for a time. As a lesbian, Batwoman also became DC's first major LGBTQ character.

CABLE
The epitome of the 1990s X-Men era, dominated by artist Rob Liefeld, Cable was actually Nathan Summers, the grown son of X-Men leader Cyclops and a time traveler from the future who joins the team to prevent future calamity. Victim of a strange virus, Summers had been sent into the future for treatment, and returned as a fierce warrior. Introduced by Liefeld and Louise Simonson in *New Mutants* #87 (March 1990), he later became leader of the mutant team X-Force. In 2018, he was killed off and replaced by a younger version of himself named Kid Cable.

THE CROW
One of comics' darkest characters, the Crow was the creation of James O'Barr, first appearing for independent publisher Caliber Press in 1989. After he and his fiancée are murdered by thugs, a young man named Eric is resurrected by a supernatural bird and transformed into a figure of vengeance, hunting down those responsible. His trademark dark hair and makeup have made him a cultural icon, whose adventures are even better known from the acclaimed 1994 motion picture adaptation starring Brandon Lee.

DEADPOOL
Perhaps the most popular Marvel character to appear in more recent decades is Deadpool, created by Rob Liefeld and Fabian Nicieza. He started out as a villain when he first appeared in *New Mutants* #98 in February 1991—a disfigured mercenary with the almost limitless mutant power

of regeneration. He would eventually evolve into a figure of comedy and a classic antihero, while retaining his extremely violent practices. Today, he is best known from the smash-hit *Deadpool* movies starring Ryan Reynolds.

HELLBOY

One of the most unorthodox heroes of recent decades is Mike Mignola's demonic paranormal investigator who first appeared in a San Diego Comic Con special magazine in 1993. Conjured up as a baby devil from the depths of hell by Nazi occultists during World War II, he was rescued by Allied Forces and raised by the kindly Professor Bruttenholm, who teaches him to resist his evil nature. He eventually goes to work with Bruttenholm as part of the mysterious Bureau of Paranormal Research and Defense, battling supernatural threats to humanity.

MILES MORALES

Of all the characters created for Ultimate Marvel, the alternate universe created by Marvel in the 2000s to modernize its traditional characters, there has been none as popular or enduring as Morales, who took on the Spider-Man role in the Ultimate Universe following the 2011 death of that universe's Peter Parker. Created by Brian Michael Bendis and Sarah Pichelli, he first appeared in *Ultimate Fallout* #4 but became part of the main Marvel Universe after the 2015 discontinuation of the Ultimates line. Morales was featured in the Oscar-winning 2018 animated film *Spider-Man: Into the Spiderverse* and its 2023 sequel, *Spider-Man: Across the Spiderverse*.

THE SAVAGE DRAGON

The reptilian police officer with the mysterious origin holds the distinction of being the star of the longest-running color comic book by the same writer and artist, that being Erik Larsen, who first introduced the character in 1992 for the groundbreaking Image Comics, the company that broke from tradition by allowing creators to own their own creations. Along with Todd McFarlane's Spawn, the Savage Dragon is one of only two original Image characters in continuous publication in the company's thirty-year history.

STEEL

In the fallout of the "Death of Superman" story line in 1993, John Henry Irons was one of several characters who emerged to try and take the place of the departed Man of Tomorrow. A brilliant engineer who builds a mechanized suit of armor that replicates Superman's powers and bears his insignia, he later joins forces with his inspiration when Supes is brought back from the dead. Created by writer Louise Simonson and artist Jon Bogdanove, Steel first appeared in *Adventures of Superman* #500.

WAR MACHINE

James "Rhodey" Rhodes was originally conceived by John Byrne and David Michelinie as a fighter pilot shot down in Vietnam who encounters Tony Stark in his prototype armor and becomes his close friend and ally. Stark's personal pilot and a Stark Industries engineer, at times he would even take on the Iron Man armor himself, until he was given his own unique armored suit and identity. Although Rhodes first appeared in 1979, he did not debut as War Machine until *Avengers West Coast* #94 in 1993.

THE WATCHMEN

Alan Moore, with the help of artist Dave Gibbons, revolutionized the entire superhero concept in the late 1980s with his innovative miniseries that presented characters like the deranged vigilante Rorschach, the omnipotent Dr. Manhattan, the washed-up and out-of-shape Owl, and the arrogant, megalomaniacal Ozymandias, who challenged traditional notions of comic book superheroics. These characters set the tone for the modern era of superheroes and have informed nearly all adaptations of comic book characters since.

Bruce Wayne even further into dark territory, redefining him as a borderline psychotic figure utterly obsessed with the death of his parents and at times separated from his insane archvillains only by his unwillingness to kill.

But all that was a dress rehearsal for what Alan Moore did with his revolutionary *Watchmen* limited series for DC in 1986 and 1987. Moore, not long after penning the final "classic" Superman story prior to the *Crisis* reboot ("Whatever Happened to the Man of Tomorrow?") approached DC with the idea of writing a gritty, deconstructionist, and R-rated take on newly acquired characters from Charlton Comics such as the Question, Captain Atom, and the Blue Beetle. Reluctant to sacrifice its new intellectual property, DC asked Moore to create new characters, and the result was the ultimate dystopian take on the superhero oeuvre. Set in a future where superheroes are banned and corruption reigns, *Watchmen* challenged readers' preconceived notions of superheroes with characters like the rapist Comedian, the sociopath Rorschach, and the coldly detached yet all-powerful Dr. Manhattan. Moore had grown up on the Silver Age heroes and relished the chance to view that Silver Age sensibility through an unforgiving, grown-up viewpoint. The result was perhaps the single most influential take on superheroes of the past forty years.

The comic book collecting craze had been growing since the 1950s, but probably reached its ultimate fever pitch in the 1990s, and companies responded in kind, pumping out more books than ever before, with limitless gimmicks including foil covers, multiple covers, holographic covers, and all manner of story line publicity stunts. It was a flooded market, and consumers were inundated with a glut of superhero content. There was even a third major company that took shape. Image Comics was founded by former Marvel and DC creator Todd McFarlane, joined by other disgruntled creators like Rob Leifield, Erik Larsen, Jim Valentino, Jim Lee, Marc Silvestri, and Whilce Portacio. Seeking to escape the work-for-hire system and to gain both creative and financial control of their work, they set up a haven for writers and artists that also resulted in a whole wave of entirely new characters like Spawn, the Savage Dragon, WILDCATS, Pitt, the Maxx, and Shadowhawk. Suddenly, the comics industry had more competition than ever, and other startups like Dark Horse and Valiant shook up the DC/ Marvel dynamic even further.

Collector's Items: Landmark Issues
of the Late Twentieth Century

GREEN LANTERN #76, APRIL 1970
DC attempted to tackle real-life social issues for the first time through its pairing of Green Lantern and Green Arrow. This groundbreaking story of urban blight and the disadvantages of poverty-stricken African Americans is a classic example.

AMAZING SPIDER-MAN #121, JUNE 1973
The infamous death of Peter Parker's girlfriend Gwen Stacy at the hands of his archnemesis the Green Goblin brought an unforgettable edge of real-life consequences to the usual hero versus villain comic book paradigm.

INCREDIBLE HULK #181, NOVEMBER 1974
Len Wein's Wolverine crashes onto the scene for the first time in this highly coveted issue. Before joining the X-Men, he does battle here with the Hulk in the wiles of Canada. The most valuable comic of the Bronze Age, near-mint copies have sold for as much as $23,000.

GIANT-SIZE X-MEN #1, MAY 1975
This is the comic book that single-handedly saved the X-Men series. The first new X-Men story published in five years, it featured a slew of new characters from Len Wein and artist Dave Cockrum that would define the team for years to come, including Wolverine, Storm, Colossus, and Nightcrawler.

UNCANNY X-MEN #141, JANUARY 1981
One of the most revered story lines of all time, Chris Claremont and John Byrne's "Days of Future Past" debuted in this issue, featuring the mutants attempting to derail a dystopian future in which all their kind are being exterminated.

DAREDEVIL #181, APRIL 1982
The early 1980s run of writer/artist Frank Miller redefined Daredevil and his world to great acclaim. This issue, featuring the death of the assassin

Elektra at the hands of the villainous Bullseye, provided part of the inspiration for the 2003 *Daredevil* movie.

SPIDER-MAN #1, AUGUST 1990
With his highly unorthodox artistic approach to the beloved Wall-Crawler, Todd McFarlane had become the talk of the industry, and received carte blanche with his own brand-new Spidey title, the first issue of which became the highest-selling comic of all time.

SPAWN #1, MAY 1992
Falling out with Marvel, McFarlane founded his own company, Image Comics, kicking things off with the first appearance of his own original character. Spawn would become the most popular non-Marvel/DC character of the modern era.

SUPERMAN #75, JANUARY 1993
Selling six million copies, this heavily hyped issue, sealed in its unforgettable black bag with bloody logo, featured the murder of Superman by the maniacal Doomsday. Often maligned as a publicity stunt, the character's death (thankfully) proved temporary.

BATMAN #497, JULY 1993
Only a few months after the death of Superman, Batman had his back broken by hulking new archenemy Bane. Forced to retire, he was replaced by the crazed vigilant Azrael, until recovering from his injuries and returning to action the following year.

As the twentieth century drew to a close, it was clear that comic books—and superheroes in general—were no longer the province of children but had captivated several generations of adults who found them fascinating and completely relevant to their lives and their world. New works like 1994's *Marvels* and *Kingdom Come*, both from the minds of writer Kurt Busiek and the brilliant painter Alex Ross, catered to those who had grown up with the characters of Marvel and DC, and those readers responded positively

Landmark Series: Stories that Changed the Course of Comics

As the modern age of comics started, it brought with it the graphic novel craze, and the rise of the limited series, usually with far-reaching ramifications. Here are some of the most memorable.

SECRET WARS (1984–1985)

The first series of its kind from Marvel, this story from editor-in-chief Jim Shooter brought all the superheroes and supervillains of the Marvel Universe to a mysterious planet, where they were forced to battle each other by the omnipotent being known as the Beyonder. Part of a lucrative toy tie-in, it was followed by *Secret Wars II* and other reboots in later years.

CRISIS ON INFINITE EARTHS (1985–1986)

Faced with decades of confusing chronologies and alternate realities, DC decided to clean house with this mega-event from Marv Wolfman and George Perez. The multiverse is laid waste by the all-powerful Anti-Monitor, as his nemesis the Monitor enlists the help of DC superheroes to stop him. In the end, DC was left with one universe, and one chronology (which they've since remuddied).

THE DARK KNIGHT RETURNS (1986)

From the mind of Frank Miller came this bold reimagining of Batman, set in a future in which an aging Bruce Wayne has hung up the cape but must come out of retirement in a fascist America to face the renewed threats of the Joker and Two-Face, not to mention a corrupt Superman. Its grim and revisionist take on DC characters has influenced Batman's depiction ever since.

THE INFINITY GAUNTLET (1991)

The culmination of a long cosmic story arc, masterminded by Marvel's Jim Starlin, this tale of the genocidal Thanos and his accumulation of the gems he will use to wipe out half the population of the universe became the basis of an epic multifilm story line in the Marvel Cinematic Universe, reaching its conclusion in the movies *Avengers: Infinity War* (2018) and *Avengers: Endgame* (2019).

to such intelligent and nuanced storytelling, as well as the reimagining of heroes who had by now become cultural touchstones.

In fact, something interesting and perhaps inevitable would happen as the new century dawned. These characters had often been adapted into cinematic form over the years, but nothing would compare to the explosion of cinematic superheroes that was about to occur. Decades of evolution had developed these characters to such a degree of realism and maturity that they were ready to leap en masse from the page to the screen, to the point that it could be argued that the movies would even supplant comic books as the primary home of superheroes, and the medium through which most of the public would encounter them. To be sure, comics would continue to be published, but in the twenty-first century, the superhero movie would rule supreme—not only over comic books, but over the movie industry itself. It made perfect sense. These characters we had all come to love so dearly were taking their next logical step in dominating popular culture.

ICONS #7

The Amazon Princess

Creators: William Moulton Marston and H. G. Peter

First Appearance: *All Star Comics* #8, December 1941/January 1942

Alter Ego: Diana Prince

Powers: superhuman strength, invulnerability, superspeed, flight, bullet-proof bracelets, magic lasso of truth, elite fighting skill, healing factor, communication with animals, astral projection

Archenemies: Cheetah, Giganta, Maxwell Lord, Circe, Baroness Paula von Gunther, Ares, Dr. Psycho, Silver Swan, Veronica Cale, Dr. Poison

The last of DC Comics' "Holy Trinity" of cultural icons to emerge at the beginning of the Golden Age of Comics, **WONDER WOMAN** takes her place alongside Superman and Batman at the highest echelon of superhero royalty. She is without question the most well-known and revered female superhero of all time, with her name and likeness recognized worldwide. In a medium long dominated by male characters, male creators, and aimed at a male readership, she stands out as an icon of female empowerment and, like other cornerstones like Superman and Batman, has grown to transcend the comic book medium and the realm of superhero fiction, becoming a powerful archetype along the way.

THE ORIGIN

In her original Golden Age version, Wonder Woman began her life as Princess Diana of Paradise Island (later named Themyscira), the realm of the mighty Amazon warrior women. Her existence changes forever when American military pilot Steve Trevor crashes his aircraft on the island. A competition is held to determine which Amazon will return to the human world with Trevor and help him battle the forces of the Axis Powers. Against her mother, Queen Hippolyta's, wishes, Diana disguises herself, enters the contest, and wins. Despite her disapproval, the queen must abide by the rules and thus outfits her daughter with a special uniform and weapons, and Diana/Wonder Woman embarks on a mission of peace into the mortal world, along with Trevor, who soon becomes her romantic interest.

THE CREATION

Troubled by the overt masculinity and violence of the emerging superhero comic book form, author and psychologist William Moulton Marston (pen name Charles Moulton) was approached by National Periodicals publisher Max Gaines to create a different kind of superhero. This one would be guided by love and peace and represent traits Marston—a devout feminist and believer in the superiority of women—identified with the female sex. Guided by his wife, fellow psychologist Elizabeth Holloway Marston, as well as companion Olive Byrne, who shared a polyamorous relationship with the couple, he designed her as a woman of godlike powers, and with the help of artist H. G. Peter, gave her a look that combined ancient Hellenic themes and the red, white, and blue emblematic of the patriotic heroes of the World War II era.

FEMINIST SYMBOL

From the very beginning, Wonder Woman was meant to be a symbol of female liberation in the modern world. It's therefore not surprising that she has been generously co-opted for this purpose over the years, and her likeness stands today as a literal embodiment of this concept. Marston felt strongly that women were destined for much more power in modern society, but that they just lacked appropriate role models, and the ability to revel in their own strength without giving up traditional notions of nurturing and kind-heartedness. Her stories have often demonstrated her attainment of power over men, and regularly rejecting the notion of the "damsel in distress."

OF SUPERHUMAN BONDAGE

To varying degrees, overt sexuality has also played a role in Wonder Woman's character. Marston and others often depicted her in chains or otherwise restrained, reflecting Marston's belief in the virtues of bondage/submission practices. Her escape from bondage became a common device in her stories, as well as her imposing bondage on others, as she does with the magic lasso that compels its captives to tell the truth. Her Golden Age stories were ambiguous about the character's sexuality, and it was sometimes hinted that she was lesbian or bisexual. Although these aspects were toned down during the ensuing decades, later creators like George Perez and Grant Morrison chose to reemphasize them, and Wonder Woman's transcending of heteronormative gender roles and conventional sexuality is now a given.

A CHANGING FIGURE FOR CHANGING TIMES

Wonder Woman's origins have changed over the years, often dramatically. During the Silver and Bronze Ages of the 1950s–1980s, she was described as having been molded from clay, and bestowed powers from the Greek gods. She possessed an invisible plane, later jettisoned when she gained the ability to fly. In more contemporary incarnations following DC reboots like Crisis on Infinite Earths and The New 52, she became the biological child of Hippolyta and Zeus. Her costume has been altered, removing American color schemes to make her more universal, and desexualizing and further militarizing her uniform to tone down the fetishization Marston built into the character, while also—sometimes controversially—making her into more of a warrior than Marston intended.

THE GODDESS IN OTHER FORMS

Unlike Superman and Batman, Wonder Woman wasn't adapted into other media until the 1970s. It began in 1973 with her inclusion in the long-running Saturday morning cartoon *Super Friends*. The following year, Cathy Lee Crosby played her in a made-for-TV movie. But it would be Lynda Carter who'd make the role her own in the ongoing TV series that ran from 1975 to 1979, set partly during World War II and partly in contemporary times. More recently, a new iconic big screen Wonder Woman has emerged in Israeli actress Gal Gadot, who portrayed Diana in a 2017 motion picture—the first for the character—as well as a sequel, *Wonder Woman 1984*, and other DC films like *Batman v Superman: Dawn of Justice* and *Justice League*.

THE ULTIMATE SUPERHEROINE

"Now the world is ready for you, and the wonders you can do. Make a hawk a dove, stop a war with love, make a liar tell the truth." So went the unforgettable theme song of the 1970s *Wonder Woman* TV show, with lyrics that perfectly capture what the character was intended to be, and what she has meant to so many for so long. And although there are many more female superheroes today than there were when Wonder Woman first left Paradise Island, she has always remained at the top of the list—a fascinating anomaly in a medium populated by hypermasculine fantasies, and a symbol of both power and peace in equal parts.

8

YOU WILL BELIEVE A MAN CAN FLY

DC at the Movies

Today, it's easy to forget that motion pictures based on costumed comic book characters were once extremely few and far between. But even during the late twentieth century, when such films were scarce, the characters who enjoyed by far the lion's share of the attention on the silver screen were the iconic characters of DC Comics, who for so many years had been working their way into the fabric of popular culture and public consciousness. It was the archetypal DC heroes who led the way in the gradual superhero take-over of Hollywood. Even currently, at a time when superhero movie output is finally more diverse and varied, they are still there—only now they have to fight a little harder for the public's attention against Marvel, their long-time rival on the printed page.

However, those who grew up in a time when there wasn't a new super-hero movie coming out every few months will recall that in those olden days it was largely the "big two"—Superman and Batman—who kept showing up on the silver screen. In fact, there were several different itera-tions of both the Man of Steel and the Caped Crusader that were adapted for motion pictures before more characters of the DC Universe started to finally be given more cinematic attention well into the twenty-first century. In the past decade or so, thanks to what has become known as the DC Extended Universe, there has for the first time been an attempt, though a flawed one, to create a fully realized movie version of the kind of interconnected fictional world that DC Comics readers have enjoyed for three-quarters of a century.

Naturally, Superman would be the first superhero to get feature film treatment. He had previously come to life, as many superheroes had, in the form of movie chapter serials. It was in fact just one year after the second and final Superman serial, *Atom Man vs. Superman*, that the Last Son of Krypton would be adapted for his first standalone movie. Whitney Ellsworth was a longtime DC Comics writer and editor with connections to the entertainment world. He had been a writer and consultant on the Superman serials and the radio series of the 1940s and had worked on some of those radio shows with another writer, Robert Maxwell. Under the combined pseudonym of "Richard Fielding," they pooled their talents to pen a script for a feature-length theatrical Superman film, which they hoped to use as a springboard for an eventual series in the brand-new medium of television.

The result of their efforts was *Superman and the Mole Men*, the first superhero feature film ever made. Released in 1951, it starred the beefy and amiable George Reeves, a long-struggling bit player in Hollywood whose career had stalled after World War II. Having resorted to digging cesspools for a living, Reeves was plucked from obscurity to play the Man of Steel, a role that would change his life, particularly when the film did lead to a full-fledged TV series, as Maxwell and Ellsworth had hoped. Reeves was joined by Phyllis Coates as Lois Lane, a role she would reprise for the first season of the *Adventures of Superman* TV series.

The 1950s was the decade that saw the enormous success of Superman on TV, and for a time, DC's film presence would continue to be linked to its dominance of the small screen. When another DC TV series, *Batman*, took the nation by storm a decade later, it would lead to the first feature appearance of a second DC icon. *Batman* TV series producer William Dozier had wanted to make a feature film even before his series hit the air on CBS, but 20th Century Fox was unconvinced of the project until the TV series became an enormous hit during its initial early 1966 season. Production on *Batman: The Movie* was greenlit in spring of 1966 and the movie was put together in a mere month in order to get it into theaters by the summer and before the autumn debut of the series' second season.

The cast of the TV show also appear in the film, with the unforgettable Adam West and Burt Ward, the Dynamic Duo, matching wits against the combined forces of Batman's most nefarious enemies. Burgess Meredith, Cesar Romero, and Frank Gorshin reprise their respective roles as the Penguin, the Joker, and the Riddler, with Lee Meriwether as the one-time replacement for the unavailable Julie Newmar, who played Catwoman on the TV show. Written by series mastermind Lorenzo Semple Jr., it continued his campy take on the Batman mythos, which in fairness was not that far off from the DC comics of the era. And although very different from the Batman films that would come in later decades, it remains the Dark Knight's first feature foray.

However, most would agree that DC movies, and superhero movies in general for that matter, didn't really reach maturity for yet another decade. This development was helped along in a big way by the 1969 purchase

Visionaries: The Creators Who
Helped Shape DC on the Silver Screen

LORENZO SEMPLE JR.

Known for the campy sensibility he brought to Batman, inspired largely by the comics of the 1940s and 1950s, Semple was a struggling playwright and fiction writer who found a home in Hollywood, mainly writing for television. After his success with Batman, he continued to apply his tongue-in-cheek approach to iconic fantasy characters with scripts for *King Kong* (1976), *Flash Gordon* (1980), and *Sheena* (1984). He also contributed to the scripts of films like *Papillon* (1973), *The Parallax View* (1974), and the James Bond film *Never Say Never Again* (1983).

RICHARD DONNER

Also making his name initially in television, Donner broke in as a director on such 1950s and 1960s TV shows as *The Man from UNCLE*, *The Fugitive*, and *The Twilight Zone* (including the classic episode "Nightmare at 30,000 Feet"). After his blockbuster success with the 1976 horror film *The Omen*, he was given the reins for the first *Superman* movie in 1978. Although he departed the franchise over creative differences during production on the sequel, he went on to tremendous acclaim helming such major hits as *The Goonies* (1985), *Scrooged* (1988), and the *Lethal Weapon* franchise.

TIM BURTON

The unorthodox Burton got started in the film industry by making quirky short films at Disney, but really got going thanks to the cult success of *Pee-Wee's Big Adventure* (1985) and horror comedy *Beetlejuice* (1988), which is also where he encountered the comic actor he'd tap to play his Batman, Michael Keaton. Burton went on to perhaps the greatest critical acclaim of his career with the unforgettable biopic *Ed Wood* (1994) starring Johnny Depp. *Mars Attacks!* (1996), *Sleepy Hollow* (1999), *Big Fish* (2003), *Alice in Wonderland* (2010), and *Frankenweenie* (2012) are among his diverse and interesting films.

JOEL SCHUMACHER

Starting out as a production and costume designer, Schumacher always retained his aesthetic sensibilities later in his career, eventually making the leap to writing and directing, making a splash in the 1980s with youthful flicks like *St. Elmo's Fire* (1985), *The Lost Boys* (1987), and *Flatliners* (1990). Although his work on the Batman film franchise was divisive, it was also financially successful, and led to further success with films like the legal thriller *A Time to Kill* (1996), the Nicolas Cage noir *8mm* (1999), and the movie adaptation *The Phantom of the Opera* (2004).

CHRISTOPHER NOLAN

One of the most important filmmakers of the past twenty-five years, Nolan is known for his starkly realistic, visually washed out, and foreboding style. His entrance into the rebooted Batman movie franchise was facilitated by breakout success first with the highly acclaimed *Memento* (2000) and then the thriller *Insomnia* (2002). His films continued to push boundaries, and later works like *The Prestige* (2006), *Inception* (2010), *Interstellar* (2014), *Dunkirk* (2017), and *Tenet* (2020) have proven hugely influential groundbreakers.

ZACK SNYDER

Perhaps no other active filmmaker is as polarizing as Snyder, which carried over into his work in the DC Extended Universe of films—nevertheless, his influence on the direction of DC's current movie output cannot be denied. With a dynamic, visually arresting, and action-oriented style that is unmistakably his, Snyder has been a natural for such pulpy material as the zombie remake *Dawn of the Dead* (2004), the ancient Roman epic *300* (2007), and his first foray into the realm of superheroes, *Watchmen* (2009). More recently, he further demonstrated his knack for high-octane action with *Army of the Dead* (2021).

of DC Comics by Warner Bros. Both the comic book company and the movie studio were hurting at the time, and it was thought that they could somehow help each other out. In particular, Warner Bros. wanted to make a movie about the most valuable property that it now owned and do it in a way in which superheroes had never been treated before on screen. They wanted a movie that would address the more serious, majestic side of super-heroes, but had trouble getting a project off the ground due in part to how thoroughly the *Batman* TV series had established superheroes as figures of camp and parody.

After years of development hell, Warner Bros. finally put a project into production after being approached by Alexander and Ilya Salkind, a father-son duo of Mexican film producers who purchased the film rights to Super-man in 1974. After his tremendous success directing the 1976 horror film *The Omen*, Richard Donner was brought on board by the Salkinds and as screenwriters added the talented likes of *Godfather* scribe Mario Puzo and Hollywood legacy Tom Mankiewicz. The idea was to treat the subject straight and with respect, and to do that they hired perhaps the most per-fectly cast superhero actor of them all, Christopher Reeve, in the role of the Man of Steel. With Margot Kidder as Lois Lane, and heavy hitters Gene Hackman and Marlon Brando as Lex Luthor and Jor-El, respectively, the film became the talk of the entertainment industry.

When it came out in 1978, it became the talk of the world. *Superman: The Movie* perfectly captured the spirit of comics' most famous character and did it in a way that was in no way disrespectful to the source material. For the first time, a superhero was not relegated to a low-rent, B-movie pre-sentation, but was given big-budget, blockbuster treatment, with a quality script and special effects that had audiences believing a man could fly, as the film's famous tagline declared. It was far and away the most ambitious superhero film that had ever been mounted and would set the tone for Hol-lywood's future relationship with the genre. It also led to a series of sequels, which was also a first: *Superman II* (1981) continued the high quality of the original, with the Man of Steel battling the notorious Phantom Zone vil-lains led by General Zod (Terence Stamp). As the 1980s wore on, the series

Christopher Reeve: The Greatest
Screen Superhero of Them All

The prospect of portraying a superhero on film can be a daunting one—both for actors and for fans with high expectations. But arguably no actor more completely embodied and inhabited a comic book hero to the degree that Christopher Reeve did in his four appearances as Superman, in a film franchise stretching from 1978 to 1987. Particularly in the first two films of the series—*Superman: The Movie* and *Superman II*, but even in the lesser installments of the series, which were lesser through no fault of his, Reeve became the physical translation of the Man of Steel, in appearance and in manner. And for legions of fans, he achieved the ultimate goal of any superhero actor—to be almost completely identified with the character to the point that it's nearly impossible to imagine one without the other.

Born September 25, 1952, in New York, he was a relative unknown, a recent Juilliard graduate who had mainly appeared on stage, when he was selected by director Richard Donner and executive producers Alexander and Ilya Salkind to portray the most famous and beloved superhero of all time. But from the first test shots, it became apparent that the tall, distinguished, and strikingly handsome Reeve was the man for the job. Donning a perfectly realized comic book-accurate red and blue costume, Reeve seemed to have walked right out of the pages of *Action Comics*, delivering his earnest dialogue without a trace of irony, making Superman as believable as possible without ever coming off as corny or insincere. And in a masterstroke, he played Clark Kent as a bumbling, awkward goof—an innovation at the time that helped audiences believe that no one would ever dream he was really Superman.

Reeve immediately became the idol of millions thanks to the role, and would forever be associated closely with it, even though he continued to enjoy a prosperous career in such films as *Somewhere in Time* (1980), *Deathtrap* (1982), *Street Smart* (1987), *The Remains of the Day* (1993), and *Speechless* (1994)—in which he starred alongside movie Batman Michael Keaton. But unthinkable tragedy struck in 1995 when Reeve, an accomplished equestrian, suffered a devastating neck injury while riding, leaving him a quadriplegic. He continued to inspire millions with his activism and fervent efforts to walk again, and even continued to take on occasional acting roles, including a memorable return to the Superman mythos in 2003 with a guest role on the TV series *Smallville*. But after a nine-year battle, Reeve at last succumbed to complications from his paralysis, passing away on October 10, 2004, at the age of fifty-two.

Although some like Hugh Jackman and Robert Downey Jr. have come close, never before or since has a superhero actor so perfectly fulfilled fans' expectations and become so inextricably linked to the role he played. Quite simply, Christopher Reeve was more than "the actor who played Superman." For millions, Christopher Reeve *was* Superman—and always will be. He made us believe a man could fly, and so much more, and his contributions will never be forgotten.

petered out with the critically panned *Superman III* (1983) and the abysmal failure *Superman IV: The Quest for Peace* (1987), but nevertheless, the Christopher Reeve Superman series set the bar for all superhero movies to come.

The success of the Superman movie franchise even led to a *Supergirl* movie in 1984. And DC even managed to bring its dark avenger Swamp Thing to the screen in 1982 with a future cult classic directed by horror mastermind Wes Craven. But now that it had experienced success with Superman, Warner Bros. really set its sights on giving that other DC warhorse of the screen, Batman, the proper movie treatment. The big-time producing team of Jon Peters and Peter Guber was brought on board, and they enlisted quirky director Tim Burton, fresh off his breakthrough success with *Pee-Wee's Big Adventure* (1985) and *Beetlejuice* (1988). Burton was hardly the kind of director fans had in mind for a Batman movie, and that attitude only continued when it was announced that comic actor Michael Keaton would be donning the batsuit.

However, all doubt was washed away with the record-breaking, worldwide success of *Batman* in 1989. The film became a bona fide cultural phenomenon, and Keaton became indelibly linked to the Batman role, becoming just as iconic as Jack Nicholson's memorable turn as the Joker.

The Men Behind the Bat

No other superhero has been played on screen by more people than the Dark Knight. Here's a rundown of the many actors who have taken on the cape and cowl in live-action films over the decades.

LEWIS WILSON
Batman (1943)

Tapped by Columbia to star in its first fifteen-chapter Batman movie serial, Wilson became the first actor to play Bruce Wayne/Batman. It was his first credited film role, and the only starring turn he'd ever have. After appearing in a string of B-pictures during World War II, most notably the early William Castle western *Klondike Kate* and the Cary Grant vehicle *Once Upon a Time*, he relocated from Massachusetts to California and focused on community theater, eventually making his final film appearance in the noir thriller *Naked Alibi* in 1954.

ROBERT LOWERY
Batman and Robin (1949)

With Wilson out of the business, Columbia turned to thirteen-year movie vet Lowery for its second serial. A versatile B-movie bit player, he'd appeared in three Charlie Chan films, as well as *Tarzan's Desert Mystery* (1943) with Johnny Weissmuller, *Mr. Moto in Danger Island* (1939) with Peter Lorre, and Universal's *The Mummy's Ghost* (1944), in addition to prestige films like *The Mark of Zorro* (1940) with Tyrone Power and 1939 Henry Fonda vehicles *Young Mr. Lincoln* and *Drums Along the Mohawk*. He became a fixture in westerns, last appearing with Doris Day in *The Ballad of Josie* in 1967.

ADAM WEST
Batman (1966)

Best known for his campy, self-aware portrayal of the Caped Crusader in the late 1960s *Batman* TV series, West also took on the part in the feature film based on the series, which was released after the first season of the TV show. Known mainly for his TV work prior to Batman, he became the first actor whose career was defined by the role. In fact, he was able to make part of his living through personal appearances both in and out of costume for many years afterward. He was rumored to have turned down the role of Thomas Wayne in Tim Burton's 1989 *Batman* film.

MICHAEL KEATON
Batman (1989), *Batman Returns* (1992), *The Flash* (2023)

The first actor to reprise the role of Batman in a second motion picture appearance, Keaton was a controversial casting choice made by director Tim Burton, mainly because he had only been known up to that point for comedies, such as *Night Shift* (1982), *Mr. Mom* (1983), *Johnny Dangerously* (1984), and *Beetlejuice* (1988). But Keaton made the part his own in both memorable appearances, and even got to riff on the role in the 2014 drama *Birdman*, for which he was nominated for an Oscar. He returned in a cameo as an elderly Bruce Wayne in the recent DC Extended Universe film *The Flash*.

VAL KILMER
Batman Forever (1995)

Burton's departure as director from Warner Bros.' Batman film franchise led to the recasting of Batman for the third film. New director Joel Schumacher put his mark on the project by casting Kilmer, more classically handsome than Keaton and known for both comedies like *Real Genius* (1985), as well as impressive dramatic roles in *Top Gun* (1986), *Tombstone* (1993), and *The Doors* (1991), in which he memorably played front man Jim Morrison. Notoriously difficult to work with, Kilmer left the franchise after just one film. His career plateaued in the late 1990s. He was the subject of the 2021 documentary, *Val*.

GEORGE CLOONEY
Batman & Robin (1997)

The actor who first rose to fame in the early 1990s as Dr. Doug Ross on the hit NBC medical drama *ER* was perhaps the most suited to the role of the modern Bruce Wayne, which is ironic since he played the part in the silliest of all modern Batman films. Nephew of noted stage actor Jose Ferrer and legendary jazz singer Rosemary Clooney, he won a Best Actor Oscar for his performance in *Syriana* (2006). One of the most famous leading men in Hollywood for years, he's also known for films like *From Dusk Till Dawn* (1996), *O Brother Where Art Thou?* (2000), *Ocean's Eleven* (2001), and *The Descendants* (2011).

CHRISTIAN BALE
Batman Begins (2005), *The Dark Knight* (2008), *The Dark Knight Rises* (2012)

The first actor to star as the Caped Crusader in three feature films, the English performer was the lynchpin of Christopher Nolan's landmark "Dark Knight" trilogy, perhaps best remembered for his deep-voiced portrayal of the crimefighter, as well as his faithful interpretation of Wayne as a thoughtless and superficial playboy. Introduced to audiences at age thirteen in Steven Spielberg's *Empire of the Sun* (1987), he went on to gain great acclaim as the killer Patrick Bateman in *American Psycho* (2000) and won a Best Actor Oscar in 2010 for *The Fighter*.

BEN AFFLECK
Batman v Superman: Dawn of Justice (2016), *Justice League* (2017), *The Flash* (2023)

Ironically, Affleck had already played Daredevil in 2003, making him the first actor to play both a Marvel and DC superhero on screen. He got his start with director Kevin Smith in films like *Mallrats* (1995) and *Chasing Amy* (1997), but it was in *Good Will Hunting* (1997), a film he cowrote and starred in with childhood friend Matt Damon, that he cemented his superstardom. He has also achieved success as a director, most notably with the 2012 thriller *Argo*, in which he also starred. Affleck enjoyed a brief postcredits cameo as Bruce Wayne in *Suicide Squad* (2016).

ROBERT PATTINSON
The Batman (2022)

To an entire generation of fans, he will always and forever be known as the dreamy, misunderstood vampire Edward Cullen in the blockbuster smash *Twilight* movie series of 2008–2012. Even before that, he had become known to a different subsection of genre film fans as the ill-fated Cedric Diggory in *Harry Potter and the Goblet of Fire* (2005), the fifth installment in that other blockbuster series. One of the most high-profile (and highest paid) actors in the world, he has recently impressed viewers in Robert Eggers's horror film *The Lighthouse* (2019) and Christopher Nolan's spy picture *Tenet* (2020).

Blending the campy sensibilities of the past with the darker, more gothic feel that permeated Batman comics of the 1980s, the film struck a perfect note, casting all skepticism aside. Burton and Keaton stayed on board for a sequel, *Batman Returns* (1992), which added Danny DeVito as the Penguin and Michelle Pfeiffer as a wonderfully realized Catwoman. But the film's dark tone troubled some viewers (not to mention studio executives), leading to Burton's replacement as director by the more camp-minded Joel Schumacher for the next two films in the series: *Batman Forever* (1995) and *Batman & Robin* (1997). Although also hugely successful, these two later installments took the series in a direction that more closely resembled the 1960s TV series and have divided audiences to this day.

And yet, the trend continued of Superman and Batman being the only viable DC characters to successfully translate to the screen, a reality further highlighted by the underwhelming *Steel* (1997) starring Shaquille O'Neal and even the financially successful *Constantine* (2005), an adaptation of DC's mature-readers title *Hellblazer*, starring Keanu Reeves, that garnered mixed reception from critics. With the Peters/Guber/Burton Batman franchise having run its course by the end of the twentieth century, Warner Bros./DC returned to their two most reliable characters yet again in the new decade. One endeavor was *Superman Returns* (2006), a high-prestige project that attracted comics-enthusiast director Bryan Singer (who abandoned his duties as director of the *X-Men* franchise for the honor) and attempted to continue the legacy and continuity of the Richard Donner/Christopher Reeve Superman films of the previous generation. Although Singer and company made a valiant effort, with Brandon Routh as the new Supes and Kevin Spacey filling Gene Hackman's shoes as Luthor, the film was seen as overly faithful to the past films, and an unnecessary retread that fell short of the original.

This was not the case at all with the rebooted Batman franchise. The brilliant director Christopher Nolan had a specific vision of what he wanted to do with the Dark Knight, which was to take him in an even grimmer, more reality-based direction than what Burton had done. With Christian Bale under the cowl, Nolan's vision intrigued audiences beginning with *Batman Begins* in 2005, telling an effective origin story for the first time. Then, with 2008's *The Dark Knight*, Nolan surpassed his first achievement and created a movie that many fans believe is the greatest superhero movie ever made. Featuring a harrowing Heath Ledger in one of his final performances as a totally maniacal Joker, and Aaron Eckhart as the tortured Harvey Dent/Two-Face, the film is epic in ambition and scale, in many ways the most "grown-up" of all superhero movies. Nolan's trilogy was completed with *The Dark Knight Rises* (2012), a film which, although it doesn't equal its predecessor, introduces Tom Hardy as a memorable Bane and provides a satisfying conclusion to Bruce Wayne's story.

By this time, Marvel was in full swing with its efforts to create its own cinematic universe, and rumblings began to emerge of similar ambitions within the Warners/DC machine. In the meantime, the output continued to be erratic. There was 2009's *Watchmen*, which adapted the groundbreaking Alan Moore graphic novel with mixed results and represented action director Zack Snyder's introduction to the (extended) DC catalog, as well as the disastrous and forgettable *Jonah Hex* (2010) starring Josh Brolin as the supernatural cowboy. There was even the first feature film adaptation of Green Lantern in 2012, which also marked the first time a major DC character beyond Superman or Batman had been adapted for the silver screen. But although developed by Greg Berlanti (who would later have great success with his DC TV properties), helmed by James Bond director Martin

Campbell, and starring the eminently likeable Ryan Reynolds as Hal Jordan, *Green Lantern* was both a critical and financial disappointment.

The launch of the DC Extended Universe began in 2013 the only way it could, with a return to the tried-and-true Superman territory. This time, David Goyer, who had experienced great success scripting Nolan's Batman films, not to mention Marvel's *Blade* series, was brought on as screenwriter, while the controversial Zack Snyder took the director's chair. British actor Henry Cavill became the newest screen Superman, as Warner Bros. partnered with Legendary Entertainment, a company known for its big-budget blockbusters, to bring *Man of Steel* to theaters. The result was quite different in tone from the Christopher Reeve Superman films, with an emphasis on action and a decidedly more downbeat perspective. Gone was the All-American wonder, optimism, and charm of the Donner films, and in its place a more brooding Superman that seemed more in line with the darker turn that comic books had taken in recent decades.

It wasn't everyone's cup of tea, and it seemed the DC Extended Universe was off to a rocky start. *Man of Steel* was just the beginning of the plan. It was followed by *Batman v Superman: Dawn of Justice* (2016), which once again teamed Synder, Goyer, and Cavill, this time adding Ben Affleck as the Dark Knight, and placing the two beloved characters at odds for the first time on screen. Critical response was negative and audience response was mixed. Box office receipts fell a bit short of studio hopes. But the DC Extended Universe was off and running nevertheless, with the supervillain teamup picture *Suicide Squad* (2016) from David Ayer representing DC's off-beat and darkly humorous answer to Marvel's *Guardians of the Galaxy*. Nevertheless, despite the memorable turn of Margot Robbie as Joker's girlfriend Harley Quinn, the film was the worst-received DC movie thus far, attracting none of the goodwill that

Guardians had. Five years later, DC would correct this problem by bringing in the *Guardians* writer/director himself, James Gunn, to write and direct *The Suicide Squad*, a sequel/reboot that kept the best aspects of the first film (including Robbie), while injecting much-needed levity and slapstick ultraviolence, including a star-making performance by former wrestler John Cena as the jovial but deadly Peacemaker.

But all this was devised so a film could be made that would combine the major DC superheroes into an eventual Justice League as an answer to Marvel's Avengers films. The last step of the journey was the movie that remains perhaps the most well-received of all the DC Extended Universe films, *Wonder Woman*, starring Gal Gadot as the Amazonian princess, with acclaimed director Patty Jenkins adding an appropriately female perspective to the world's most beloved female superhero. The film was a major hit with critics and fans, but there were still many who felt that the *Justice League* project was being rushed and wasn't coming together as organically as Marvel's efforts.

These feelings were further strengthened by the creative conflicts taking place behind the scenes. Director Zack Snyder left the project due to personal issues, but creative differences also seemed to play a part, with DC and the studio losing patience with the pessimistic, gloomy approach to their heroes that seemed to be alienating audiences. *Avengers* director Joss Whedon was brought in to replace Snyder and maybe bring along some of that Marvel magic, but this seemed only to further muddy the waters. The resulting *Justice League* film, which came out less than half a year after *Wonder Woman*, was a major disappointment for DC, especially considering the wondrous and continued success of the Marvel Cinematic Universe. Not even the combined forces of Batman, Wonder Woman, Aquaman (Jason Momoa), Flash (Ezra Miller), and Cyborg (Ray Fisher) and their mission to resurrect Superman (killed by Doomsday in the previous film) was enough to make the film work, and it soon became common knowledge that the entire DC Extended Universe project was in disarray.

As grassroots support for previous director Snyder and his vision for *Justice League* grew, DC continued to produce entries in the franchise to continued mixed results. In 2018, Momoa starred in the first-ever *Aquaman* film, which coasted along even more on the natural charisma of Momoa than it did on the talents of veteran horror director James Wan and longtime DC comics creator Geoff Johns. The following year, *Shazam!*—aka the original Captain Marvel—was brought to the screen for the first time in almost sixty years with a whimsical effort starring the charming and funny Zachary Levi as the childlike superhero. The film was embraced by fans as a break from the DC Extended Universe's typical doom-and-gloom. The same could not be said for *Wonder Woman 1984*, the mishandled 2020 sequel to the 2017 original that squandered much of the goodwill the first movie had built.

Finally, in 2021 DC put out the so-called Snyder Cut of *Justice League* as part of Warner Media's newly launched HBO Max streaming service. With Snyder brought back to reshoot and reedit the film he had originally been hired to make, the film was expected to fix the mistakes of the original version and be an overall more satisfying experience. However, all it did was further polarize fans. Fervent supporters of Snyder's work and philosophy ate it up, while most other fans were even more turned off by it than they had been by the Whedon film. It has been reported that Warners and DC were so displeased with the direction of the DC Extended Universe that they decided to use the new *Flash* standalone movie, set for release in June 2023, as a way of completely resetting the DC film continuity and starting from scratch. Nevertheless, this hasn't completely stopped the production of further films in the various franchises, as 2023's *Shazam! Fury of the Gods* and *Aquaman and the Lost Kingdom* would attest.

This detachment from established continuity was further enforced by the spring 2022 release of *The Batman*—the eleventh film to star the Caped Crusader, featuring a brand-new Bruce Wayne/Batman, Robert Pattinson, the seventh actor to play the part. Having nothing to do with the DC films of the past decade, and darker even than the Nolan *Dark Knight* trilogy, the product of science fiction director Matt Reeves (who first came to fame with the 2008 monster movie *Cloverfield*) established Batman once again in his own fictional world, separate from other DC heroes.

As of this writing, the future of DC superhero films seems to be at a crossroads. Despite being the most traditionally popular and loved superheroes of all time, they have had a rough time of it as of late on the silver screen. Some have even argued that the iconic images of DC superheroes, which took decades of cultivation to develop, have been tarnished by recent cinematic outings. Nevertheless, it's a safe bet that there will always be a place for Superman, Batman, and the rest of the DC pantheon in movie theaters and on streaming platforms the world over. From George Reeves to Henry Cavill and from Adam West to Robert Pattinson, DC characters have carved a historic path worthy of their cultural status, and today there is an entire generation of fans that has enjoyed them even more for their adventures on the screen than on the pages of comic books. These superheroes are the definition of "larger than life," and unsurprisingly, have found a fitting home in a medium that makes them larger than ever, both literally and figuratively.

Batman and Beyond: Animated DC Films

Going back to the classic Fleischer shorts of the 1940s, DC has had a proud history of bringing its characters to the big screen in animated form. And yet, DC did not get to produce its first animated feature-length, theatrically released film for another half-century. Building on the phenomenal success of Bruce Timm and Paul Dini's *Batman: The Animated Series* on TV, Warner Bros. produced *Batman: Mask of the Phantasm* in 1993. A noirish thriller that boasts the excellent voicework of Kevin Conroy as Batman and Mark Hamill as the Joker (as heard on the TV series), *Mask of the Phantasm* explored more mature themes than the TV version would typically allow and is often regarded as among the very best of all Batman films, animated or otherwise.

Perhaps owing to the success of *Batman: TAS* and *Mask of the Phantasm*, a disproportionate number of DC animated film releases have been Batman-related, including *Batman: The Killing Joke* (2016), which adapted the seminal 1988 Alan Moore/Brian Bolland graphic novel; and *Return of the Caped Crusaders* (2016), based on the 1966 TV series and even using original stars Adam West, Burt Ward, and Julie Newmar. Even many direct-to-home-video animated film releases have starred Batman, including *Batman & Mr. Freeze: SubZero* (1998), *Batman: Year One* (2011), *The Dark Knight Returns* (2012), and *Batman: Hush* (2019), most of which have also adapted beloved story lines from the comics. Other of DC's animated features have done the same, including *Superman: Doomsday* (2007), *Green Lantern: First Flight* (2009), *All-Star Superman* (2011), and *Justice League: The Flashpoint Paradox* (2013).

The general high quality of DC's animated feature releases has caused them to be held in high regard by fans. In recent years, more lighthearted fare has also made its way to the big screen, such as *Teen Titans Go! To the Movies* (2018), based on the successful Cartoon Network TV series, as well as *DC League of Super Pets* (2022)—the only theatrically released DC animated films to date that have not starred Batman.

ICONS #8

Clobberin' Time!

Creators: Stan Lee and Jack Kirby

First Appearance: *The Fantastic Four* #1, November 1961

Alter Egos: Reed Richards (Mr. Fantastic), Sue Storm-Richards (Invisible Girl/Woman), Johnny Storm (Human Torch), Benjamin Grimm (Thing)

Powers: elasticity (Mr. Fantastic); invisibility and force-field projection (Invisible Woman); flame projection, flight, fire absorption, and manipulation (Human Torch); rock-hard skin, superhuman strength (Thing)

Archenemies: the Mole Man, Dr. Doom, Kang the Conqueror, Galactus, the Super Skrull, Annihilus, Psycho-Man, the Frightful Four, Molecule Man, the Mad Thinker

The Marvel Age of comics that kicked off in the early 1960s had many key characters, but the group that truly led the charge was the wonderful, dysfunctional, quirky, and for their time truly groundbreaking quartet known as the **FANTASTIC FOUR.** The brainchildren of the brilliant and indispensable creative duo of Stan "the Man" Lee and Jack "King" Kirby, the team comprised the professorial Reed Richards, aka Mr. Fantastic; the maternal Sue Storm, aka the Invisible Girl, Reed's eventual wife; Sue's brother Johnny, the hotshot Human Torch; and Benjamin Grimm, the irascible and ever-lovin' Thing. Their cosmic adventures have helped redefine the superhero medium for more than sixty years.

THE ORIGIN

When genius scientist Reed Richards builds a rocket ship to attempt the first-ever voyage into deep space, he enlists his best friend, skilled pilot Ben Grimm, in addition to his girlfriend Sue and her teenage brother Johnny as crew. But the experimental ship is blasted with cosmic rays and forced to make an emergency landing on Earth. It's there that they discover that the rays have bestowed fantastical powers upon them: in the case of Grimm, whose rock-like transformation is permanent, the accident is a source of guilt for Richards. Still, the four decide to use their new powers for good, setting up shop in the Baxter Building in Midtown Manhattan (later replaced by Four Freedom Plaza, then a second Baxter Building).

THE CREATION

Although the two men would later dispute the details and who, if either, was more responsible, it was Stan Lee, then the longtime editor in chief of Marvel Comics under various corporate names, and Jack Kirby, the most talented and influential artist in the bullpen, who created the Four at the behest of publisher Martin Goodman, who wanted a team of superheroes to rival DC's Justice League of America. The result would mark Marvel's return to the superhero genre after largely abandoning it like most companies did

Protosuperhero Heracles (later known as Hercules in the Roman tradition) does battle with the river god Achelous in this 1824 bronze sculpture by Francois-Joseph Bosio. (Louvre Museum, Paris)
CREDIT: ROB OO FROM NL / WIKIMEDIA COMMONS

The medieval figure Robin Hood, as depicted here in a 1912 illustration by Louis Rhead, had a direct influence on the development of the concept of costumed crusaders and vigilantes. (*Bold Robin Hood and His Outlaw Band*) CREDIT: BY LOUIS RHEAD / WIKIMEDIA COMMONS

The 1920 silent film classic *The Mark of Zorro*, starring Douglas Fairbanks in the title role, implanted the masked avenger in the imaginations of a generation of future comic book creators. CREDIT: DOUGLAS FAIRBANKS PICTURES CORPORATION / UNITED ARTISTS / WIKIMEDIA COMMONS

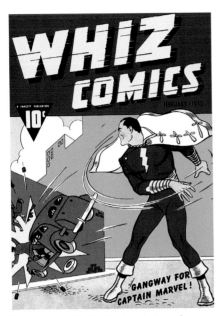

The creation of C. C. Beck with Pete Costanza and Bill Parker, the original Captain Marvel (later known as Shazam) makes his first appearance on the cover of Whiz Comics #2.

Plastic Man and The Spirit, drawn here by Gill Fox for this January 1943 issue, were Quality Comics's two great contributions to the Golden Age of superheroes.

The January 1943 issue of Detective Comics, in which the Dynamic Duo contend with their greatest foe. During the 1940s, Bob Kane, Bill Finger, and Jerry Robinson created the template for Batman and his world.

The 1944 Captain America serial from Republic Pictures represented the first time a character from Marvel Comics (then known as Timely Comics) was adapted for the big screen.

Emerging from the world of radio and pulp novels, The Shadow, seen here in an original painting by Charles Joseph Coil, was a classic superhero who predated the rise of comic books. CREDIT: BY CHARLES JOSEPH COLL / WIKIMEDIA COMMONS

Wonder Woman's popularity was so strong that she was one of the few superheroes whose comic books continued to be published when superhero comics died out in the early 1950s, as demonstrated by this February 1951 retelling of her origin story. CREDIT: DC COMICS INC./PHOTOFEST ©DC COMICS INC.

Superman's adventures became decidedly silly and strange during the Silver Age, as typified by this infamous September 1964 issue that came out in the wake of the Beatles. CREDIT: FLAB/ALAMY STOCK PHOTO

The *Batman* TV series starring Adam West and Burt Ward enjoyed three smash seasons in the late 1960s, lampooning Silver Age comics' wackiness and setting the standard for the Caped Crusader for decades. CREDIT: 20TH CENTURY STUDIOS/PHOTOFEST ©20TH CENTURY STUDIOS

Bob Kane, co-creator of Batman (who took full credit for many years), enjoyed celebrity status when the *Batman* TV show became a hit and spent his time creating a line of original Batman paintings. CREDIT: PHOTOFEST

Dr. Doom tangles with the Fantastic Four in this typically trippy cover by Jack "King" Kirby for the March 1967 issue of "The World's Greatest Comic Magazine" from the height of the Marvel Age.

CREDIT: MARVEL COMICS GROUP/PHOTOFEST

A bona fide Mexican sensation, the legendary masked luchador El Santo battled the forces of evil in a series of fifty-one movies made between 1959 and 1981, sometimes with Blue Demon by his side, as in 1972's *Santo and Blue Demon vs. Dracula and The Wolf Man*. CREDIT: PICTURELUX/ALAMY STOCK PHOTO

Super Friends was a Saturday morning cartoon institution from 1973 to 1985, bringing a simplified version of the Justice League into the homes of little Gen Xers everywhere.

CREDIT: HANNA-BARBERA PRODUCTIONS/PHOTOFEST

©HANNA-BARBERA PRODUCTIONS

Christopher Reeve forever immortalized himself as the definitive Man of Steel in the blockbuster *Superman: The Movie* (1978) and its three sequels. CREDIT: ALL STAR PICTURE LIBRARY/ALAMY

Before he was The Phantom of the Opera on Broadway, Michael Crawford was Condorman, perhaps the unlikeliest of heroes, in Disney's obscure 1981 offering. CREDIT: PICTORIAL PRESS/ALAMY STOCK PHOTO

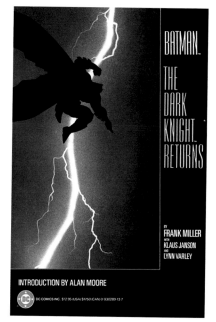

The iconic cover of *The Dark Knight Returns*, which helped redefine comic books and comic book heroes for the Modern Age.
CREDIT: DC COMICS INC./PHOTOFEST ©DC COMICS INC.

Michael Keaton comes face-to-face with Jack Nicholson in this unforgettable moment from Tim Burton's *Batman*, the runaway hit of 1989.
CREDIT: WARNER BROS./PHOTOFEST ©WARNER BROS.

Brought to life by the Jim Henson Studio, the Turtles chow down on their favorite food in this scene from *Teenage Mutant Ninja Turtles II: The Secret of the Ooze* (1991).
CREDIT: NEW LINE CINEMA/PHOTOFEST ©NEW LINE CINEMA

Though not as well-known today as his creative partner Stan Lee, Jack Kirby was just as responsible (if not more so) for the explosion of Marvel Comics characters that were created in the 1960s. CREDIT: BY SUSAN SKAAR, KIRBYMUSEUM.ORG / WIKIMEDIA COMMONS

Brandon Lee became a tragic figure after being accidentally killed on the set, but his 1994 performance as Eric Draven in Alex Proyas's *The Crow* is one of the most celebrated in the history of comic book movies.
CREDIT: MIRAMAX FILMS/PHOTOFEST ©MIRAMAX FILMS

Hugh Jackman brought Wolverine to life to an uncanny degree in a string of X-Men movies and spin-offs, including Brett Ratner's *X-Men: The Last Stand* (2006). CREDIT: 20TH CENTURY STUDIOS/PHOTOFEST ©20TH CENTURY STUDIOS

Spider-Man 2 marked Tobey Maguire's second turn as Peter Parker. The 2004 film is often cited as the very best of the Spider-Man movies. CREDIT: SONY PICTURES/ PHOTOFEST ©SONY PICTURES

The living embodiment of Marvel Comics, Stan Lee (seen here at the 2014 Phoenix Comi Con) was not only one of its greatest creators, but also its greatest goodwill ambassador.

CREDIT: BY GAGE SKIDMORE / WIKIMEDIA COMMONS

James Gunn's *Guardians of the Galaxy* (2014) was Marvel Studios' most unexpected mega-hit, and its snarky tone and pop culture self-awareness changed the way superhero movies were made. CREDIT: WALT DISNEY STUDIOS MOTION PICTURES/PHOTOFEST ©WALT DISNEY STUDIOS

Wonder Woman (Gal Gadot), Batman (Ben Affleck), and the Flash (Ezra Miller) join forces for the first time on screen in *Justice League* (2017). CREDIT: WARNER BROS./PHOTOFEST ©WARNER BROS.

T'Challa, the first Black comic book super-hero, comes to life in the form of the late Chadwick Boseman in Ryan Coogler's Oscar-nominated *Black Panther* (2018). CREDIT: WALT DISNEY STUDIOS MOTION PICTURES/ PHOTOFEST ©WALT DISNEY STUDIOS

After eleven years, the Marvel Cinematic Universe's epic Infinity Gauntlet saga came to its star-studded conclusion in *Avengers: Endgame* (2019), which set a new record for all-time highest grossing movie. CREDIT: WALT DISNEY STUDIOS MOTION PICTURES/PHO-TOFEST ©WALT DISNEY STUDIOS

John Cena became an overnight sensation as the star of the darkly comical *Peacemaker*, the current HBO Max series based on the character originally created by Joe Gill and Pat Boyette for Charlton Comics in 1966 (but now a part of the DC Extended Universe). CREDIT: HBO MAX/PHOTOFEST ©HBO MAX

at the start of the 1950s. Given creative freedom, the two men sought to write a comic book and build a team that would stand out from superheroes of the past.

A NEW KIND OF SUPERTEAM

Marvel Comics became known for more down-to-earth, relatable characters in comparison to the more two-dimensional DC icons. That reputation began with the creation of the Fantastic Four. Bickering, disagreeing, and holding grudges, they couldn't be more different from the Justice League, whose members were always in perfect harmony and seemed to have no personal hang-ups. The Thing started out very bitter over his transformation, which became a source of friction between himself and Richards. Such themes continued over the years, including a memorable 1980s story line in which Johnny begins a relationship with (and eventually marries) Ben's girlfriend Alicia Masters, after Ben exiles himself temporarily on a planet that gives him the ability to revert to human form. The Fantastic Four also made history as the first major comic book superheroes who didn't hide their identities and were fully known to the public.

THE WORLD'S GREATEST COMICS MAGAZINE

The near decade run of Lee and Kirby on *Fantastic Four* is one of the all-time legendary creative collaborations in comics history, with Lee's science fiction sensibilities perfectly complementing Kirby's bold and exciting line work. Like any great comic book, there were dramatic changes over the years, with new creative teams and even new members joining. The late 1970s through mid-1980s were marked by the influence of writer and artist

John Byrne, who helped modernize the team and added She-Hulk during the temporary absence of the Thing. The late 1990s was another fertile period for the Fantastic Four, with legendary former X-Men scribe Chris Claremont and gifted Spanish newcomer Salvador Larocca at the helm.

THE SAGA OF THE SURFER

One of the most memorable Fantastic Four story lines took place in the midst of Lee and Kirby's tenure and gave rise to another of Marvel's most enduring heroes. The arrival of the mighty Galactus, intent on absorbing Earth for nourishment, leads to the world-eater's mysterious alien herald, the Silver Surfer, standing against his master when the Fantastic Four—with help from Alicia Masters, who bonds with the Surfer—convinces the herald of the moral wrong of what Galactus is doing. Galactus would remain a thorn in the Fantastic Four's collective side for years, and the Surfer remained on Earth (for a time), his space-faring powers temporarily stripped from him by Galactus, who felt betrayed by him.

SOME LESS-THAN-FANTASTIC ADAPTATIONS

Despite its important status, the Fantastic Four's translation to the big screen hasn't been the most memorable. A notorious low-budget film was made by B-movie master Roger Corman in 1994 that was never released but can be found in bootleg versions. Film production studio 20th Century Fox produced two Fantastic Four films in the 2000s, the second of which included the Silver Surfer and Galactus (sort of). Although critically panned, the films were highlighted by excellent performances from Michael Chiklis as the Thing, and Chris "Captain America" Evans as Human Torch.

A 2015 reboot fared even worse. In 2019, it was announced that thanks to Disney's acquisition of 20th Century Fox, the Fantastic Four would finally be brought into the Marvel Cinematic Universe.

MARVEL'S FIRST FAMILY

Perhaps what has caused the Fantastic Four to resonate with fans for all these decades is the genuine feeling of camaraderie—flawed and strained though it may be—that exists among them. Reed, Sue, Johnny, and Ben (and later Reed and Sue's mutant son, Franklin) are a family first and foremost. Before the X-Men, before Spider-Man, before Hulk, before Iron Man, and even the Avengers, they were the ones who ushered in the modern era of superheroics that is still with us. What started as Lee and Kirby's creative experiment has set the standard for how we now expect superheroes to be characterized. "World's Greatest Comics Magazine" is a bold moniker, but it just may well have been the most influential.

9

MAKE MINE MOVIES

Marvel's Bumpy Road to the Big Screen

Marvel's colorful and iconic characters are more culturally inescapable than ever since being featured in the movies in recent years. Through the success of the most lucrative film franchise to ever exist, Marvel has become ubiquitous, its heroes affecting millions of people who may never have even picked up a comic book in their lives. Marvel's superheroes are no longer characters whose primary home is on the printed page. They have become full-fledged movie stars who live and breathe in the hearts and minds of at least one entire generation of fans that has grown up with their domination of the silver screen. The Marvel Cinematic Universe has eclipsed even *Star Wars* as the epicenter of our popular culture, and along the way it transformed Marvel Comics into Marvel Studios.

Through a process that's been nearly a half-century in the making, Marvel has made incredible strides in the world of motion pictures. The establishment of Marvel Studios' Marvel Cinematic Universe is only the latest and most high-profile chapter in that fascinating story. While

Marvel movies haven't been with us as long as DC's movies, they have now unseated DC from its long-held position as the trendsetter in superhero films, causing the venerable home of Superman and Batman to now try to play catchup and follow in the shadow of Iron Man and Spider-Man. With its outlandish characters and trippy story lines, Marvel has long seemed perfect for the movie medium; all it took was for special effects technology to catch up with the imaginations of Stan Lee, Jack Kirby, Steve Ditko, Chris Claremont, Jim Starlin, Todd McFarlane, and the rest of Marvel's brilliant comic creators.

At first, Marvel wasn't a player in the movie world. Despite existing about as long as DC, it hadn't been able to match the success DC was having, especially in crossing over its two biggest characters, Superman and Batman, to the screen, which DC had been doing since the 1940s. With the exception of an early Captain America theatrical serial made in the days when the company was still known as Timely Comics, Marvel fans were stuck with having to imagine what their favorite heroes would look like in the movies, which was ironic, considering how colorful and entertaining Marvel comic books were during the Silver and Bronze Ages compared to their more staid and static DC counterparts.

Part of the reason may have been that Marvel wasn't actively pursuing having its characters adapted for the big screen. Original owner Martin Goodman didn't seem to be able to see beyond the world of comic books, and the company he sold it to, Perfect Film & Chemical Corporation, had little interest, at first, in capitalizing on the growing cultural cache of the characters it owned. It took editor in chief Stan Lee to make things happen by the middle of the 1970s, pitching Marvel's characters to studios and trying to get them better seen. For example, it was Lee's maneuverings that got TV deals for both Spider-Man and the Incredible Hulk to be developed into series. In the case of the Hulk, the show was a tremendous success and quickly made him into one of Marvel's most well-known characters.

In those days, it seemed like the more modest medium of television was the only place where Marvel characters could make the transition. In fact, although the TV version of *Spider-Man* was less successful than that of *The Incredible Hulk*, it did lead to the first Marvel feature film ever made. The ninety-minute pilot for *Spider-Man*, which only aired in the United States as a TV movie, starring Nicholas Hammond as the Wall-Crawler, enjoyed a limited theatrical release elsewhere throughout the world—a humble beginning for what would eventually become a mighty film empire. Lee worked out a similar deal with Japanese movie studio Toei to produce a *Spider-Man* TV series that led to a one-off theatrical short subject. Lee's wheeling and dealing in the late 1970s also led to a poorly received 1978 TV movie based on Dr. Strange, which failed to get picked up as an ongoing series by CBS, as well as two Captain America TV movies in 1979, *Captain America* and *Captain America II: Death Too Soon*, which bore very little resemblance to the Cap who fans knew and loved. A big part of the problem was that Marvel itself had very little power or leverage beyond licensing its characters, especially creatively. If Lee and company wanted their characters adapted, any hope for faithfulness to the source material was tenuous at best.

Nevertheless, Marvel remained a treasure trove of intellectual property, needing only the right individuals with enough creative vision to come along. But the first feature film based on a Marvel character to see wide theatrical release would do little to encourage anyone that this would ever happen. Just as Marvel Comics and its parent company Marvel Entertainment Group were being prepped for a sale to media production and distribution entity New World Entertainment, none other than George Lucas, fresh off the success of the original *Star Wars* trilogy and the first two *Indiana Jones*

The Men Behind the Spider

Throughout Marvel's history, its most enduringly popular and adaptable superhero has been Spider-Man, played on screen by more actors than anyone else. Here's a look at those who've spun webs and crawled walls over the years (and that's even without including the infamously unauthorized Turkish version).

NICHOLAS HAMMOND
Spider-Man (1977)

Launching to fame as one of the singing Von Trapp children in the 1965 classic *The Sound of Music*, Hammond would, a dozen years later, become the first person to portray Spider-Man on screen. Although his screen debut as the Wall-Crawler was intended as a feature-length pilot for the television series that was to follow, it did get a theatrical release internationally, and was aired in the United States as a television movie. In more recent years, Hammond can be seen in Quentin Tarantino's *Once Upon a Time in Hollywood*, in which he has a memorable turn as the eccentric director Sam Wanamaker.

SHINJI TODO
Spider-Man (1978)

The least-known actor to play Spidey (at least in the United States) would be Todo, who portrayed him in a bizarre TV series in Japan that was part of a short-lived deal between Marvel Comics and Japanese movie studio Toei. Todo's career was just starting when he took on this role. He would go on to much success in Japanese *tokusatsu* (science fiction) television, including recurring roles in the various *Super Sentai* series, which later reached Western shores as *Mighty Morphin Power Rangers*. In the summer of 1978, Todo appeared in a special theatrical Spider-Man short released as part of Toei's "carnival" series of theatrical packages for kids.

TOBEY MAGUIRE
Spider-Man (2002), Spider-Man 2 (2004), Spider-Man 3 (2007), Spider-Man: No Way Home (2021)

A child actor during the late 1980s and early 1990s, he made his feature film debut with a supporting role in the Leonardo DiCaprio vehicle *This*

Boy's Life (1993), which led to a lifelong friendship between the two. Leading parts in *Pleasantville* (1998), *The Cider House Rules* (1999), and *Wonder Boys* (2000) helped propel him to stardom and put him on Sam Raimi's radar when it came time to cast his Spider-Man. He received acclaim for his role in the Oscar-nominated *Seabiscuit* (2003), and in 2013 reunited with DiCaprio when he played Nick Carraway in Baz Luhrmann's ambitious version of *The Great Gatsby*.

ANDREW GARFIELD
The Amazing Spider-Man (2012), *The Amazing Spider-Man 2* (2014), *Spider-Man: No Way Home* (2021)

Enjoying shared citizenship due to his British and American parents, Garfield grew up in the United Kingdom and got his start on British television, including a guest spot on *Doctor Who* in 2007. He achieved notoriety in the United States due to his performance in Aaron Sorkin's *The Social Network*, which led to his being cast as Spider-Man. He is the only actor to play Spider-Man who has been nominated for an Oscar (for *Hacksaw Ridge* in 2017 and *tick, tick . . . BOOM!* in 2022) as well as a Tony (for *Angels in America* in 2018). He also appeared alongside Adam Driver in Martin Scorsese's *Silence* (2016).

TOM HOLLAND
Captain America: Civil War (2016), *Spider-Man: Homecoming* (2017), *Avengers: Infinity War* (2018), *Avengers: Endgame* (2019), *Spider-Man: Far from Home* (2019), *Spider-Man: No Way Home* (2021)

The closest in age to the young Peter Parker of all screen Spider-Men, Holland has also played the part more times than anyone else. First discovered for his dancing skills while still a child, he achieved notoriety in his native United Kingdom in the stage production of *Billy Elliot: The Musical*, as well as the 2012 film *The Impossible*, which also gained him attention in America. Just prior to being cast as Spider-Man, he infamously flopped in his audition to play Finn in *The Force Awakens*. He recently nabbed the starring role in an upcoming biopic on the life of Fred Astaire.

movies, set about producing a motion picture adaptation of *Howard the Duck*, a quirky Marvel property from the unconventional mind of writer Steve Gerber, which Lucas had been interested in since he first discovered it back in the 1970s. Ambitious in scale, with an all-star cast and the full power of Lucasfilm behind it, *Howard the Duck* (1986) was nevertheless a failure—and not just your run-of-the-mill bomb, but a disaster of epic proportions, often considered among the very worst movies ever made. For what's generally considered the first true Marvel movie, it did not bode well for the future of Marvel on film.

It was a devastating blow, and it took a couple years before anyone again saw the value in Marvel properties. Things were quiet until the end of the 1980s, when New World sold Marvel to cosmetics mogul Ronald Perelman, who took a very serious approach to viewing the comics company as a source of valuable intellectual property that could be turned into movies. Still, despite Perelman's ambitions, it was very difficult to get movie studios to view Marvel that way. While DC had its parent company Warner Bros., and was making mainstream blockbusters out of Superman and Batman, Marvel had to settle for infamous stuff like *The Punisher* (1989) starring Dolph Lundgren of *Rocky IV* fame as Frank Castle (sans his trademark skull emblem), and a decidedly low-rent *Captain America* (1990) starring Matt Salinger—son of *Catcher in the Rye* author J. D. Salinger—as the Star-Spangled Avenger (complete with inexplicably fake ears on his rubbery costume and a Red Skull, who was Italian instead of German). Confidence in either project was so low that they didn't even receive an initial domestic theatrical release, instead coming out internationally first and then going straight to home video in the United States many months later.

It was a baffling situation for a company whose comic books at the time were the best-selling in the industry. Rumors of possible projects abounded, including a Spider-Man film directed by horror-meister John Carpenter and an Iron Man starring Tom Cruise as Tony Stark. But nothing came to pass—many at the time attributed the problems partially to the fact that movie special effects, up to that point, simply weren't advanced enough to do justice to the Marvel superheroes. But that definitely began to change during the 1990s, and so did Marvel's fortunes in the motion picture business. Perelman sold the company to Toy Biz in 1997—together, Toy Biz owner Isaac Perlmutter, along with Marvel head Avi Arad, set about changing the Marvel movie approach by working to creatively partner with film studios to which they would license their characters, thus avoiding the surrender of creative control that had plagued them in the past.

The first result of this new approach was Marvel's first breakout theatrical movie success, a partnership with New Line Cinema, which ironically was centered around a character who was never a major figure in the Marvel Universe. Marv Wolfman and Gene Colan's Blade wasn't even really a superhero, but rather a vampire-hunting vampire who originated from Marvel's 1970s dalliances in horror comics. But audiences didn't care: the film, written by David S. Goyer, directed by Stephen Norrington, and starring action hero Wesley Snipes as Blade, was a runaway hit in 1998, and even produced two sequels and a TV series. Finally, Marvel had made a splash on the big screen—even if most moviegoers probably didn't even realize Blade was a Marvel character.

The success of *Blade* made studios begin to take an interest in other Marvel properties. Major Hollywood powerhouse 20th Century Fox took aim at the X-Men, which was then Marvel's most popular comic book. *Blade* notwithstanding, this was the first time a true big-budget blockbuster was being built around one of Marvel's main properties, and really the first time a major film about a team of superheroes had ever been attempted. Richard

Donner, director of *Superman: The Movie*, had long been attached to a proposed X-Men film, and in the end his production company did play a role, but the film would instead be helmed by acclaimed director Bryan Singer. An all-star cast was put together, with Halle Berry as Storm, Famke Jansen as Jean Grey, Ian McKellen as Magneto, Patrick Stewart as Charles Xavier, and Anna Paquin as Rogue.

But it was the casting of relatively unknown Australian actor Hugh Jackman as the X-Men's most popular member, Wolverine, that became the film's crowning achievement. Although a bit tall for the famously short Wolvy, Jackman embodied the character as no actor had done for a superhero since Christopher Reeve's Superman, and when the movie was released in 2000, fans were sold largely on the power of his iconic performance. It told them that the studio had taken the property seriously, which was a major break from Marvel movies of the past. *X-Men* was a resounding mega-hit and was responsible for proving to studios that movies about Marvel superheroes could be extremely lucrative. In fact, most point to *X-Men* as the start not just of the Marvel movie era, but of the extensive modern-day superhero movie craze that has been ongoing ever since.

A veritable franchise was kicked off, with the superior sequel *X2* hitting theaters in 2002, when it was joined by an even bigger Marvel icon who finally made his way to the big screen after forty years. Earlier, Columbia Pictures had snagged the rights to Spider-Man and kicked their project into motion with Sam Raimi as director and the baby-faced Tobey Maguire tapped to play the young Wall-Crawler himself, opposite Willem Dafoe as the deranged Green Goblin. There was some concern over the credentials of Raimi, previously known mainly for the *Evil Dead* series and quirky fare like *Darkman* (1990) and *The Quick and the Dead* (1995). But he was more than up to the task; *Spider-Man* smashed *X-Men*'s previous box office numbers, and for the first time there were multiple Marvel movies vying for audiences' attention.

It was the age of licensed Marvel movies, and they were coming fast and furious. Adding to its *Spider-Man* franchise, Fox put out *Daredevil* (2003) starring Ben Affleck as Matt Murdock and Michael Clarke Duncan as the Kingpin. Taking its story from Frank Miller's memorable "Death of Elektra" arc, it was the first comic book movie to be based directly on a specific comic book story line. Universal Pictures, traditionally known as the classic monster studio, brought the first film adaptation of the Hulk to the big screen the same year, bringing in Ang Lee, visionary director of *Crouching Tiger, Hidden Dragon* (2000). Though many felt it missed the mark creatively, *Hulk* featured innovative panel editing that resembled actual comic book pages, and was far more faithful to the source material than the 1970s TV series. Also that year, the Punisher finally got a proper treatment after the 1990 debacle, with Thomas Jane in the lead. Even characters like Man-Thing were getting into the act.

But despite the turnaround, folks at Marvel still felt they could do even better. Some subpar licensed adaptations, such as the 2005 *Fantastic Four*, an erratic take on Marvel's first family that captured little of the spirit of the World's Greatest Comics Magazine, and the unintentionally campy *Ghost Rider* (2007) starring the histrionic Nicolas Cage as Johnny Blaze, began to convince Marvel to take an even bigger role. Arad's wunderkind Kevin Feige had been put in charge of the Marvel Studios branch of the company that had been founded some years earlier to oversee film production. Feige and others envisioned the role of Marvel Studios differently. With enough capital, it was felt that Marvel Studios could become an actual movie studio, producing its own films with its own characters, free of outside studio tampering. Additionally, with that kind of creative control, Feige hypothesized

The Ultimate Multiverse: Animated Marvel Films

Although Marvel's live-action features have somewhat overshadowed DC's in recent years, that has not quite been the case in the area of animated feature films. Marvel doesn't have as much of a successful and long-running track record as its distinguished competition in that department. But although they got off to a bit of a later start, Marvel's output has been catching up, especially in recent years with the blockbuster success of *Spider-Man: Into the Spider-Verse*, which won the Oscar for Best Animated Feature in 2019 and dazzled fans worldwide with its astonishing computer animation and clever incorporation of so many of Spidey's incarnations.

Marvel's forays into animated features began in 2006 with the Marvel Animated Features project, an eight-picture deal between Marvel Entertainment and film studio/distributor Lions Gate. This partnership kicked off with two animated features centering on the *Ultimate Avengers* line, and also included such titles as *The Invincible Iron Man* (2007), *Doctor Strange: Sorcerer Supreme* (2007), *Planet Hulk* (2010), and *Thor: Tales of Asgard* (2011). As with most Marvel animated features, these films were released direct-to-home video, and later distributed to television.

Other more recent direct-to-video or streaming titles include the *Heroes United* series, intended to capitalize on the success of the live-action Marvel Cinematic Universe. But it wasn't until *Into the Spider-Verse* that Marvel really came into its own as a force in the animated feature department, and led to two sequels, *Spider-Man: Across the Spider-Verse*, released theatrically in 2023, and *Spider-Man: Beyond the Spider-Verse*, set to be released in 2024. Prior to this, Marvel's greatest animated success may have come from *Big Hero 6*, a property only tangentially related to the mainstream Marvel comics universe, and turned into a popular Disney animated feature in 2014 thanks to Marvel's incorporation into the House of Mouse.

the creation of an actual cinematic universe to rival the Marvel Universe that comics fans had enjoyed for decades, with interconnected story lines and characters crossing over into each other's movies—a fictional world just as fully conceived and developed as the one it was adapting. The Marvel Cinematic Universe was about to be born.

ICONS #9

The Green Goliath

Creators: Stan Lee and Jack Kirby

First Appearance: *The Incredible Hulk* #1, May 1962

Alter Ego: Bruce Banner

Powers: near-limitless strength and invulnerability; advanced healing; ability to leap great distances

Archenemies: the Leader, the Abomination, the Absorbing Man, Glenn Talbot, Thunderbolt Ross, Wendigo, Juggernaut, the Maestro, the Gray Gargoyle, Rhino

Part King Kong, part Frankenstein's monster, part Jekyll and Hyde, **THE INCREDIBLE HULK** has long been a character that defies description, treading the boundary between superhero and monster, a cautionary tale about man's tampering with nature and the universal struggle to contain the demons within us all. He has long been one of Marvel's most widely known characters, thanks in large part to his memorable portrayal on both the 1970s television series *The Incredible Hulk*, as well as in a string of Marvel Cinematic Universe films decades later. In all his various forms, he has enthralled readers and viewers with his endless struggle for dominance with his alter ego Bruce Banner, an ultimate power fantasy of inner rage and brutal force unleashed.

THE ORIGIN

A nuclear scientist reluctantly working on a gamma bomb, Dr. Bruce Banner is exposed to a powerful dose of gamma radiation when, in a selfless act of protection, he throws himself on Rick Jones, a young thrill-seeker trespassing on the test site. As a result, he's transformed into the gigantic and powerful Hulk. Initially, the creature is gray, and the transformation occurs at sunset, but soon, he morphs into his more familiar form—a green, simple-minded giant whose transformation is triggered whenever Banner becomes angry or agitated. On the run from the military led by General Thaddeus "Thunderbolt" Ross—the father of his great love, Betty—Banner goes into hiding, working to find a cure for his condition while attempting to restrain the beast within.

THE CREATION

Inspired by the Thing, who had quickly become readers' favorite member of the Fantastic Four, Stan Lee set about creating a new monster-type superhero, this time taking his cue from some of the greatest monsters of fiction, including the misunderstood Frankenstein Monster, the sympathetic Quasimodo, and most notably Dr. Jekyll and Mr. Hyde, which is where he got the concept of transformation and the unleashing of his protagonist's repressed id. Lee also cited inspiration from the Jewish legend of the Golem, as well as the common Cold War-era trope of radiation-produced monsters.

As designed by Jack Kirby, Hulk was originally gray, but printing led the two creators to switch to a more vibrant green color.

THE DESERT WANDERER

The Hulk became a charter member of the original Avengers when the team was first formed in 1963—although he quickly exited the group due to his cantankerous nature and desire for solitude. As years went on, the "Jade Giant" was portrayed in a less articulate, more childlike fashion, his vocabulary reduced to simple sentences, a la Frankenstein Monster in *Bride of Frankenstein*. In his classic 1970s period, drawn by seminal artist Herb Trimpe, Hulk could usually be found in self-imposed exile in the deserts of the Southwest, avoiding human society as much as possible, yet constantly tormented by the government and a whole host of fantastical enemies. A gentle being at heart, he could be provoked into violent wrath, and only got stronger as he got angrier.

JOE FIXIT AND FRIENDS

Few characters in comics have gone through so many dramatic mutations and transformations as the Hulk. One of the more notable occurred during the legendary run of writer Peter David in the early 1990s, when Hulk morphed back into his gray form and became the Las Vegas leg-breaker "Mr. Fixit"—his childlike innocence replaced with sardonic cynicism, as he kept Banner imprisoned within his mind. Over the years, he and Banner have actually been separated into two beings, and at other times the Banner and Hulk personas have even been merged into peaceful coexistence, combining the power of the latter with the mind of the former. In fact, this version could even be seen in *Avengers: Endgame* (2019).

DON'T MAKE HIM ANGRY, MR. McGEE

Without question, what rocketed the character into the stratosphere in mainstream culture was the hugely popular *Incredible Hulk* TV series that ran on CBS from 1978 to 1982, featuring *My Favorite Martian* star Bill Bixby as David Banner (the name was changed by TV executives, according to Stan Lee, because "Bruce" sounded "gay"), and bodybuilder Lou Ferrigno as the green-skinned goliath. Patterned on the 1960s series *The Fugitive*, it featured Banner hiding out in different towns each week, always running into trouble while searching for a cure, stalked by the determined reporter Jack McGee. Due to TV budgets and limited special effects, it was a very scaled-down version of Hulk, but at the same time it humanized him, making the show that much more relatable.

THE THREE MOVIE BANNERS

The character finally made it to the big screen in the 2003 film titled simply *Hulk,* directed by Ang Lee. Predating the Marvel Cinematic Universe, it starred Eric Bana as Bruce Banner, Jennifer Connelly as Betty Ross, and Sam Elliott as Thunderbolt Ross, with Nick Nolte as Banner's abusive father and a villain reminiscent of Absorbing Man. Five years later, Hulk was incorporated into the Marvel Cinematic Universe with the reboot *The Incredible Hulk*, starring Edward Norton as Banner, Liv Tyler as Betty, William Hurt as Ross, and Tim Roth as the Abomination. Marvel later recast Banner/Hulk with Mark Ruffalo, who truly made the role his own in the *Avengers* series of movies, as well as hilarious turns alongside Chris Hemsworth in *Thor: Ragnarok* (2017) and Tatiana Maslany in the 2022 TV series *She-Hulk: Attorney at Law*.

THE STRONGEST ONE THERE IS

Superheroes, at their essence, let us live vicariously through their powerful characters, and often allow us to let out our secret frustrations in a safe fashion. From this point of view, the Hulk may be the purest superhero there is, especially to children—who were, of course, the original target audience for comic books, and who still adore superheroes to this day. Tapping into primal themes found not just in human psychology but in how that psychology has played out in some of our most iconic literature and mythology, it's easy to understand why the public has latched on to the Hulk for so long, and why he remains one of Lee and Kirby's most enduring creations.

10

THE MARVEL CINEMATIC UNIVERSE

How the House of Mouse and the House of Ideas Took Over the World

As Marvel Studios, with Kevin Feige leading the way, set out to enact its grandiose plans to create a vast and interconnected fictional universe akin to the Marvel Comics Universe, the immediate problem it was facing was where to begin. Two of Marvel's biggest properties were already licensed out to other studios—*Spider-Man 2* (2004) and *Spider-Man 3* (2007) had continued Columbia's franchise, while *X-Men: The Last Stand* (2007) had rounded out Fox's trilogy, with a prequel/reboot, *X-Men: First Class*, in the works. The decision was made to focus on the formation of the Avengers, Marvel's elite superteam, beginning with individual films on the lynch-pin characters of the classic Avengers: Iron Man, Thor, Hulk, and Captain America. Although Marvel Studios retained the rights to all these charac-ters, they were also characters whose "coolness" factor had faded in recent years in the wake of the 1980s and 1990s popularity of Spider-Man and the X-Men, and so Feige and company had their work cut out for them.

Looking to kick things off with a bang, Marvel chose Iron Man as the starting point for the whole operation, encouraged especially by the acquisition of enthusiastic fan-boy Jon Favreau as director. But Favreau's choice for Tony Stark was a controversial one: seemingly washed-up actor Robert Downey Jr., whose troubles with addiction and the law had made him almost untouchable in years past. Yet there were others who felt that Downey's life experience would actually lend gravitas to his interpretation of the troubled and conflicted Stark. Those instincts turned out to be correct, as it was arguably Downey's performance that helped knock *Iron Man* (2008) out of the park. Just like that, Iron Man became the hottest character in the Marvel Universe, and even the comic book version began to mimic Downey's trademark dry wit and quirky behavior. The success of the brand-new Marvel Cinematic Universe seemed assured.

And the teaser scene at the end of the credits—featuring Samuel L. Jackson as SHIELD's Nick Fury proposing the formation of the Avengers to Stark—laid the foundation of all that was to come, as those end-credit scenes became a hallmark of Marvel movies ever after. In what was considered "Phase One" of the MCU, further character introduction films were rolled out. Working out a deal with Universal, which still partly owned the license on the Green Goliath, Marvel Studios took their own shot at *The Incredible Hulk* (2008), written by *X-Men* cowriter Zak Penn and starring Edward Norton as Bruce Banner and Tim Roth as the Abomination. Next was *Thor* (2011), helmed by Oscar-nominated British director Kenneth Branagh and featuring Chris Hemsworth as the God of Thunder, Anthony Hopkins as his father Odin, and Tom Hiddleston stealing the show as the devilish Loki. And rounding things out was *Captain America: The First Avenger* (2011), the first faithful treatment of one of Marvel's oldest and most beloved heroes, starring Chris Evans (who had previously played the

Robert Downey Jr.: The Heart and Soul of the MCU

It's entirely plausible to say that the entire success of the planned Marvel Cinematic Universe depended on the choice of who would play Tony Stark/Iron Man, the first superhero to be introduced when things were kicked off in 2008. And in that, Kevin Feige and Marvel could not have hoped for better than with Robert Downey Jr., a man whose effortless charm, quirky performance style, irresistible humor, and undeniable charisma endeared him to millions of fans worldwide, and helped put a beloved (not to mention handsome) face to what would become the world's most successful film franchise. And perhaps the best part of it all was just how much of a redemption story it was for an actor who once seemed a has-been before even hitting his prime.

The son of noted actor and director Robert Downey Sr., he grew up in New York's Greenwich Village surrounded by creative people. Unfortunately, he also grew up surrounded by booze and drugs, which would eventually take their toll on him from his formative years onward. He initially rose to fame in the 1980s as a member of the notorious "Brat Pack" of teen and twenty-something stars, appearing in films like *Weird Science* (1985), *Less Than Zero* (1987), and *Johnny Be Good* (1988), and even spending a season on *Saturday Night Live* (1985–1986). He seemed to be maturing as an actor when he got the title role in the critically acclaimed *Chaplin* (1992), but the specter of addiction began to drag him down, and a series of arrests and trips to rehab looked like they had doomed his once-promising career.

But something happened after he achieved sobriety in 2003—he began to build himself back up, and his inspiring "second act" included impressive parts in films like *Zodiac* (2007) and *Tropic Thunder* (2008), earning an Oscar nomination for his memorable role as vapid method actor Kirk Lazarus in the latter. These successes led to Marvel and director Jon Favreau taking a chance on him when it came time to launch the MCU with *Iron Man* (2008). That choice proved a smart one, as he went on to anchor the MCU for eleven years, playing Iron Man in nine different movies—more times than any other actor had ever played a superhero. The profoundly moving worldwide response to the death of his character in *Avengers: Endgame* (2019) is a testament to the irreplaceable role he played in making Marvel into a movie juggernaut.

Human Torch in *Fantastic Four*) as Cap and Hugo Weaving of *Matrix/Lord of the Rings* fame as the Red Skull.

Meanwhile, as the seeds of the MCU were being planted, Marvel's outside licensed properties continued to pull in the bucks. Jackman became such a breakout star as Wolverine that Fox made him the star of his own spin-off film series, beginning with *X-Men Origins: Wolverine* in 2009. Troubled by the creative and box office underperformance of *Spider-Man 3*, Sony/Columbia removed Sam Raimi from the series and rebooted it completely, beginning in 2012 with *The Amazing Spider-Man*, recasting Andrew Garfield as the Webhead, with Emma Stone's Gwen Stacy replacing Kirsten Dunst's Mary-Jane Watson as Peter Parker's main squeeze. The film would spawn its own 2014 sequel, but both failed to escape the shadow of Raimi's series, particularly the first two excellent films.

Marvel Studios had been putting all the pieces in place for its first *Avengers* movie, but along the way something had happened that would change the course of the company's history and bring the MCU even greater attention and prestige. At the end of 2009, with the first two Marvel Studios films already released, Disney had purchased Marvel Entertainment from Toy Biz for $4 billion, bringing under its massive umbrella controlling power over some of the world's most recognizable and enduring characters. Arguably, this had been part of the play behind Marvel Studios' launching of the MCU in the first place, to make the company that much more desirable to such a bidder. As Phase One drew to a close, Disney began gradually taking over the reins—Marvel Studios would continue to exist, but the House of Mouse was now at the top of the food chain. The first film to be released under the Disney banner, perhaps appropriately, would be *Iron Man 2* (2010), the first sequel to the first MCU movie.

And the takeover seemed to happen at just the right time, as Marvel put all its might behind making *Avengers* (2012) the grandest spectacle in the history of superhero movies up to that point. With the limitless Disney coffers at its disposal and genre fave Joss Whedon at the helm, *Avengers* teamed up Hulk, Cap, Iron Man, and Thor, also adding Jeremy Renner's Hawkeye and Scarlet Johansson's Black Widow to the team. Hiddleston's Loki led the charge as the charismatic main baddie, while the closing moments would introduce a new supervillain, Thanos, who would play an even greater role in future MCU phases. The message was clear: Phase One was just the beginning.

Fox's X-Men franchise rolled along with *The Wolverine* (2013), another Logan standalone that saw the clawed one travel to the Orient, and *X-Men: Days of Future Past* (2014), a bold and innovative sequel that saw director Bryan Singer return to the fold to adapt a popular 1980s Chris Claremont time-travel story arc and do what he could to streamline the increasingly convoluted past/present timelines of the mutant movie series. Meanwhile, with Disney fully in the driver's seat, Marvel Studios launched headlong into "Phase 2," intended to lead the way to the first *Avengers* sequel, *Age of Ultron* (2015), featuring one of the World's Mightiest Heroes' oldest and greatest adversaries. Along the way, the God of Thunder returned in *Thor: The Dark World* (2013), Tony Stark faced the mysterious Mandarin in *Iron Man 3* (2013), and Steve Rogers clashed with his presumed-dead former sidekick Bucky Barnes in *Captain America: The Winter Soldier* (2014), a taut espionage thriller directed by brothers Anthony and Joe Russo that welcomed none other than Robert Redford into the fold of distinguished Marvel bad guys.

But the most influential and biggest surprise hit of Phase 2 would be a film based on one of Marvel's least known superteams that was directed by a largely unknown B-movie director. James Gunn's *Guardians of the Galaxy* (2014) was a game changer, incorporating self-effacing metahumor and a killer rock n' roll soundtrack to totally reinvent the superhero movie. The wonderful ensemble of Chris Pratt (Star-Lord), Zoe Saldana (Gamora), Dave Bautista (Drax the Destroyer), and Bradley Cooper and Vin Diesel as the respective voices of Rocket and Groot, gelled to create gold. The chemistry and vibe of the film would lead to several imitators both within the world of Marvel and beyond.

With Disney charting the course, the Marvel Cinematic Universe was steadily expanding. New titles were announced and the vast, interconnected web of story lines came together with greater clarity. The initial dream of Kevin Feige was very much a reality, and a fictional world unlike any the motion picture industry had seen before was firmly in place, erasing all previous expectations of how comic books could be translated to the big screen. And yet, as Phase 3 went into effect, and the Marvel heroes' eventual confrontation with Thanos emerged on the horizon, 20th Century Fox continued to make the most of the characters it had licensed from Marvel in years past, and which Marvel Studios was still unable to incorporate into its plans, much to fans' chagrin. A woefully misguided attempt to reboot Marvel's original superteam with *Fantastic Four* (2015), which made the previous attempts palatable by comparison, caused Fox to give up on successfully adapting the Baxter Building's famous residents. The mutant train kept rolling along with *X-Men: Apocalypse* (2016) and later *X-Men: Dark Pheonix* (2019), the second film adaptation of Chris Claremont and John Byrne's most famous collaboration.

Although the X-Men series seemed to be finally petering out after a nearly twenty-year run, Fox had some notable success with more solo features from the X-Men world. In 2016, clearly inspired by the irreverent and

Visionaries: The Creators Who Helped Shape Marvel on the Silver Screen

DAVID S. GOYER

Bridging the gap between Marvel and DC, Goyer was screenwriter for the Blade franchise and the second Ghost Rider film, and later did the same for Christopher Nolan's Batman films as well as the early stages of the DC Extended Universe. A graduate of USC's film school, he sold his first screenplay right out of college, the 1989 Jean-Claude Van Damme vehicle *Death Warrant*. A "script doctor" in high demand, he's also known for his work on the underrated *Dark City* (1998) from *The Crow* director Alex Proyas. His most recent projects are the Apple+ TV series *Foundation*, and the reboot of the horror classic *Hellraiser*.

BRYAN SINGER

The superhero movie renaissance was largely kicked off by the X-Men franchise, and Singer's approach to the material helped it succeed. Known to that point for "serious" dramas like *Apt Pupil* (1998) and his acclaimed *The Usual Suspects* (1995), Singer was the first die-hard comics fan given the reins to a superhero film franchise. After directing the first two X-Men movies, he stepped away for another dream project, DC's *Superman Returns* (2006), but later returned to the X-Men series with *Days of Future Past* (2014) and *Apocalypse* (2016). His 2018 Freddie Mercury biopic, *Bohemian Rhapsody*, was nominated for Best Picture.

SAM RAIMI

Little would anyone have suspected that Raimi, the horror maestro behind the grisly and darkly comic *Evil Dead* series, had what it took to bring Spider-Man to the big screen in all his glory. But like Singer, Raimi was an unabashed comics geek, with special fondness for the Spider-Man comics of the 1960s and 1970s. Raimi also had some superhero film experience, albeit on the bizarre, horror-tinged *Darkman* (1990), featuring Liam Neeson as the deranged and burned avenger. Raimi returned to horror with the cult flick *Drag Me to Hell* (2009) and made his MCU debut with *Doctor Strange in the Multiverse of Madness* (2022).

KEVIN FEIGE

No one else is more directly responsible for the Marvel Cinematic Universe than Kevin Feige, who's been president of Marvel Studios since 2007, one year before the franchise kicked off. A USC film school grad like Goyer, Feige came into the orbit of producer Lauren Schuler-Donner (wife of the late *Superman* producer/director Richard Donner) at the start of the 2000s, and was an assistant to Marvel chief Avi Arad, getting some of his earliest production credits on the *X-Men* and *Spider-Man* films of that decade. The success of the MCU films has made him the highest-grossing movie producer of all time.

JON FAVREAU

To get the MCU started, Marvel turned to prolific actor/producer/director Favreau, whose closest affiliation with superheroes was playing Foggy Nelson in the 2003 *Daredevil* movie. But it was his humor and knowledge of the source material that helped set the tone for the entire MCU with the first *Iron Man* movie. He also directed the sequel and served as executive producer for all four *Avengers* films. His portrayal of the bumbling Happy Hogan in numerous MCU entries has endeared him to fans—as has his creation of the hugely successful *Star Wars* TV series *The Mandalorian* and *The Book of Boba Fett*.

JOSS WHEDON

The genre wunderkind behind the runaway success of movie/TV franchises *Buffy the Vampire Slayer* and *Firefly/Serenity* helped put an exclamation point on the Marvel Cinematic Universe by writing and directing the first two *Avengers* films, tying together all the story lines that had led up to that point. He also developed the ABC spinoff TV series *Agents of SHIELD*. He may have continued to guide the *Avengers* franchise, but parted ways with Marvel over creative differences. Although he also contributed to the DC Extended Universe with his work on *Justice League*, he has since alienated much of his fan base due to allegations of abusive behavior.

THE RUSSO BROTHERS

Essentially picking up where Whedon left off were Anthony and Joseph Russo, two brothers from Cleveland, Ohio, whose initial claim to fame came from their work on the popular TV sitcoms *Arrested Development* and *Community*. They won over the hearts of fans and executives with their gritty take on Captain America in *The Winter Soldier*, and after deftly managing a major superhero crossover in *Captain America: Civil War*, they were given control over the third and fourth *Avengers* films, chronicling the epic cosmic war with Thanos and the fallout from his infamous finger snap.

JAMES GUNN

Getting his start in the business with Lloyd Kaufman's B-movie juggernaut Troma Studios, Gunn was a lifelong fan of all things horror and science fiction, and first rose to fame as the screenwriter behind the first two live-action *Scooby-Doo* movies, not to mention collaborating with Zack Snyder on the 2004 remake of George Romero's *Dawn of the Dead*. His comic sensibilities and irreverent approach to the *Guardians of the Galaxy* films helped change the course of Marvel's film output into a more lighthearted, humorous direction, which he also did for DC with *The Suicide Squad* (2021).

snarky tone of *Guardians of the Galaxy*, the studio released *Deadpool* starring Ryan Reynolds as the unkillable mercenary with a twisted sense of humor. Drenched in bloodshed and violence, the darkly comical film marked a milestone: it was the first major film based on a comic book superhero to receive an R-rating. Despite the rating, or perhaps because of it, the movie was a runaway hit, expanding the possibilities for superhero films and spawning an equally crowd-pleasing sequel. Continuing the trend, Fox produced *Logan* (2017), the ultimate coda for Hugh Jackman's Wolverine that had all the R-rated violence of *Deadpool* but replaced the humor with grim gravitas. The result was a film that many fans placed right alongside some of the year's best straight dramas.

But rumors were swirling that Disney was on the verge of buying Fox, which would thereby eventually return to Marvel's control all those characters it had licensed to Fox years earlier. And even before that happened, Disney and Marvel were laying the groundwork for bringing all their characters home when they worked out a deal with Sony/Columbia for use of arguably their most beloved character of all, and one who had been conspicuously absent from the MCU thus far. In *Captain America: Civil War* (2016), part of Marvel's Phase 3, fans were finally introduced to the newest incarnation of Spider-Man, played by Tom Holland, and got to see him fight right alongside—and against—all the other heroes of the MCU. It was a momentous event, and only ratcheted up the excitement heading toward *Avengers: Infinity War* (2018), the first of a two-part saga in which our heroes grappled with the universe-ending powers of Thanos in a story line based on Jim Starlin's highly successful "Infinity Gauntlet" comics arc of the 1990s.

Phase 3 also meant the 2016 motion picture debut of Stan Lee and Steve Ditko's Dr. Strange, played by award-winning British chameleon actor Benedict Cumberbatch. It followed shortly after the most unlikely of all Avengers-member adaptations, *Ant-Man* (2015), with the size-changing hero played to great lighthearted effect by Paul Rudd. The *Guardians of the Galaxy* influence was clearly in effect as Marvel continued to turn up the humor and merge it with its already established penchant for mind-blowing action in not only the 2017 sequel to *Guardians*, but also in the madcap *Thor: Ragnarok* (2017), a stupendously fun comic book come to life written and directed by cult director Taika Waititi, best known for the underground vampire comedy *What We Do in the Shadows* (2014).

In the months leading up to *Infinity War*, Marvel Studios finally pulled off what had once seemed impossible—giving Tom Holland's new MCU Wall-Crawler his own vehicle in the suitably titled *Spider-Man: Homecoming* (2017), featuring Michael Keaton as the maniacal Vulture. And then there was *Black Panther* (2018), bringing the Prince of Wakanda to the screen for the first time in the form of Oscar-nominated actor Chadwick

Boseman. Ushering the latest Avenger into the fold, the film also netted Marvel its first-ever Academy Award nomination for Best Picture. It was a coming-of-age moment for Marvel, and for superhero movies in general. The genre once considered the exclusive domain of children was achieving maturity and gaining respect.

If Disney and Marvel hadn't already fully captivated the imaginations of the movie-viewing public, then *Infinity War* was the clincher. With its cliff-hanger ending, in which Thanos, portrayed by Josh Brolin, appears to wipe out half the population of the universe with the snap of a finger—including half of all the Marvel superheroes—the movie and its aftereffect became a part of pop culture consciousness. Thanos and his finger snap became a meme, and audiences waited in desperate anticipation to see how it would all resolve in the finale and last piece of Phase 3, *Avengers: Endgame* (2019). The Paul Rudd sequel *Ant-Man & The Wasp* (2018), uniting two old-school Avengers cornerstone members, was a much-needed levity break allowing fans to catch their breath. Brie Larson's turn as cosmic hero Captain Marvel (2019) provided 1980s-era nostalgia and introduced viewers to the charac-ter teased at the very end of *Infinity War*, and who would play an integral role in *Endgame*.

Living up to expectations and then some, *Avengers: Endgame* drew mov-iegoers in droves around the globe, taking in a staggering $2.7 billion world-wide, and providing a satisfying conclusion to the Avengers saga that had been gradually building for over a decade. Thanos became a movie villain for the ages, and Tony Stark's ultimate sacrifice tugged at the heartstrings of Marvel's loyal fan base, as did the touching fate of Captain America. But despite the closure it provided, *Endgame* would of course not be the end of the MCU—not when these films were reigning supreme over the box office in such dominant fashion.

In the wake of the Avengers swansong, Spider-Man emerged as the most prominent character in the MCU, with the sequel *Spider-Man: Far from Home* showing Peter grappling with the loss of his mentor Stark. However, there were also signs that perhaps audience fatigue following *Endgame*, not to mention the withering and lingering effects of the global COVID-19 pandemic and lockdown, were having a negative impact on the once bulletproof MCU. The long-awaited standalone movie *Black Widow* (2021), Marvel's first post-lockdown release, was also considered by many to be the first major disappointment for the franchise. It was then followed by two more entries that were met with relative apathy: *Shang-Chi and the Legend of the Ten Rings* (2021), based on the 1970s martial arts comic *Master of Kung-Fu*, and *Eternals* (2021), which failed to find an audience for its new superteam.

The impact of COVID-19 was changing the entire movie landscape, with streaming from home largely surpassing movie theater patronage in terms of how audiences watched new movies. The movie to finally shake off not only the doldrums of post-*Endgame* Marvel output, but also the general doldrums of moviegoers no longer interested in leaving their homes, was one that some argue surpassed even *Endgame* itself—*Spider-Man: No Way Home* (2021). Introducing the concept of the multiverse—set to play an important role in future MCU films—*No Way Home* was a Marvel fan's fantasy come true, bringing together Holland's Spider-Man with the previous Spider-Men played by Andrew Garfield and Tobey Maguire. Through a unique arrangement with Sony/Columbia, Disney and Marvel crafted a story that brought all the Spidey timelines together, including previous villains Green Goblin (Willem Dafoe), Doctor Octopus (Alfred Molina), Sandman (Thomas Haden Church), Electro (Jamie Foxx), and the Lizard (Rhys Ifans). The movie pulled off an incredible feat, becoming one of the highest-grossing films of all time, and the first major release to draw crowds to theaters in the post-COVID-19 world. It was a rare sign that perhaps the motion picture exhibition business wasn't dead, and another example of the unifying power of superhero cinema, not to mention the enduring popularity of Stan Lee's greatest creation.

Phase 4 continued, as audiences were wowed by such releases as *Doctor Strange in the Multiverse of Madness* (2022), furthering the exploration of Marvel's alternate realities; *Thor: Love and Thunder* (2022), the historic fourth installment in the Thunder God's franchise; and *Black Panther: Wakanda Forever* (2022), moving that series beyond the tragic 2020 passing of Chadwick Boseman. The beginning of 2023 saw the MCU's Phase 5 kick off with *Ant-Man & The Wasp: Quantumania*, introducing Jonathan Majors as the Marvel Cinematic Universe's next franchise-defining supervillain, Kang the Conqueror; followed by *Guardians of the Galaxy 3*, bringing James Gunn back to the series. Other installments coming include *The Marvels* (2023), featuring the return of Brie Larson's Captain Marvel; *Blade* (2023), rebooting the vampire hunter and bringing him into the MCU; *Captain America: New World Order* (2024), the fourth film in the Cap series; and *Thunderbolts* (2024), marking the debut of a new superteam. And with Disney's acquisition of Fox, more of those previously licensed characters, like the Fantastic Four and the X-Men, have finally become able to take their place among their peers in the Marvel Cinematic Universe.

Fifteen years later and still going strong, the MCU continues to enthrall audiences. With these latest developments, the possibilities do indeed seem to be very exciting. Young fans today are much more likely to have discovered Spider-Man, Captain America, Hulk, or the X-Men via a movie than a comic book, which although it might be bittersweet for longtime comics lovers, ensures that these characters will endure and continue to transcend any one medium, even the medium of their origin. Marvel may have taken several decades to truly find its footing in the realm of motion pictures, but when it did, it took hold of that realm like nothing before or since, laying claim to it and transforming it in the process. Thanks in large part to Marvel and the MCU in particular, the superhero genre has become the one most associated with the entire movie industry—a feat that would've been unimaginable in the days of the Captain America serials of the 1940s.

ICONS #10

The Wall-Crawler

Creators: Stan Lee and Steve Ditko

First Appearance: *Amazing Fantasy* #15, August 1962

Alter Ego: Peter Parker

Powers: proportionate strength of a spider, "Spider-sense," ability to cling to walls and ceilings, self-made wrist web-shooters, enhanced speed and reflexes, spider-tracer homing beacons

Archenemies: the Green Goblin, Dr. Octopus, Venom, the Sandman, the Lizard, Electro, the Kingpin, Carnage, Mysterio, the Vulture

His red webbed mask is the virtual face of Marvel Comics. DC may have Superman and Batman constantly vying for supremacy with fans, but when it comes to Marvel, there is one character who has stood above the rest for most of the past sixty years: **SPIDER-MAN**. And although Avengers mainstays like Iron Man and Captain America may have challenged that spot thanks to the Marvel Cinematic Universe, now Spidey is a part of that as well, and so all is well with the world again. With his affable charm, everyman real-world problems, fantastic powers, and unflappable sense of humor, his universal appeal is easy to understand, as is his ability to be kept fresh despite changing tastes.

THE ORIGIN

Bitten by a radioactive spider in a laboratory, high school science wiz Peter Parker finds that he has gained amazing spider-like abilities, including clinging to walls, preternatural senses, and vastly increased strength. Using his powers for personal gain, he becomes arrogant, at one point refusing to help stop an escaping burglar even though he easily could. When that criminal later murders his beloved Uncle Ben, who has raised Peter as a son, young Parker learns the hard lesson that his uncle tried to teach him: with great power comes great responsibility. Crafting a suit to hide his identity and adding homemade liquid web-shooters to his arsenal, he becomes a watchful guardian for his native New York City.

THE CREATION

Seeking to continue the reinvention of the superhero genre he'd begun with the Fantastic Four, Marvel editor in chief Stan Lee wanted a teen hero to appeal to teen readers, but one that wouldn't be patronizing or inferior to other heroes. Inspired partly by 1930s/1940s pulp hero the Spider, as well as a character prototype developed in the 1950s by Jack Kirby and Joe Simon, Lee originally worked with Kirby on the new character, but rejected the direction Kirby wanted to take the character, artistically speaking. He turned to the offbeat and eccentric Steve Ditko, who gave him the unorthodox design he was looking for. The character made his first appearance in the final issue of sci-fi comic *Amazing Fantasy*, which after that point became *Amazing Spider-Man*.

THE ICONIC SPIDER-ARTISTS

In addition to Ditko, who first conceived the character and his look, many talented illustrators have left an unmistakable mark on Spidey over the years. After Ditko's departure, for much of the 1960s and 1970s, John Romita, known for his clean line work, gave Spider-Man his definitive look. The late 1980s saw Spider-Man completely redefined by Todd McFarlane, with a highly exaggerated style that gave Spidey enlarged eyes, anatomically impossible poses, and a new look for his webbing. McFarlane influenced many who came after, most directly his immediate successors like Erik Larsen and Mark Bagley. In the twenty-first century, John Romita Jr. has left his mark on Spidey comics, as has Umberto Ramos, the most prolific Spider-Man artist of recent years.

SPIDEY'S UNFORGETTABLE ADVENTURES

So many classic stories have captured the essence of Spider-Man. They include "The Master Planner Saga" (*Amazing Spider-Man* #30–33, 1965), whose inspirational climax, with Spidey trapped under a ton of debris, was re-created in *Spider-Man: Homecoming*. "Kraven's Last Hunt" played out in all three Spider-Man titles in the fall of 1987, and memorably featured Kraven the Hunter burying his mortal foe alive. "The Death of Gwen Stacy" (*Amazing Spider-Man* #121–122, 1973) shocked readers, as Green Goblin's evil plot resulted in the demise of Peter's girlfriend. With Peter giving up his heroic role, "Spider-Man No More!" (*Amazing Spider-Man* #50, 1967) served as a direct inspiration for the movie *Spider-Man 2*. And of course, 1990s fans recall the infamous "Clone Saga," which revealed that the Peter we knew and loved had been replaced with a doppelganger (later revealed to be a trick).

MILES MORALES AND OTHER SPIDER-FOLK

More than most superheroes, Spider-Man has had a few other iterations over the years. Although Peter Parker is by far the definitive Spider-character, they've all played an important role in the Spider-saga. Chief among them in recent times is Miles Morales, the teenager who has ascended to the role of Spider-Man in Marvel's Ultimate Universe, and who was the star of the animated *Spider-Man: Into the Spider-Verse*. There is also the recent Spider-Woman, who is actually Gwen Stacy from an alternate universe. She was preceded by the original Spider-Woman, Jessica Drew, most popular in the late 1970s/early 1980s. Miguel O'Hara is the Spider-Man of the futuristic Marvel 2099 Universe. And of course, there's everyone's favorite parody, Peter Porker, the Amazing Spider-Ham.

THE SPIDER ON THE SCREEN

With different film versions portrayed by Tobey Maguire (2002–2007), Andrew Garfield (2012–2014), and Tom Holland (2016–2021), Spider-Man has been well-represented over the course of eleven movie appearances thus far, even if he was a little late to the game. He was also played by Nicholas Hammond in a short-lived TV series of the late 1970s, and there was even a Japanese TV adaptation around the same time. And when it comes to the many animated versions of Spidey, there is perhaps none as beloved as the late 1960s cartoon series with its classic earworm theme song, although 1980s fans of "Spider-Man and His Amazing Friends" may disagree.

FRIENDLY NEIGHBORHOOD SPIDER-MAN

Perhaps Marvel's greatest contribution to popular culture, Spider-Man has embedded himself into our society and become just as much of an archetype as DC's top two heroes. But even more than them, we're enthralled by his humanity, vulnerability, and by how he feels like he's just one of us, something that Clark and Bruce could never claim. Complete with the petty J. Jonah Jameson, the gorgeous Mary-Jane Watson, the doting Aunt May, and one of the greatest rogue's galleries of all time, his lived-in world holds a unique attraction. The fictional web spun by Lee and Ditko continues to reel us right in, and likely will for many years to come.

11

THE INCREDIBLE, UNBREAKABLE MYSTERY MEN

"Other" Superhero Movies That Kick-Ass

As with the comic books they came from, the genre of superhero films has traditionally been dominated by Marvel and DC. And yet, just as every now and then a major character (or characters) might emerge from one of the smaller publishers, so have there been some impressive movies over the years featuring superheroes that didn't originate at the House of Ideas or its Distinguished Competition. Some of them might be based on characters from other comics, and in some cases, they might be entirely original creations, developed purely for the movie screen but based on some of the common tropes of superhero fiction. No matter where they came from, these movies are proof that there can be much more to the rich world of superhero cinema than just the Avengers, the Justice League, and their assorted friends and colleagues. Here's a look at some of the greatest independent superhero movies and how they helped make the genre what it is today.

FLASH GORDON (1980)

From the irreverent mind of Lorenzo Semple, the mad genius behind the 1960s *Batman* TV series, came this camp classic based on the legendary comic strips of Alex Raymond, and the Buster Crabbe serials based on them. With a bonkers soundtrack by Queen, a performance for the ages by Max von Sydow as the deliciously evil Ming the Merciless, the gorgeous Ornella Muti as his flirtatious daughter Princess Aura, Brian Blessed chewing up the scenery as Prince Vultan of the Hawk Men, and so much more, it's a visual feast that never takes itself too seriously. Although it wasn't a huge success when it first came out in the wake of *Star Wars*, it found an audience in later years among those who enjoy their superhero adventures a bit on the wacky and trippy side.

ROBOCOP (1987)

Set in a dystopian future Detroit, where criminals run the city and the police run for cover, director Paul Verhoeven's perverse vision gave us the ultimate science fiction look at law enforcement. When decent policeman Alex Murphy (Peter Weller) is mercilessly gunned down by a vicious street gang, a shady corporation brings him back from the dead as the cyborg Robocop, programmed to clean up the streets and look into Detroit's rampant crime—but not so far up the ladder as to discover the nefarious doings of the corporation that built him, headed by the unscrupulous Dick Jones (Ronny Cox). With a twisted sense of humor and graphic violence galore, it's an R-rated extravaganza that spawned two sequels, a 1994 TV series, and a subpar 2014 remake.

TEENAGE MUTANT NINJA TURTLES (1990)

At the start of the 1990s, there was nothing more popular in the world than the "heroes on a half-shell," and this debut feature film took that popularity to a whole new level. The film combined elements of the darker, original Eastman & Laird stories first published by Mirage Comics, as well as the more kid-friendly adaptation that had been appearing in TV cartoons in the late 1980s and in the pages of Archie Comics. Released by New Line Cinema, it told the origin story of the Turtles, who were brought to life with the magic of the Jim Henson Creature Shop. Naturally, the movie was a monster hit, and led to two direct sequels, *Teenage Mutant Ninja Turtles II: The Secret of the Ooze* (1991) and *Teenage Mutant Ninja Turtles III* (1993); followed by the animated film *TMNT* in 2007; as well as a 2014 reboot and the reboot sequel *Teenage Mutant Ninja Turtles: Out of the Shadows* in 2016.

DARKMAN (1990)

Before he ever tackled Spider-Man, Sam Raimi's first foray into superhero cinema was this grim and offbeat cult classic—and before he became the Oscar-nominated star of *Schindler's List*, Liam Neeson played the titular dark and disfigured avenger. Bringing his quirky and comical horror sensibilities to bear in adapting his own short story, Raimi told the tale of Peyton Westlake (Neeson), a scientist burned and brutalized by the evil Durant (Larry Drake) and his goons, who recovers through a process that grants him superhuman abilities but also renders him mentally unstable and psychotic. A revenge story based somewhat on the old Universal monster flicks of the 1930s, it came about after Raimi had failed to secure the rights to either Batman or The Shadow, and so came up with his own character. It was followed by two direct-to-video sequels, sans Neeson and Raimi.

THE ROCKETEER (1991)

A classic example of a superhero movie that should've been more success-ful, Joe Johnston's *The Rocketeer* was overwhelmed in a summer 1991 box office bonanza dominated by movies like *Terminator 2* and *Robin Hood: Prince of Thieves*. Based on the Pacific Comics character created by Dave Stevens a decade prior, the Disney film featured Bill Campbell as Cliff Sec-ord, a 1930s stunt pilot who uses a rocket jetpack to combat Nazis and their sympathizers, including a Hollywood actor inspired by Errol Flynn and played by Timothy Dalton. Also featuring Jennifer Connelly as Secord's Bettie Page-inspired girlfriend Jenny Blake, the film—much like the orig-inal comic—takes major inspiration from 1930s and 1940s movie serials like *Commando Cody* and *King of the Rocket Men*.

THE CROW (1994)

Few, if any, superhero movies not based on Marvel or DC characters have built such a devoted following as this bold and innovative movie from director Alex Proyas, which features Brandon Lee, son of action movie icon Bruce Lee, as the resurrected angel of vengeance Eric Draven. Based on the character created by James O'Barr for Caliber Comics in 1989, *The Crow* was unlike any superhero film made before or since, and ahead of its time for its dark tone and striking visuals. Sadly, the film was marred by the accidental death of Lee on the set due to the misfire of a prop gun. A 1996 sequel, *The Crow: City of Angels*, introduced a new Crow character, and was followed by a series of sequels, and a Canadian TV series. A reboot had been stuck in developmental hell for years, but finally began shooting in 2022, with a planned release sometime in 2023 as of this writing.

THE SHADOW (1994)

Continuing the amazing trend of superhero movies in the summer of 1994, this memorable and somewhat underrated film adapted one of the originators of the modern costumed crimefighter, the creation of William Gibson, best known for his pulp fiction and radio adventures of the 1930s and 1940s. Set during that original time, the movie features a screenplay by *Jurassic Park* scripter David Koepp, and stars Alec Baldwin as The Shadow. The character's direct influence on Batman can be keenly felt throughout the film, most notably by the effective musical score created by Jerry Goldsmith, which is reminiscent of the scores Danny Elfman had composed for Tim Burton's two Batman films a few years earlier.

THE MASK (1994)

Rounding out the summer was this enormously successful vehicle for Jim Carrey, then on a tear as the king of the American box office (he would play the Riddler in *Batman Forever* just one year later). Loosely based on the Dark Horse comics of the late 1980s and early 1990s, *The Mask* took the deranged and ultraviolent character created by Doug Mahnke and John Arcudi and adapted him for the broad physical comedy of Carrey, turning him into a Tex Avery cartoon come to life. Donning a magical mask possessed by the spirit of Loki, god of mischief, Carrey's Stanley Ipkiss becomes a wisecracking, reality bending dynamo who makes major trouble for the underworld of Edge City. An animated series followed, as well as the dismal *Son of the Mask* in 2005.

SPAWN (1997)

Just as Todd McFarlane had done when he created the character for his company Image Comics in 1992, *Spawn* represented something refreshing and new after decades of Marvel and DC superhero movies dominating the public consciousness. The first Black actor to play a major superhero in a major motion picture, Michael Jai White portrayed Al Simmons, the murdered CIA agent who returns to life thanks to a deal with the devil. With Martin Sheen as corrupt CIA director Jason Wynn and comic actor John Leguizamo with an unforgettable turn as the demonic Violator/Clown, the film almost received an R-rating for its violence and imagery but was toned down by New Line Cinema to qualify for PG-13. A sequel has been in development but has yet to see the light of day.

MYSTERY MEN (1999)

One of the first movies to take an irreverent and meta look at the superhero genre was this unique comedy based on the Dark Horse Comics work of Bob Burden, best known for the groundbreaking *Flaming Carrot Comics* of the 1980s. The movie follows the bizarre adventures of an amateur band of quasi-superheroes with the most unorthodox of "powers," including the Bowler, Shoveler, Spleen (with startling flatulent abilities), Invisible Boy (who can only turn invisible if no one is looking), Blue Raja (a weapons master who throws all manner of cutlery except knives), and Mr. Furious. Featuring a who's who of 1990s stars like William H. Macy, Ben Stiller,

Janeane Garofalo, Geoffrey Rush, Greg Kinnear, and Hank Azaria, the movie nevertheless failed to find an audience despite its clever wit.

UNBREAKABLE (2000)

On the surface, it doesn't even initially seem like a superhero film at all, but M. Night Shyamalan's haunting movie is actually steeped in superhero and comic book lore and takes perhaps the most reality-based approach ever taken by any superhero movie. Bruce Willis plays David Dunn, a security guard who survives a massive train derailment to discover that he is inexplicably impervious to all physical harm. Guiding him on the path to using his power heroically, comic shop owner Elijah Price turns out to be his physical opposite, a man whose extreme frailty has earned him the nickname "Mr. Glass" and made him deranged, secretly causing disasters in order to find someone like Dunn. Years later, Shyamalan revisited the world of *Unbreakable* with *Split* (2016) and *Glass* (2019).

HELLBOY (2004)

One of the most fascinating comics creations of the 1990s, Mike Mignola's *Hellboy* first came to the screen thanks to visionary writer/director Guillermo del Toro, and the landmark performance of Ron Perlman as everyone's favorite trench coat-clad devil-spawn. With John Hurt as his adopted father Trevor Bruttenholm, Selma Blair as psychic love interest Liz, Doug Jones as the amphibious Abe Sapien, and Jeffrey Tambor as the put-upon director of the Bureau of Paranormal Research and Defense for which Hellboy works, the film is a wild ride with a Lovecraftian bent and imagination to spare. It was followed by the superb *Hellboy II: The*

Golden Army (2008), and a disappointing 2019 reboot that replaced Perlman with *Stranger Things*' David Harbour.

THE INCREDIBLES (2004)

With influences ranging from *Fantastic Four* to *Watchmen*, this wonderful, animated entry from Pixar may have been marketed as a kids' movie but has so much more to offer for viewers of all ages, providing one of the most satisfying and thoughtful—not to mention original—superhero portrayals of all time. In a world in which superheroes have been outlawed, the superpowered couple of Mr. Incredible (Craig T. Nelson) and Elastigirl (Holly Hunter) have settled down to mundane lives in the suburbs, raising children who are all developing powers of their own. When a mysterious figure from the past begins hunting down "supers," the whole family gets called into action. One of Pixar's most beloved movies, it produced a long-awaited sequel in 2018.

SKY HIGH (2005)

The influence of *The Incredibles*, not to mention the growing explosion of superhero movies in general, was already showing with this movie—a teen-friendly comedy that centers on a high school for young future superheroes. Kurt Russell and Kelly Preston play the Commander and Jetstream, two famous and powerful heroes, whose son, Will, must navigate freshman year while discovering his own emerging powers, which equal the combined abilities of his parents. With several knowing nods to superhero film/TV culture—including the casting of Lynda "Wonder Woman" Carter as the principal—the movie is a good example of how the superhero film genre was growing to the point of being able to support different subgenres and produce movies that appealed to different age groups.

HANCOCK (2008)

Ambitious in its own way, yet not quite hitting the mark, this interesting film from Columbia Pictures was a direct result of the more realistic and "grounded" approach to superheroes explored in Christopher Nolan's *Batman Begins*, and the earliest Marvel Studios' efforts. Will Smith plays a reckless vigilante superhero who tries to use his powers for the good of all, but whose alcoholism and personality flaws make him a dangerous liability. Jason Bateman's character, whose life had previously been saved by him, works to help improve Hancock's image and get his life on track. More nuanced than typical superhero fare and benefiting from using an original character never before seen in comics, the movie nevertheless overreaches a bit, unable to fully pay off on the provocative themes it introduces.

THE SPIRIT (2008)

Judging by the success and quality of *Sin City* (2005), a film Frank Miller had written and codirected based on his popular noir crime thriller comic series, it would've seemed that his adaptation three years later of Will Eisner's seminal superhero comic strip *The Spirit* was also destined for greatness. Sadly, nothing could've been further from the truth. Although visually gripping and hyperexpressionistic like his previous effort, the movie was a critical and box office failure, despite the best efforts of Gabriel Macht as the masked vigilante and Samuel L. Jackson as his deranged nemesis, the Octopus. Losing vast sums of money, it effectively spelled the end of Miller's directorial career (such as it was), aside from the 2014 *Sin City* sequel, *A Dame to Kill For*.

KICK-ASS (2010)

The meta-trend arguably kicked off a decade earlier by *Mystery Men* continued with what is ostensibly a "Marvel" movie, based as it is on the Mark Millar/John Romita Jr. comic originally published under Marvel's Icon imprint. Yet the subject matter has no connection to the Marvel Universe. It's darkly comic treatment of superhero tropes, set in a world in which superpowers do not exist, put it in a class by itself. Aaron Johnson is memorable as Dave Lizewski, an inept teenager who sets out to become the crime-fighting vigilante Kick-Ass, only to get himself pulled into the real world of organized crime, and cross paths with the unlikeliest of crime-fighters, brutal eleven-year-old vigilante Hit-Girl (Chloe Grace Moretz). A sequel, *Kick-Ass 2*, was released in 2013.

CHRONICLE (2012)

Yet another subgenre of the superhero craze was explored in this, the first "found-footage" superhero movie, tracking the exploits of a group of high school seniors who develop telekinetic powers, including the power of flight, after a bizarre encounter with a mysterious object. After enjoying their powers like most teenage boys would, one in the group decides to use them for darker purposes. Belonging to the category of films that includes such similar shaky-cam, reality-driven efforts as *Paranormal Activity* (2007) and *Cloverfield* (2008), its surprise smash success gave its director, Josh Trank, the chance to helm Fox's doomed *Fantastic Four* reboot. Trank has been vocal about his opposition to a sequel, but as of 2021, a female-led second film was in the works.

DREDD (2012)

Righting the wrongs of the notoriously reviled 1995 film *Judge Dredd* starring Sylvester Stallone, this revamped adaptation of the British character created by John Wagner and Carlos Ezquerra was grittier, more violent in tone, featured Karl Urban as the titular law enforcement officer, and did *not* feature Rob Schneider, the eye-rolling comic relief of the 1995 bomb. Serving as judge, jury, and executioner in the dystopian Mega-City One, Judge Dredd and his assistant Judge Anderson (Olivia Thurlby) collide with drug lord Ma-Ma (Lena Headey). Perhaps in an effort to avoid the camp comedy of Stallone's movie, this version jettisoned most of the satirical content of the original comic strip, which appeared for years in British comic magazine *2000 AD*.

BIG HERO 6 (2014)

Another tangential Marvel creation, *Big Hero 6* started as a comic series in the late 1990s, whose characters have generally been kept apart from the regular Marvel Universe. Featuring a team of superpowered teens, the movie focuses on Hiro Hamada, a young boy in the fictional city of San Fransokyo who forms a team with Baymax, the robot created by his late brother, for the purpose of hunting down his brother's murderer. Eventually, they are assisted by a group of his brother's friends, who use their technological prowess to develop enhanced abilities of their own. A Disney animated feature, the movie was made possible by Disney's acquisition of Marvel a few years prior and represented the company's first animated superhero effort.

ICONS #11

The God of Thunder

Creators: Stan Lee, Larry Lieber, and Jack Kirby

First Appearance: *Journey into Mystery* #83, August 1962

Alter Egos: Donald Blake, Eric Masterson

Powers: superhuman strength and invulnerability; flight; ability to harness lightning and create storms; wields the unbreakable hammer Mjolnir, which can harness his power and be hurled at enemies

Archenemies: Loki, Kurse, the Destroyer, Midgard Serpent, Hela, Surtur, Ulik, Malekith, the Enchantress, Skurge the Executioner

Unlike most other comic book superheroes, the Mighty **THOR** can trace his origins long before comics were even invented—many centuries before, in fact. If mythological heroes and deities were the original superheroes, then perhaps it's only fitting that one of their kind would find his place among the most iconic of all Marvel characters. Many gods and heroes of legend have found their way into comics over the years, but none has been so thoroughly reinvented and reimagined as Thor, son of Odin. In fact, thanks to Marvel Comics, and the blockbuster films of the Marvel Cinematic Universe, it's safe to say that these days, Thor is even better known in his superhero form than originally worshipped by the Vikings long ago.

THE ORIGIN

In the original version of the story, disabled surgeon Dr. Donald Blake discovers Mjolnir, the hammer of Thor hidden in a Norwegian cave, while taking refuge from an alien invasion. When he strikes the hammer, it transforms him into the thunder god himself. However, some years later it was revealed that Blake had always been Thor, and that Thor's father Odin, Lord of Asgard, had erased his memory and incarnated him in feeble human form to teach him a lesson in humility. As the son of Odin, Thor is a prince of Asgard, and part of a superpowered alien race worshipped by the ancient Norse as gods. Developing an affinity for his new home of Earth, he vows to protect it and its people.

THE CREATION

Having just created the Hulk, the strongest human imaginable, Lee decided to go one step further by coming up with a character who wasn't human at all, but a god. Rather than using more commonly known Greek and Roman myths, Lee delved into Norse mythology and chose to adapt Thor, the fierce warrior god. Jack Kirby had already worked on a Thor character in the 1950s while working for DC and used some of the original elements in reinventing and modernizing Thor for the Marvel Universe. Both men had an affinity for myths and legends and used Thor as the new lead feature for *Journey into Mystery*. Eventually, the character took over the entire book and became a charter member of the Avengers.

MIGHTY MJOLNIR

Forged by the dwarven race in days of old for Asgard's fiercest warrior, the mystic Uru hammer is Thor's greatest weapon. In Norse mythology, Mjolnir is described as being made of red-hot stone and having a very short handle, while Marvel's version is more utilitarian, making it easier for the thunder god to hurl at opponents. The hammer always returns to his hand, and can only be lifted by Thor himself, or the rare individual as pure of heart as he is. While the hammer is not the source of his power, and in the comic's version he still retains most of his powers without it, it does help him focus those powers, and he is demoralized when separated from his fabled weapon for any length of time.

TALES OF ASGARD

Much of the classic Norse pantheon is represented in Marvel's version of Thor's world, including his father Odin; his diabolical brother Loki; Heimdall, the guardian of Asgard's Rainbow Bridge; the virtuous Balder the Brave; Thor's sometime-love interest Sif; Hela, ruler of the underworld, and others. There is also the unique Marvel creation of the Warriors Three, a sentimental favorite among Thor fans whose adventures have often been chronicled in side features within Thor's comic books. The group is made up of the rotund Volstagg, the dashing Fandral, and the Vanir warrior Hogun. As for the magical realm of Asgard, it is represented as being on another plane of existence entirely, making the Asgardians a race of powerful aliens.

ALIENS, MORTALS, AND WOMEN

Among the most popular of Thor's supporting characters has been Beta-Ray Bill, an extraterrestrial from the planet Korbin introduced by Walt Simonson in 1983. Bill is notable for being the first non-Asgardian capable of wielding Thor's hammer and becomes a staunch ally of the thunder god. Eric Masterson, introduced by Tom DeFalco and Ron Frenz in 1988, was a human also revealed to be worthy, and even spends some time taking on the mantle of Thor himself, before adopting the unique superheroic identity of Thunderstrike. In 2014, Thor's mortal paramour Jane Foster actually took on the role of Thor herself after lifting the hammer, a time during which the original Thor went under the name of Odinson, before reclaiming his birthright.

THE ASGARDIAN ON FILM

Australian actor Chris Hemsworth has made the role of Thor his own, playing the character in eight Marvel films, including four in his own series: *Thor* (2011), *Thor: The Dark World* (2013), *Thor: Ragnarok* (2017), and *Thor: Love and Thunder* (2022)—the longest ongoing series of any of the Avengers' central four heroes. He has proven adept with both drama and comedy, making Thor a much more lighthearted figure than longtime Marvel comic readers would've ever expected. Eric Allan Kramer was the first to play the thunder god on screen, taking on the role for the 1988 television movie, *The Incredible Hulk Returns*. In the 1960s, the Mighty Thor was also featured in the *Marvel Super Heroes* animated series.

WHOSOEVER HOLDS THIS HAMMER . . .

If any character has ever demonstrated the direct link between ancient heroes of myth and legend, and the modern-day superheroes of comic books and film, it would have to be the Mighty Thor, who quite literally has spanned the centuries to be reinvented for the twentieth century and beyond. He is also proof that the qualities that have always drawn us to superpowered saviors, such as bravery, honor, compassion, determination, and the willing-ness to use their might and power to protect and defend, are truly universal. These qualities can be endlessly readapted and applied to our modern world just as much as in days long ago. Perhaps even more human and noble than his sometimes-hot-tempered Norse inspiration, Marvel's Thor represents heroism in its purest form.

12

TELEVISION TITANS

Superheroes on the Small Screen

For as much as costumed heroes have triumphed at the movies and become box office gold, it's entirely possible that the history of superheroes on television is even richer, deeper, and more varied. From the very beginning of the medium in the middle of the twentieth century, caped crimefighters and swashbuckling do-gooders were right there, leaping off the comic book page and sometimes out of the radio speaker, and making that crucial transition to the format that would change the world in so many ways. Perhaps it originally owed to the fact that superhero stories were not taken terribly seriously in the beginning, and so were considered much more suitable to TV, which was seen as more disposable, low-rent, and less prestigious than the cinema, where entertainment was seen as a more grown-up affair.

Whatever the reasons, superheroes thrived on the tube from the very start, and their hold in that format has only gotten stronger, particularly in the past ten to fifteen years, thanks to spillover from the ongoing superhero explosion in movie theaters. In fact, superheroes have had such success on television that this chapter has been divided into two sections, one devoted to live-action and the other to animated TV series and specials. In this way, the seventy-five-year relationship between superheroes and television can be fully chronicled.

FROM GEORGE REEVES TO JOHN CENA: LIVE-ACTION EVOLUTION

The 1950s

In the earliest days of television, the brand-new medium was almost like an extension of the radio days that had preceded it. Many concepts came either from radio or from the movie serials and short subjects that had been so popular in theaters in the 1930s and 1940s. *The Lone Ranger* was the first major adaptation, coming to ABC in 1949, taking direct inspiration from the long-running radio series in presenting the exploits of the masked Western avenger. There was also the science fiction kids' adventure show, *Captain Video and His Video Rangers*, famously lampooned on an episode of *The Honeymooners*. And even Disney got into the act with its first superhero-themed TV series, *Zorro*, which aired on ABC in the latter part of the decade.

That decade, however, was defined by *The Adventures of Superman*, the smash hit series that ran in syndication from 1952 to 1958. Starring George Reeves in the title role, and Lois Lane played first by Phyllis Coates and then Noel Neill (who had previously played the role in the Superman movie serials), the show was one of early TV's biggest successes, inspiring a generation of little kids and setting the tone for the character for decades to come. It was also the first TV series based on a comic book superhero—thus setting the bar rather high right from the start.

The 1960s

Following the end of the Superman series, things were quiet for a few years until DC's other iconic character, Batman, made his way to television in 1966 in a big way. Taking advantage of the color-TV breakthrough of the mid-1960s, *Batman* brought to life the Caped Crusader and the Boy Wonder in all their Silver Age wackiness, with a campy, parodic approach that made it one of TV's most popular shows for three seasons. With a rotating cast of colorful villains played by some of Hollywood's biggest stars, it was a whole lot of fun, even if it did set a standard for superheroes as the objects of spoof comedy, which took many years for the genre to shake.

The success of *Batman* also led to *The Green Hornet*, developed by the same creators and originating as a spin-off, beginning with an episode where the Dynamic Duo cross paths with the Hornet and his sidekick Kato (played by a young Bruce Lee). Meanwhile, on the other side of the world, an entire superhero TV genre in Japan was taking shape thanks to Tsuburaya Productions' *Ultraman*, which grew out of the supernatural anthology series *UltraQ*. With numerous iterations over the years, it kicked off a craze that flourished in the 1970s and beyond.

The 1970s

The third of DC's triumvirate of major characters, Wonder Woman, finally came to TV in 1975, with the beautiful Lynda Carter in the title role. It ran for three seasons, first on ABC and then on CBS, with stories that took place both during World War II and in the "present day" of the 1970s. And after over a decade of infiltrating pop culture, Marvel Comics also made it to TV late in the decade, first with the short-lived *Amazing Spider-Man*, but much more importantly with *The Incredible Hulk*, CBS's huge hit starring Bill Bixby as Banner and Lou Ferrigno as Hulk. Though loosely based on the comics, it ran well into the 1980s, and even got a series of TV movies after going off the air.

The Six-Million-Dollar Man hit the airwaves in 1973, with Lee Majors playing Steve Austin, a man who suffers a terrible accident and has his body reconstructed with bionic technology. A bona fide TV sensation, it was the first major TV superhero who hadn't come from the pages of a comic book, but who was created strictly for television. It also got a female-led spin-off, *The Bionic Woman*, starring Lindsay Wagner. Other shows proliferated in the 1970s, including DC's *Shazam!*, as well as *The Secrets of Isis*, and *Electra Woman & Dyna Girl*. In Japan, the trend started by *Ultraman* continued with *Kamen Rider* and *Super Sentai*. Even Buck Rogers, one of the first protosuperheroes of the early twentieth century, got new life thanks to a hit series starring Gil Gerard.

The 1980s

The 1970s had been a bonanza for superhero TV, but things cooled down a bit during the next decade, and in fact the only show featuring any popular comic book characters would be *Superboy*, which took strong inspiration from the popular Christopher Reeve-led *Superman* film franchise that was just winding down. But before that, the 1980s would boast its greatest TV contribution to superhero culture, and the first show to deconstruct the genre and create something truly unique and original.

The Greatest American Hero focused on a bumbling schoolteacher, Ralph Hinkley (William Katt), who is given a supersuit by extraterrestrial visitors.

Unfortunately, he loses the instructions for the suit, and so must clumsily navigate his many new powers in comedic fashion, discovering new ones from week to week. Aided by FBI agent Bill Maxwell (Robert Culp), he reluctantly attempts to use the suit for good, while learning how to handle his powers along the way. Running for three seasons on ABC, it even produced a hit single, "Believe It or Not," the opening theme of the show, performed by Joey Scarbury.

The 1990s

DC returned to TV in the early 1990s with its fourth major character, the Flash, which became an instant cult classic. Starring John Wesley Shipp as Barry Allen, it was influenced by the first Tim Burton *Batman* film, featuring a sculpted rubber suit for the Scarlet Speedster and theme music from Bat-composer Danny Elfman. It only ran one season but made quite an impression. It was followed a couple years later by the TV return of Superman for the first time since the 1950s. *Lois and Clark: The New Adventures of Superman* featured Dean Cain as the Man of Steel and Teri Hatcher as Ms. Lane, focusing more on their romance and relationship than on Clark's superheroics.

DC also had a minor hit at the start of the decade with its *Swamp Thing* TV series. Combining superhero, horror, and crime genres was *Forever Knight*, a Canadian series about an eight-hundred-year-old vampire who becomes a homicide detective to atone for his centuries of preying on humans. Meanwhile, the ongoing Japanese sci-fi superhero subgenre had eventually led to the American sensation known as *Power Rangers*, which was basically a reedited and repurposed version of the *Super Sentai* series that had been running in Japan since the 1970s and distributed for Western consumption by American-Israeli production company Saban Entertainment.

The 2000s

With the superhero movie craze taking off with the dawn of the new century, renewed interest in comic book characters and their adventures began to spill over into television and result in some fresh, interesting takes on tried-and-true formulas. The WB's *Smallville* brought Clark Kent back to TV, but with a new spin, acting as a prequel of sorts, with Tom Welling playing a young Clark discovering his abilities, as well as his young friend Lex Luthor (Michael Rosenbaum), and how their relationship became estranged. And *Heroes* became the first show to take the "prestige television" approach to the genre, for four seasons chronicling the interactions of a group of seemingly ordinary people all over the world who begin to develop superpowers.

Networks were taking chances, like what Fox did with *The Tick*, starring *Seinfeld*'s Patrick Warburton as Ben Edlund's parody superhero, using the same creative team responsible for the hit animated *Tick* series of the 1990s. The live-action show wasn't as successful as the cartoon however, lasting only nine episodes. The WB added *Birds of Prey* to its lineup, a DC show set in a future timeline in which an all-female team led by the Huntress (daughter of Bruce Wayne and Selina Kyle) and Barbara Gordon protect a Gotham city abandoned by Batman. And Marvel finally returned to TV with *Blade: The Series*, its first show since *The Incredible Hulk* had ended twenty years earlier.

The 2010s

Just as it did in movie theaters, the superhero craze really busted wide open on television in the 2010s with a bumper crop of shows from multiple companies and on multiple platforms the likes of which had never been seen. Through the efforts of show-runners Greg Berlanti and Andrew Kreisberg, The CW put together a collection of related DC shows casually known as "The Arrowverse," beginning with *Arrow* starring Stephen Amell as Green Arrow and *The Flash* starring Grant Gustin as Barry Allen, with later Arrowverse shows added like *Legends of Tomorrow*, *Supergirl*, *Black Lightning*, and *Batwoman*. And this didn't even include *Gotham*, a prequel show similar to *Smallville* that told the story of a very young Bruce Wayne coming into his own, with the help of idealistic cop Jim Gordon.

Not to be outdone, Marvel carried over the popularity of the MCU with a slate of tie-in shows, beginning in 2013 with Joss Whedon's *Agents of SHIELD* on ABC, followed by *Agent Carter*, covering the 1940s exploits of Peggy Carter after the disappearance of Steve Rogers/Captain America. Netflix joined the party with an interconnected network of shows that kicked off with *Daredevil*, then continued with *Jessica Jones*, *Luke Cage*, and *Iron Fist*, culminating in *The Defenders*, an eight-episode miniseries that brought all four heroes together. Even the *Punisher* got his own Netflix series, starring *The Walking Dead*'s Jon Bernthal as Frank Castle.

Premium cable got into the act for the first time with HBO's fascinating *Watchmen* series, a sequel to Alan Moore's groundbreaking 1985 graphic novel that takes place in the present day, thirty-four years after Ozymandias's catastrophic attack on New York City. Amazon Prime took a very Alan Moore-like approach as well, with its dark and dystopian prestige drama

The Boys, featuring a group of vigilantes who have taken it upon themselves to protect the world from rogue superheroes who are abusing their powers. With an increased level of sophistication but a loss of innocence, superhero TV had certainly come a long way from George Reeves and Noel Neill.

The 2020s

DC has only continued the expansion of its Arrowverse in recent years with the debut of *Superman & Lois*, featuring Tyler Hoechlin and Elizabeth Tulloch as comic books' leading couple. And with the launch of the streaming platform Disney+, a barrage of highly buzz-worthy new Marvel shows further expanded the MCU. Taking things a step further than the Netflix shows of the previous decade, series like *WandaVision*, *Loki*, *The Falcon & the Winter Soldier*, and *Hawkeye* tied directly into the happenings of the Marvel films, featuring established stars and characters. HBO Max, with rights to the DC characters, fired back with *Peacemaker*, a bitingly irreverent and satirical series starring former pro wrestler John Cena as his self-righteous, egotistical, and unstable vigilante character from *The Suicide Squad* (2021).

And the hits will just keep on coming as superheroes look to be a fixture on TV for some time to come. In 2022, *Moon Knight* starring Oscar Isaac, *Ms. Marvel* starring Iman Vellani, and *She-Hulk: Attorney at Law* starring Tatiana Maslany all enjoyed short series runs on Disney+, designed to set the characters up for future inclusion in the MCU. Greg Berlanti is slated to produce a Green Lantern series for HBO Max. And even Colin Farrell's Penguin is set to receive his own spin-off series on that platform, fresh off the success of Matt Reeves's *The Batman* (2022). More and more, the worlds of superhero movies and TV are colliding and connecting, giving fans more entertainment and richer stories than ever before.

FROM COURAGEOUS CAT TO CAPTAIN UNDERPANTS: ANIMATION EVOLUTION

The 1960s

During the 1950s, the first decade of television, most animation on the airwaves consisted of second-run material that had previously been seen in theaters accompanying feature films—Bugs Bunny, Woody Wood-pecker, Popeye, Tom & Jerry, and the like. It wasn't until the 1960s that the first wave of original animated series hit, including the first explosion of superhero cartoons. The first was a creation of Bob Kane, *Courageous Cat & Minute Mouse*, which ran in syndication for two years starting in 1960 and intended to lampoon his famous Batman & Robin duo. William Hanna and Joseph Barbera, animators who made their names working for MGM in the 1940s and 1950s, produced a series of original superhero-themed cartoons in the 1960s. Some, like *Space Ghost, Birdman & the Galaxy Trio*, and *The Herculoids*, took a serious comic book approach, while others were more comedic and kid-oriented, like *Atom Ant* and *Frankenstein Jr. & the Impossibles*.

The two major comic book companies got into the act as well. In 1966, Marvel Comics licensed its characters for *The Marvel Super Heroes*, a rather crude production using illustrations from original comics, and featuring the adventures of Thor, Sub-Mariner, Captain America, Iron Man, and the Hulk, each with its own memorable theme song. And speaking of memorable theme songs, there was also the revolutionary *Spider-Man* cartoon of the late 1960s, which has influenced nearly every iteration of the Wall-Crawler since, as well as a *Fantastic Four* cartoon from Hanna-Barbera. There was also the collection of animated series produced for DC Comics by Lou Scheimer's Filmation studio, including *The New Adventures of Superman*, *The Adventures of Superboy*, *The Superman/Aquaman Hour of Adventure*, *The Adventures of Batman*, and *The Batman/Superman Hour*, highlighted by the voice of Olan Soule as the Caped Crusader, and Bud Collyer, who had voiced the Man of Steel since the radio series of the 1940s.

The 1970s

Perhaps the most fondly remembered and iconic superhero cartoon show of them all—at least as far as Generation Xers are concerned—debuted in 1973 as Hanna-Barbera's *Super Friends*, featuring a streamlined version of DC's Justice League that included Superman, Batman & Robin, Wonder Woman, and Aquaman, along with goofy sidekicks Wendy, Marvin, and Wonder Dog. The series transformed over the course of the decade: *The All-New Super Friends Hour* added the Wonder Twins and their space monkey Gleek, while *Challenge of the Super Friends* had an expanded Justice League doing battle with the supervillain team of the Legion of Doom, led by Lex Luthor. DC and the Ruby-Spears cartoon studio also teamed up for *The Plastic Man Comedy/Adventure Show*.

Marvel's contributions included a revamped *New Fantastic Four* series from DePatie-Freleng Enterprises (producers of the Pink Panther cartoons) that replaced the Human Torch with Herbie the robot, as well as a short-lived *Spider-Woman* series that featured Joan Van Ark as the voice of Jessica Drew. Hanna-Barbera continued to lead the way in original animated superhero programming, adding silly Saturday morning fare like *Dynomutt,* the unforgettable *Captain Caveman,* and *The Super Globetrotters,* in which the Harlem Globetrotters were suddenly bestowed with super-abilities.

The 1980s

The *Super Friends* franchise was a Saturday morning institution that continued well into the 1980s. It had later iterations like *The Legendary Super Powers Show,* which added Firestorm and the villainous Darkseid, as well as *Galactic Guardians,* which added the hero Cyborg and Adam West as the voice of Batman. It was tied into DC's popular "Super Powers" toy line of the mid-1980s. Filmation and DC teamed up again for *Kid Super Hour with Shazam* featuring Captain Marvel and company. Marvel Productions joined with Japanese animation house Toei to produce a new *Spider-Man* series in the early 1980s, along with *Spider-Man and His Amazing Friends,* which teamed up Spidey with Iceman and a new original character, Firestar.

The 1980s' greatest independent comics creations, the Teenage Mutant Ninja Turtles, got their own animated series, which debuted in 1987. It ran for nine years, doing even more than the original comic to popularize the "heroes on a half shell" with young audiences. Popular original TV cartoon heroes included the space faring *SilverHawks* from Rankin/Bass, bumbling cyborg detective *Inspector Gadget* from the DIC animation studio, and of course Filmation's *He-Man and the Masters of the Universe,* leading the wave of 1980s cartoons based on toy lines. And in the decades' most unlikely teaming, Marvel and Stan Lee conceptualized *Defenders of the Earth,* a show joining classic comic strip adventurers Flash Gordon, the Phantom, and Mandrake the Magician.

The 1990s

There are those who still hold the opinion that the greatest screen interpretation of Batman, better than any motion picture, was the groundbreaking *Batman: The Animated Series* written by Paul Dini and designed by artist Bruce Timm. Debuting in 1992 on the Fox Network in the wake of Tim Burton's *Batman Returns*, it took its inspiration partly from the Fleischer Studios' Superman cartoons of the 1940s, with the unmistakable voice of Kevin Conroy as the Dark Knight. Although it only ran for three years, it spawned all manner of animated films and spin-offs, not least of which was *Batman Beyond*, the bold late 1990s show that featured an elderly and retired Bruce Wayne of the future passing his mantle to teenager Terry McGinnis. Other spin-offs included *Superman: The Animated Series* and *Superman/Batman Adventures*.

Marvel's greatest triumph of the decade was the fan-favorite *X-Men* animated series that ran for five years. The Incredible Hulk, Spider-Man, and even Silver Surfer all got their own series, not to mention *The Marvel Action Hour* featuring Iron Man and the Fantastic Four. And for the first time, new competitor Image Comics burst on the scene with MTV's *The Maxx*, USA Network's *The Savage Dragon*, and most notably, *Todd McFarlane's Spawn* on HBO. Dark Horse properties *Duckman* and *The Mask* received animated treatment, as did the independent comic *The Tick*.

Cartoon Network gave us perhaps the most memorable original animated superhero creation of the 1990s in *The Powerpuff Girls*, Genndy Tartakovsky's precious team of cute-yet-powerful poppets on a never-ending mission to protect Townsville from Mojo JoJo and his ilk. Other memorable series included Ted Turner's environmentally conscious Earth guardian

Captain Planet, Disney's *Darkwing Duck*, a satiric sendup of Batman, and the frenetic *Freakazoid*, produced by Steven Spielberg.

The 2000s

The version of the DC Universe developed by Paul Dini and Bruce Timm continued into the new century in its ultimate culmination: *Justice League*, a modernized retooling of *Super Friends* that was much more embracing of its comic book origins. It was followed by *Justice League Unlimited*, which opened the door to even more supporting DC characters. Separate from the "Diniverse," the Caped Crusader was retooled for two completely different series. One was *The Batman*, a dark and eccentric take on the well-trod Gotham territory, and the other was the clever and refreshing *Batman: The Brave and the Bold*, which returned Batman to his Silver/Bronze Age origins with weekly superhero team ups and a decidedly more lighthearted tone.

The tremendous success of Marvel's first *Iron Man* movie led directly to *Iron Man: Armored Adventures*, featuring a decidedly Robert Downey Jr.-esque Tony Stark. Prior to that, Marvel had already been experiencing its strongest animated TV presence in years, with *Spider-Man: The New Animated Series, Fantastic Four: World's Greatest Heroes*, and *Wolverine and the X-Men*, a series inspired by the successful X-Men film franchise. There was even the gentler and more kid-friendly *Super Hero Squad Show*, based on the then-popular line of stylized Hasbro action figures.

The 2010s

With the MCU explosion leading up to the first *Avengers* film, there was more demand for Marvel heroes in animated form. *Avengers: Earth's*

Mightiest Heroes coincided with the cinematic saga and gave kids all their favorite characters, focusing on the major ones portrayed in the movies. Later Marvel movie franchises received similar treatment, including *Guardians of the Galaxy*. Even *Big Hero 6*, a non-MCU property that had experienced success as a Disney animated feature, got its own Disney-produced cartoon series. On the DC front, there was the long-running *Young Justice*; *DC Super Hero Girls* featuring Wonder Woman, Zatanna, Supergirl, Batgirl, Bumblebee, and the Jessica Cruz Green Lantern; and the enormous Cartoon Network hit *Teen Titans Go!*, an irreverent and self-referential take on the classic team that has been going strong since 2013.

In recent years, the enduring appeal of superheroes for the very young has provided no shortage of original shows aimed squarely at them. *Paw Patrol* is a Nickelodeon series that follows the adventures of a group of puppies, with their many ingenious vehicles and gadgets, that rescue folks in need. *PJ Masks*, a French/British production distributed by Disney, boasts a group of kids who gain animal-like powers at night that allow them to foil the devious plots of an assortment of pesky villains. And Netflix brings us *The Epic Adventures of Captain Underpants*, based on the children's book series by Dav Pilkey, about George Beard and Harold Hutchins, two ingenious schoolkids who hypnotize their principal into becoming the titular briefs-clad hero each episode.

The 2020s

Marvel's pervasive cultural cachet has certainly insured that superheroes will continue to appear on TV in animated form. So far this decade, we've seen comedian Patton Oswalt develop the snarky *MODOK* for Hulu, taking a parodic look at one of Marvel's strangest villains; *Spidey and His Amazing*

Friends, teaming Peter Parker, Miles Morales, and Gwen Stacy in a Disney Junior series for the youngest Marvel fans; and the fascinating *What If . . . ?*, featured on Disney+ alongside the MCU films, and taking up the kind of wildly speculative stories that the long-running Marvel comic book of the same name was known for. Even the beloved *X-Men* cartoon series of the 1990s has been revived as *X-Men '97*, picking up right where the old show left off. Pliable, creative, and endlessly entertaining, these latest incarnations, and all those that preceded them, demonstrate how the animated medium is tailor-made for superhero stories.

ICONS #12

The Genius, Billionaire, Playboy Philanthropist

Creators: Stan Lee, Larry Lieber, Don Heck, and Jack Kirby

First Appearance: *Tales of Suspense* #39, March 1963

Alter Ego: Tony Stark

Powers: an immensely powerful, mechanized, and computerized suit of body armor that gives him superstrength and the ability to fly. The suit possesses a wide array of weapons, including repulsor beams in the gauntlets, a beam projector in the breastplate, and a forcefield generator.

Archenemies: the Mandarin, the Iron Monger (Obadiah Stane), Crimson Dynamo, Titanium Man, MODOK, Whiplash, the Living Laser, Blizzard, Justin Hammer, Madame Masque

Enjoying tremendous popularity especially within the past fifteen years thanks to the landmark movie performances of Robert Downey Jr., **IRON MAN** is actually one of Marvel's seminal characters and a founding member of the Avengers. He originated sixty years ago with the company's original classic line of Silver Age heroes, most of which are still with us today. With his technological prowess, limitless fortune, and the idealistic heart that beats within his sometimes-cynical exterior, Tony Stark is a fascinating character that combines our greatest escapist power fantasies with a dark edge and demonstrates—somewhat like Batman on the DC side of things—exactly what human ingenuity is capable of, even in the absence of actual superpowers.

THE ORIGIN

A wealthy industrialist and head of Stark Industries, Tony Stark is manufacturing weapons for the US military (originally during the Vietnam War, although this was updated in later years), when he is gravely injured by exploding shrapnel and captured by the villainous Wong-Chu, who forces him to make weapons for him. However, Stark, with the help of mentor and fellow captive Ho Yinsen, secretly constructs an armor suit that Tony uses to escape. Due to damage in his chest from the shrapnel, they also construct a permanent breastplate designed to regulate his heart, which must be charged regularly. He creates the secret identity of Iron Man—who the world believes is Stark's bodyguard—to fight threats to his company and to the world.

THE CREATION

Stan Lee had the ingenious idea to create a morally ambiguous hero who would be an unabashed capitalist and war profiteer at a time when the counterculture was on the rise, and such men were generally disliked by America's youth. He enlisted scripting help from Larry Lieber to flesh out this character's origin and the combined artistic input of Jack Kirby and Don Heck to come up with the look of his armor, which would be fully taken over by Heck, and would also evolve dramatically in its early years, becoming more streamlined. Stark's charisma, along with the eventual changing of his moral stance toward war profiteering, made him popular with fans in spite of his origins.

EVOLUTION OF THE ARMOR

The classic Iron Man look will always be the iconic red and gold armor that fans know and love. However, in his earliest version, Iron Man's armor was gray and bulky, looking more like a steel exoskeleton. It was gradually shrunk down in early issues to give the character greater mobility. During the 1980s, a red and silver redesigned suit was used for a few years, which Robert Downey Jr.'s character actually wears during the second Iron Man film, *Iron Man 2*. In more recent years, the armor has become less mechanical and more a product of nanotechnology, utilizing liquid metal tech to be able to conform to Tony's body shape at command—a long way from the metal suit he once wore under his business attire!

TONY'S WORST ENEMY: HIMSELF

Lee always prided himself on creating superheroes who were flawed people, and he perhaps never accomplished this as well as he did with Tony Stark/Iron Man. At times selfish, morally questionable, or downright obnoxious, he hasn't always been easy to root for, or for the other heroes to get along with, as can be seen during important story lines like *Civil War*, also adapted to great effect in the third *Captain America* film.

Downey Jr. has been effective at portraying Tony's flaws, although his worst flaw of all, his serious alcoholism, has never been fully explored in the Marvel movies. Nevertheless, it is something that has been with Tony since the 1970s—the "Demon in a Bottle" that has done more harm to him than any supervillain.

WE ARE IRON MEN (AND WOMEN)

Stark has designed a wide array of different types of armor for different purposes, including his massive "Hulkbuster" suit, created to do battle with the Green Goliath himself when necessary. An extremely weaponized suit, known as War Machine, was eventually given to Stark's old friend and pilot James "Rhodey" Rhodes, who has frequently fought by Iron Man's side. In fact, at certain times, particularly in the late 1980s when Tony was recovering from serious injuries, Rhodes temporarily took on the mantle of Iron Man himself. In addition to Rhodes, Stark is often assisted by his right-hand man Happy Hogan, and his secretary and love interest Pepper Potts.

MARVEL'S MOST BELOVED CHARACTER ON SCREEN

For years, Robert Downey Jr.'s iconic portrayal of Tony Stark was the lynchpin of the Marvel Cinematic Universe, thrusting Iron Man into the position of Marvel's most popular character for the first time. Downey Jr. played Stark in ten films (including one brief cameo in the end credits scene of *The Incredible Hulk*), more times than any other actor has ever played a superhero. He is the only actor to ever play Iron Man in a live-action capacity, although the character has been seen several times in animated form, first as part of the 1960s syndicated cartoon series *Marvel Superheroes*. He returned to animation in the 1990s as part of the *Marvel Action Hour*, and also starred in *Iron Man: Armored Adventures* in 2009.

THE COOL EXEC WITH THE HEART OF STEEL

In part due to Marvel Studios' inability to use Spider-Man or the X-Men in the movies, Iron Man had his profile greatly raised in recent years thanks to being used as the jumping-off point for the entire Marvel Cinematic Universe. Even more than Captain America (Marvel's original superhero and the actual leader of the Avengers), Iron Man became the character fans most associated with the MCU. And although his elevation was born out of necessity, Iron Man has always been one of Stan Lee's greatest creations, a fact known by comic book readers before Robert Downey Jr. was even born.

13

SUPERVILLAINS!

Say Hello to the Bad Guys

There can be no good without evil. Nowhere is this truer than in the world of superheroes. Heroes are only as worthy and as memorable as the opponents they must overcome. And even though in most superhero stories the good guys win in the end, the roles that supervillains play are integral. We probably wouldn't be fascinated with this genre as much as we are today were it not for the epic confrontations and rivalries that have defined its history. Just as with superheroes themselves, it's a history that goes back to our earliest tales and legends. There has always been a yin to the yang, a dark side to the light side, and a constant battle waged for supremacy.

Whether it's Beowulf challenging Grendel in Hrothgar's hall, the Sheriff of Nottingham plotting the downfall of Robin Hood, Dick Tracy matching wits with a host of grotesque criminals from the mind of Chester Gould, the Joker killing Batman's young ward Robin, or Thanos pursuing universal genocide, villains have always fascinated, and sometimes frightened, us, and given us the motivation we need to root for the good guys and hope for all that is right to win the day. In many cases, the bad guys tend to be the more interesting and nuanced ones, and certainly the more colorful. They are allowed to let all their inhibitions go; there is something appealing about that, something that keeps the story moving forward, keeping us reading and watching.

In fact, very often the villain is in some way a reflection of the hero or represents some other side—perhaps what the hero might have become if a different path had been chosen. This can be seen in the representation of Kill Monger, the vengeful, psychopathic, would-be mass murderer who stands in direct contrast to his more balanced, virtuous, and wise enemy, Prince T'Challa, aka Black Panther. A similar dichotomy exists between Magneto and Charles Xavier. Sometimes their origins are intertwined in a way that ensures they will forever be linked with each other. Tim Burton and screenwriters Warren Skaaren and Sam Hamm chose this route—somewhat controversially—for the 1989 film version of *Batman*, in which a young Joker, as Jack Napier, is revealed as the killer of Bruce Wayne's parents (unlike Batman's otherwise accepted origin, which maintains it was a random act by mugger Joe Chill). In *The Incredibles*, little Buddy Pine is rebuffed by Mr. Incredible when he wants to be his sidekick, and the rejection motivates the spurned youngster to morph into the mad villain Syndrome, intent on hunting down all "supers." This kind of origin story is seen often in supervillain lore.

Sometimes the villain is set up to be the diametric opposite of the hero they're meant to oppose, with the core of the conflict deriving from that difference. This can be seen in the classic Hulk archenemy the Leader, whose mind has been expanded in the same way as Banner's body, resulting in a never-ending struggle of brain versus brawn. Comics creators would famously work to come up with villains based on this "opposite" concept, which also resulted in characters like the Dark Archer (a grim reflection of

Green Arrow), Venom and Carnage (both representing twisted perversions of Spider-Man's appearance, not to mention his personality), and the most obvious of examples, Bizarro, who plays the role of the anti-Superman to often comical lengths in vintage Silver Age DC comics. Sometimes they are designed to have a power that specifically represents a particular hero's point of weakness, making him an intriguing and daunting opponent. This can be seen in much of the Flash's rogue's gallery for example, which was seemingly crafted as a collection of enemies whose abilities somehow counteract or nullify Flash's superspeed powers: Captain Cold, Weather Wizard, Mirror Master, etc.

The iterations of this endless war between good and evil are best known to us today in the form of comic books and comic book movies/television, but it's something that's occupied storytellers from when scribes first put chisel to stone or ink to parchment. In all the ancient mythologies and religions of the world, there have been evil gods and goddesses, such as the demonic Slavic deity Chernobog, also known as Diabol; the ancient Canaanite god Moloch, who demanded child sacrifice; and of course, Loki, the Norse enemy of Asgard, who has also crossed over into the world of superhero comics himself. These figures represented existential threats to humanity and existence, and it was the benevolent gods who kept them in check and preserved the natural order. In Homer's *Odyssey*, the quick-thinking Odysseus matches wits with the cyclops Polyphemus, the sorceress Circe (who later becomes the Catwoman to his Batman), and others. Hercules, in the completion of his legendary labors, must contend with monstrous threats like Cerberus, the Nemean Lion, and the Hydra, and confront powerful figures like Queen Hippolyta of the Amazons and King Diomedes of Thrace.

The earliest protosuperheroes had their nemeses, which were put in place to test their mettle. In the age of mass-produced fiction, authors quickly understood, taking a note from this historic tradition, that a solid, well-written, and even sometimes charismatic villain was key to a successful and satisfying story. In crafting his superdetective Sherlock Holmes, Sir Arthur Conan Doyle also created the criminal mastermind Professor Moriarty, who actually appears to kill Holmes in his very first appearance, the 1893 short story "The Final Problem," and who remains his greatest foe even in references made in later stories after the detective's reemergence. Sometimes, supervillains could even be created in the absence of a true superhero. Early horror fiction is rife with this concept, such as with Mr. Hyde, the unhinged alter ego of Dr. Jekyll in Robert Louis Stevenson's classic novel, who contends with the good doctor for physical and mental dominance. Count Dracula, lord of the vampires, was the ultimate supervillain, even though his opponents in Bram Stoker's novel are only "normal" mortals like Professor Van Helsing and Jonathan Harker.

Early movies and comic strips gave us Ming the Merciless, overlord of Planet Mongo, whose tyrannical schemes are thwarted by Flash Gordon; as well as Bluto, the strapping bully who at times seems even stronger than his superstrong rival Popeye—at least until the sailor eats his spinach. But when the comic book superhero floodgates opened at the end of the 1930s, that was when the supervillain phenomenon as we know it today really took hold. Suitably, the very first comic book superhero, Superman, was the first to battle supervillains shortly after his 1938 debut. But it wasn't Lex Luthor, the mad scientist who didn't make his first appearance until 1940; rather, the earliest comic book supervillain was the crippled genius known as The Ultra-Humanite. That same year, Batman battled his earliest foes—not the Joker, who first appeared around the same time as Luthor, but rather the hideous Dr. Death and the vampiric Mad Monk.

Worst of the Worst: The Hall of Infamy

LEX LUTHOR
Creators: Jerry Siegel and Joe Shuster
Archenemy: Superman

In his earliest incarnation, Luthor started out as young Clark Kent's friend. Luthor loses his hair in a freak accident and blames Clark, who couldn't save him in time. As reinvented by John Byrne in the 1980s, the maniacal scientist was transformed into a cynical and sinister business tycoon. In all versions he represents evil intelligence against Superman's righteous might.

DR. THADDEUS SIVANA
Creators: Bill Parker and C. C. Beck
Archenemy: Captain Marvel/Shazam

Patterned somewhat after the original Luthor, Sivana was a gnarled old scientist who uses ingenuity, bitterness, and whimsical technology to try to take down his nemesis, "The Big Red Cheese." He is sometimes joined by that other Marvel family adversary, the tiny yet formidable superworm known as Mr. Mind.

THE RED SKULL
Creators: Joe Simon, France Herron, Jack Kirby
Archenemy: Captain America

Nefarious Nazi agent Johann Schmidt was originally a protégé of Adolf Hitler himself, wearing a terrifying mask to strike fear in Captain America and all others who'd oppose the Third Reich. In later years, he became the leader of the secret organization HYDRA, and even suffered an accident that made his red-skull appearance all too real.

SINESTRO
Creators: John Broome and Gil Kane
Archenemy: Green Lantern

Representing the exact opposite of all that Hal Jordan and the Green Lantern Corps stand for, Sinestro was once a Lantern himself, before being corrupted by the yellow energy of fear—weakness of all Green Lanterns.

After being kicked out of the corps, Sinestro seeks his revenge against the corps and its greatest champion.

DOCTOR DOOM
Creators: Stan Lee and Jack Kirby
Archenemies: the Fantastic Four

Acknowledged for decades as the ultimate bad guy of the Marvel Universe, Victor Von Doom, ruler of the fictional Eastern European nation of Latveria, began by making life difficult for the Fantastic Four, but has since had all of Earth's heroes in his crosshairs. A brutal yet brilliant dictator, he will settle for nothing less than total domination.

THE LEADER
Creators: Stan Lee and Steve Ditko
Archenemy: the Hulk

Samuel Sterns was once a simple janitor who was exposed to gamma radiation, but instead of gaining superstrength like the Hulk, his brain expanded, and he gained superhuman levels of intelligence. Pitting his limitless brains against the Green Goliath's limitless brawn, he also commands his army of Humanoids.

LOKI
Creators: Stan Lee, Larry Lieber, Jack Kirby
Archenemy: Thor

Although portrayed merely as a "god of mischief" in Norse mythology, Lee and company transformed Loki, half-brother of Thor, into an embodiment of pure evil. With his eyes constantly on the throne of Asgard, not to mention domination of Earth, he has been locked in immortal combat with the thunder god for centuries, and was in fact the menace that first brought the Avengers together.

REVERSE FLASH
Creators: John Broome and Carmine Infantino
Archenemy: the Flash

Although there was a Reverse Flash who opposed Golden Age Flash Jay Garrick in the 1940s, it is evil time traveler from the future Eobard Thawne who is most associated with the role. Obsessed with replacing

Barry Allen in the present day, Reverse Flash, aka Dr. Zoom, would repeatedly travel from the future to try and eliminate him from existence.

MAGNETO
Creators: Stan Lee and Jack Kirby
Archenemies: the X-Men

The violent and genocidal flipside to Professor Xavier's dreams of mutant/human coexistence, Erik Lensherr was a Holocaust survivor who also happened to develop extremely powerful mutant abilities that give him control of all magnetic fields. As leader of the Brotherhood of Evil Mutants, he seeks to bind the human race to his will.

GALACTUS
Creators: Stan Lee and Jack Kirby
Archenemies: Silver Surfer, Fantastic Four

The Eater of Worlds is just about the most powerful supervillain there is—so much so that he seems to exist beyond mere concepts of good and evil. An entity older than the universe, who roams the spaceways in search of planets whose energy he may devour, he has been thwarted from doing so to Earth by the Fantastic Four, as well as his own former herald, the Silver Surfer.

DARKSEID
Creator: Jack Kirby
Archenemies: the Justice League

Developed by Kirby after the longtime Marvel creator jumped ship to DC, Darkseid grew to become the most dangerous threat to Superman and the Justice League, seeking to enslave the multiverse from his home base on the bleak planet Apokolips. Leader of the New Gods, he is assisted by his son Kalibak and henchman Desaad.

THANOS
Creator: Jim Starlin
Archenemies: the Avengers, Silver Surfer

Seen by some at the time as an imitation of Darkseid, Thanos became Marvel's chief cosmic villain, and would come into his own in the 1980s and 1990s in his quest to master the Infinity Gauntlet and wipe out half the population of the universe. In recent years, thanks to his role in the MCU, he has become arguably Marvel's most important supervillain.

SHREDDER

Creators: Kevin Eastman and Peter Laird
Archenemies: Teenage Mutant Ninja Turtles

The leader of the mysterious and diabolical organization known as the Foot Clan, clad in blade-covered samurai armor, Shredder is the chief rival of Master Splinter. Thus, it is Splinter's greatest pupils, the Ninja Turtles, who perpetually oppose Shredder and his evil plots, as well as mutant Foot flunkies like Bebop and Rocksteady.

VIOLATOR

Creator: Todd McFarlane
Archenemy: Spawn

A horrifying demon who takes the human form of a monstrous clown, Violator has served the supreme evil of Malebolgia for eons, guiding Hell-spawn on the path to servitude in his army. Since being assigned to Al Simmons, he has frequently clashed with the latest Spawn, seeking to dominate and frustrate him while Simmons seeks to reassert his humanity and resist his manipulations.

DOOMSDAY

Creator: Dan Jurgens
Archenemy: Superman

A genetically engineered killing machine from the planet Krypton, Doomsday spent ages locked up until escaping imprisonment and going on a planet-spanning rampage. He encountered the Justice League on Earth, as well as his ultimate target—Krypton's last son, Superman. Doomsday managed to kill the Man of Steel before being killed himself. Both have since been brought back from the dead.

OTHER NOTEWORTHY NEMESES

Abomination, Apocalypse, Bizarro, Black Adam, Black Manta, Bullseye, Cheetah, Dormammu, the Juggernaut, Kang the Conqueror, the Mandarin, Mephisto, the Mole Man, Sabretooth, General Zod

True to its reputation of clearcut good and evil, the Golden Age of Comics gave us rather easily defined and admittedly two-dimensional villains, some of whom, like Joker, Luthor, Scarecrow, Toyman, and Black Adam, would be further refined and given more nuance by later generations of creators. Others, like Mr. Mind and that interdimensional imp Mr. Mxyzptlk, were definitely products of a more whimsical age in comics, but who remained highly entertaining even if their genuine "menace" was at times questionable. And speaking of whimsical, the surreal and wacky Silver Age certainly took supervillains into an even more colorful and surreal place, with the likes of the bizarre giant intergalactic starfish Starro; Superman's alien space android adversary Brainiac, as well as the kryptonite-powered Metallo; not to mention Batman baddies like Mr. Freeze and the deservedly lesser known Calendar Man and Killer Moth.

As Marvel Comics entered the fray in the 1960s, it put its own characteristically creative and unique spin on things. Early prototypical Marvel villains like Goom and Finn Fang Foom, who appeared in the pages of anthologies like *Tales of Suspense* and *Strange Tales*, were more monsters than anything else, but the modern Marvel supervillain tradition really kicked off in late 1961 with the emergence of the Mole Man, the subterranean sovereign who opposed the Fantastic Four in their very first appearance. Marvel villains were edgier, more of a serious threat, as was infamously crystalized when the Green Goblin killed Peter Parker's girlfriend Gwen Stacy by tossing her off a bridge in *Amazing Spider-Man* #121. Marvel's top villain was established as Doctor Doom, a kind of enhanced European despot who, like the Red Skull before him, had an all-too real resemblance to actual megalomaniacal dictators.

Gotham's Most Wanted

Of the entire DC Universe—and possibly of the entire world of comic book superheroes—there is no hero with a deeper or more iconic rogue's gallery than Batman. Here are the Dark Knight Detective's greatest rivals.

THE JOKER

Creators: Bob Kane, Bill Finger, Jerry Robinson

Although his true identity has never been completely found out, Alan Moore's seminal *The Killing Joke* graphic novel established him as a failed comic who falls in with the wrong gang and goes mad after falling into a vat of chemicals due to Batman's interference. Ever since, the Clown Prince of Crime has been the Caped Crusader's greatest enemy, in a struggle that has spanned nearly eighty-five years.

TWO-FACE

Creators: Bob Kane and Bill Finger

District attorney Harvey Dent was a beacon of hope for Gotham, taking the fight to organized crime, until a mobster hurled acid at him while standing trial, hideously scarring one half of his face. His ensuing madness centering on that duality, he embarked on a life of crime, using a flip of his equally scarred lucky coin to guide his deranged and unpredictable actions.

CATWOMAN

Creators: Bob Kane and Bill Finger

Although very often depicted as a reluctant ally and even love interest of Batman's, Selina Kyle is still a criminal at heart, using her wits, consummate fighting skills, and dangerous clawed gloves mainly in self-serving schemes and larceny. In *Batman: Year One*, Frank Miller depicted her as a former dominatrix with a particular contempt for domineering and toxic men.

THE PENGUIN

Creators: Bob Kane and Bill Finger

Eccentric mob boss Oswald Cobblepot gained his nickname by his stocky, diminutive stature, distinctive waddle, grotesque features, and penchant for flashy tuxedoes. A powerful force in Gotham's underworld, he is also known for his many weaponized umbrellas and aristocratic bearing.

THE RIDDLER

Creators: Bill Finger and Dick Sprang

Known alternately as Edward Nigma, Edward Nygma, or Edward Nashton, the Riddler has a pathological desire to outsmart Batman, and some would argue secretly wants to get caught. How else to explain the elaborate puzzles and riddles he leaves behind, dropping clever and esoteric clues to his crimes, designed to confound both the Dark Knight and the Gotham PD?

OTHER ARKHAM ASYLUM INMATES

Bane, the Scarecrow, Poison Ivy, Mr. Freeze, Ra'as al Ghul, Clayface, Killer Croc, Man-Bat, Dr. Hugo Strange, the Mad Hatter

The explosion of supervillains that took place in the Silver Age mirrored that of superheroes as well. There were even supervillain teams taking shape, such as the Sinister Six made up of a host of Spidey villains, or the Brotherhood of Evil Mutants led by Magneto. In the 1970s, even the Super Friends (aka Justice League) did battle with the Legion of Doom on TV, composed of a who's who of DC villains. Meanwhile, in comic books, villains were becoming even grittier than ever in a reflection of the times, as well as a desire to appeal to a more mature readership. The Joker was amped up by creators like Neal Adams, Denny O'Neil, and Steve Englehart to become less a mischievous gang boss and more of a truly deranged psychopath, which would be how the character was portrayed ever after. The same could be said about most of Batman's villains—an evolution that continued through the efforts of writers like Alan Moore, Frank Miller, and particularly Grant Morrison, whose highly influential 1989 graphic novel *Arkham Asylum* made that Gotham mental institution infamous and put on full display the dangerous psychoses of even previously flimsy Bat-villains like the Mad Hatter, Killer Croc, and Maxie Zeus. In a reflection of the times, Luthor went from a mad scientist to a sophisticated capitalist robber baron. Eventually, new 1990s villain Doomsday would murder Superman, and not long after, Bane would put Batman in a wheelchair. The stakes had decidedly been raised.

The waters were being muddied, and those clear-cut divisions of good and evil weren't always so clear-cut anymore. It wasn't uncommon for heroes to do things that might be considered morally ambiguous or worse, and villains were being made more relatable and even sympathetic for a more cynical fan base that had been trained not to take anything at face value. And the villains' actions could be far more reprehensible than anything a 1940s comic book reader could've possibly imagined. Characters like the Punisher and Deadpool sometimes had readers wondering what side they were actually on. The memorable 2004 DC limited series *Identity Crisis* revealed that longtime villain Dr. Light—who had often been portrayed as a forgettable and even silly afterthought—was actually a serial rapist, and that Elongated Man's wife, Sue Dibny, had been one of his victims. Batman, without the knowledge of the rest of the Justice League, persuades Zatanna to tamper with his mind to make him less of a danger and accidentally lobotomizes him in the process.

Thanks to the superhero movie craze of the twenty-first century, supervillains have been given a greater stage than ever on which to play out their despicable schemes, and to wage war against the forces of good. Even before that craze began, early movie supervillains like Gene Hackman's Lex Luthor, Terence Stamp's General Zod, Jack Nicholson's Joker, and Michelle Pfieffer's Catwoman illustrated exactly why the villains were often the best part of the story. Willem Dafoe's Green Goblin and Ian McKellen's Magneto were among those who continued that theme in early Marvel movies, but it was in the blossoming Marvel Cinematic Universe that villains took

Tangled Web of Evil

There is no more well-developed and colorful assortment of baddies in the Marvel Universe than Spider-Man's surreal coterie of sinister adversaries. Here are just a few of the foes who make Spidey's life hell.

THE GREEN GOBLIN
Creators: Stan Lee and Steve Ditko

The most dangerous and persistent of Spider-Man's enemies, Norman Osborn was the head of Oscorp when he was exposed to an experimental chemical that gave him enhanced strength and intelligence while also driving him insane. Using his trademark glider, pumpkin bombs, and other weapons, he has hit Spidey hard over the years, even killing his girlfriend, Gwen Stacy.

DOCTOR OCTOPUS
Creators: Stan Lee and Steve Ditko

The brilliant scientist Otto Octavius builds a mechanical harness with four powerful appendages. When it becomes permanently fused to his body, he uses the unique tool/weapon to become a dangerous criminal. At times, he has been Spidey's main nemesis, especially during the period when Norman Osborn was (temporarily) dead, and he is also the leader of the formidable Sinister Six.

THE VULTURE
Creators: Stan Lee and Steve Ditko

Another Sinister Six member, gifted but unstable electronics engineer Adrian Toomes creates a bird-like suit that enables him to fly at great speed, and makes him a major threat to the Wall-Crawler in the skies above New York City. The Vulture was the first supervillain captured in a photograph by Peter Parker for the *Daily Bugle*.

THE KINGPIN
Creators: Stan Lee and John Romita Sr.

Although later becoming more closely associated with another NYC-based hero, Daredevil, Wilson Fisk first tangled with Spider-Man, and has been a thorn in his side ever since. A tough street kid from the Bronx who grew to become the city's most powerful mobster, Kingpin is also deadly in hand-to-hand combat, and his cunning once allowed him to discover Daredevil's secret identity.

VENOM
Creators: Todd McFarlane and David Michelinie

Although he came along a lot later than most of Spidey's primary foes, in recent decades Venom has arisen to become one of Web-Head's most recognizable and popular opponents. Combining the cold alien intelligence of the black symbiote suit that originally belonged to Peter with the rage and bitterness of human host Eddie Brock, Venom is a nightmare come to life.

OTHER WOULD-BE SPIDER-SQUASHERS
Kraven the Hunter, Sandman, Electro, Carnage, the Lizard, Mysterio, the Shocker, the Chameleon, the Hobgoblin, the Rhino

center stage more than ever. In fact, one could argue that the entire overarching plot of this interconnecting franchise has revolved largely around the machinations of bad guys like Tom Hiddleston's diabolically likeable Loki, and most importantly of all, the mad titan, Thanos. As played by Josh Brolin, the character—originally created by Jim Starlin in the 1970s—was at the heart of an overarching story that spanned the first three phases of the MCU, and in the end it took the combined forces of all the Marvel superheroes to thwart him.

And in what may be seen as the ultimate evolution of the ultimate comic book villain, Joaquin Phoenix wowed audiences and critics—and won an Academy Award—for his complex portrayal of the Joker in the 2019 film of the same name. It was a loosely adapted origin story that put the villain at center stage, without even a Batman to oppose him. The compelling performance highlighted the decidedly understandable societal forces that could give rise to someone like him.

The fixation and fascination that millions of fans had with Brolin's layered portrayal of Thanos, and Phoenix's tortured interpretation of Joker, were only the latest examples of how supervillains have enthralled our attention, just as they repeatedly attempt to enthrall our heroes. There's something that's almost impossible to perfectly pin down about the way we are simultaneously repelled by, and yet drawn to, these shameless scoundrels, relentless schemers, preening madmen, and unspeakable menaces. In the end, they make superheroes seem all the more "super" for having vanquished them, which is really what their primary role has always been anyway, all through the decades and even centuries of their existence. We cling to the light, represented by the valor and honor of great heroes, in our desire to fend off the encroachment of the darkness. It's a darkness that's terrified us since the days of huddling in caves and around bonfires. But now, as then, our stories give us the solace and escape that real life may not always afford. So here's to the bad guys—in losing, they do their job well.

ICONS #13

The Merry Mutants

Creators: Stan Lee and Jack Kirby

First Appearance: *The X-Men* #1, September 1963

Key Members: Professor X (leader), Cyclops, Marvel Girl/Jean Grey, Beast, Iceman, Angel/Archangel, Wolverine, Colossus, Nightcrawler, Rogue, Kitty Pryde, Polaris, Havok, Banshee, Storm, Psylocke, Gambit, Jubilee, Bishop, Cable

Powers: Members of the X-Men are all mutants—humans born with a genetic marker that causes them to develop superhuman abilities at puberty. Their powers are widely varied, and include energy projection/manipulation (Cyclops, Havok, Banshee, Rogue, Gambit, Polaris, Jubilee, Bishop), psychic abilities (Professor X, Jean Grey, Psylocke, Cable), enhanced speed/reflexes/senses/healing (Beast, Wolverine), temperature/weather manipulation (Iceman, Storm), flight (Angel), body metamorphosis/phasing (Colossus, Kitty Pryde), and even teleportation (Nightcrawler).

Archenemies: Magneto, Sabretooth, Juggernaut, Apocalypse, the Sentinels, Dark Phoenix, Mr. Sinister, the Hellfire Club, Mystique, Lady Deathstrike

With themes of social nonconformity, the struggle with prejudice, youthful insecurities, and self-discovery, it's no wonder that **THE X-MEN** have resonated with readers and viewers for so long. More than most of Stan Lee and Jack Kirby's original 1960s Marvel creations, they have shown an ability to mature and adapt with the times, becoming during the latter part of the twentieth century—and arguably right up to the beginning of the Avengers-centric Marvel Cinematic Universe—Marvel's hottest characters. Starting as a relatively simple superhero team book, their stories became more nuanced and adult over time, pushing the boundaries of comic book storytelling and bringing moral ambiguity to mainstream superhero fiction.

THE ORIGIN

In the Marvel Universe, the mutant gene causes teenagers to develop strange powers that make them different and hence, ostracized from society. Seeking to provide guidance and harness their abilities, Charles Xavier, himself a mutant with strong psychic abilities, establishes a secret school for mutants in Westchester County, New York. Among his original recruits are Scott Summers (Cyclops), Jean Grey (Marvel Girl), Tim Drake (Iceman), Warren Worthington III (Angel), and Hank McCoy (Beast). Using their powers to protect a world that hates and fears them—including the threat of evil mutants—they also fight for greater acceptance of mutant-kind, gathering many new members along the way.

THE CREATION

On a historic creative run in the 1960s, Lee and Kirby put their heads together to create a different kind of team. This time, they didn't want to create another weird explanation for how they got their powers, opting instead to explain that they'd been born with them. Thus, the concept of the mutant began, with both men deciding it would provide great material to explore, including how such characters could fit in with the rest of the world, and if their powers would be used for good or evil. Initially wanting to call the comic book *The Mutants*, they were turned down by publisher Martin Goodman, who doubted 1960s readers would know the meaning of the word.

ALL-NEW, ALL-DIFFERENT

The initial 1960s run of *Uncanny X-Men*, as it came to be called, was not exactly an overnight success. By the end of the decade, Marvel had all but pulled the plug, running reprints of older issues instead. In the 1970s, a concerted effort was made to inject new life into the X-Men, starting with *Giant-Size X-Men* #1 in 1975, in which Len Wein and Dave Cockrum introduced a new roster of global mutant heroes, including Thunderbird, Sunfire, Banshee, Colossus, Nightcrawler, Storm, and of course, Wolverine. What followed was a stellar run by Chris Claremont and John Byrne. They, among others, helped reinvent the X-Men and give them a new edge. Also, it began the pattern of continually adding and removing team members over the years, keeping things fresh.

XAVIER VS. MAGNETO

The dichotomy between Professor Charles Xavier and Erik Lehnsherr—aka the X-Men's greatest nemesis Magneto—has been likened in many places over the years to the dichotomy between Dr. Martin Luther King and Malcolm X, with one advocating tolerance and understanding through nonviolence and the other advocating the achievement of equality "by any means necessary." In the case of Magneto, a Holocaust survivor who well knows the dangers of man's intolerant tendencies, this dichotomy manifests as a desire to subjugate or even destroy the nonpowered human race, while Xavier seeks to gain its acceptance by demonstrating the basic humanity of mutant-kind. But Magneto isn't all bad, and there have even been times when he fought alongside the X-Men, only adding to the fascinating layers of the Xavier/Lehnsherr conflict.

THE WOLVERINE PHENOMENON

Despite not being among the original group, there's one X-Men member whose popularity stands out from all the rest. In fact, a case could be made that he is the most successful comic book superhero created after 1970. Developed by Marvel editor-in-chief Roy Thomas, Len Wein, and John Romita, and making his first full appearance in *Incredible Hulk* #181 (November 1974), he possesses mutant abilities that include accelerated healing, keen senses, and enhanced strength. But he's best known for the adamantium claws implanted in his arms—along with an adamantium-laced skeleton—by the top-secret Weapon X government program. Whether known as Logan or his later-revealed birth name of James Howlett, he set the standard for many of the violent antiheroes that would follow.

X-MOVIES AND MORE

Aside from the MCU itself, no superhero movie franchise has been as expansive as the X-Men series produced by 20th Century Fox, encompassing the original trilogy of *X-Men* (2000), *X2: X-Men United* (2003), and *X-Men: The Last Stand* (2006); the prequel/reboot series of *X-Men: First Class* (2011), *X-Men: Days of Future Past* (2014), *X-Men: Apocalypse* (2016), and *Dark Phoenix* (2019); not to mention the Wolverine trilogy of *X-Men Origins: Wolverine* (2009), *The Wolverine* (2013), and *Logan* (2017), as well as spin-offs *Deadpool* (2016), *Deadpool 2* (2018), and *The New Mutants* (2020). Several popular animated versions of the X-Men have also been launched, including a beloved 1990s version that ran for five years.

GIFTED YOUNGSTERS

At the time of this writing, word is that the X-Men are finally about to be incorporated into the Marvel Cinematic Universe thanks to Disney's purchase of Fox, meaning Xavier's team of superpowered youths will soon be more relevant and popular than ever. With a story that speaks to anyone who has ever felt different, who has ever longed for acceptance, and who has ever understood the double-edged sword of great talent, the X-Men reign as one of the greatest achievements of Stan Lee and Jack Kirby's incredible body of work, as well as that of Claremont, Byrne, Grant Morrison, Jim Lee, Louise Simonson, Brian Michael-Bendis, and the many other creators who lent their ideas to its sixty-year development.

14

CREDIT TO THE CREATORS

The Folks Who Wrote and Drew the Heroes You Love

Comic books do not write and draw themselves. The true origin of superheroes occurred inside the minds of highly gifted and imaginative human beings. Throughout the past eighty-five years, the heroes (and villains) we love have been brought to life by many individuals, some who may have been their original creators and others who deftly and wonderfully continued and broadened their adventures over time. Here is a look at some of the most important and influential of those people who have populated our collective imagination for generations and given our modern culture a shared mythology in the process.

NEAL ADAMS

A native New Yorker, Neal Adams got his start working for Archie Comics in the late 1950s and later enjoyed his first success on Warren Publishing's horror comic magazines. He did some work for Marvel on *X-Men* after Jack

Kirby's exodus, but it was in the 1970s at DC that Adams truly made his mark, teaming up with writer Denny O'Neil to completely revitalize Batman for the Bronze Age and beyond. Known for his realistic style, his work on *Batman* and *Detective Comics* as well as his groundbreaking run with *Green Lantern/Green Arrow* influenced the artistic direction of the industry. He helped create Bat-villains like R'as al Ghul and Man-Bat and returned the Joker to his homicidal roots.

JOHN BYRNE

Born in the United Kingdom, Byrne relocated to Canada with his family at age eight. He first achieved notoriety in 1977 as the artist partner of writer Chris Claremont on a historic run of *Uncanny X-Men* that lasted until 1981 and included such important story lines as the Phoenix Saga. In addition to his distinctive penciling style, he added writing to his skill set beginning with a memorable run on *Fantastic Four* in the mid-1980s. Jumping to DC in 1986, he literally reinvented Superman with the beloved *Man of Steel* miniseries. He took part in the creation of characters like Kitty Pryde, Emma Frost, Sabretooth, Scott Lang, and the superteam Alpha Flight.

CHRIS CLAREMONT

Another British-born creator, Claremont played a major role in adding sophistication and nuance to superhero stories, moving them beyond the sometimes-simplistic plotting of eras past. This was on full display during his record-breaking sixteen-year run as writer of *Uncanny X-Men*, in which he tackled themes never before attempted in comics. He raised the presence of strong female characters in his work, and thanks to story lines like the Phoenix Saga and Days of Future Past, he turned *Uncanny X-Men* from a flop into one of Marvel's most successful titles. Among his countless creations are Rogue, Psylocke, Mystique, Jubilee, Gambit, and the Hellfire Club.

STEVE DITKO

The eccentric, reclusive Ditko is behind only Stan Lee and Jack Kirby as far as the role he played in the early years of Marvel Comics. A native of Johnstown, Pennsylvania, he came to New York in the early 1950s and studied under Batman artist Jerry Robinson before working for Kirby and Joe Simon's studio, developing his quirky artistic style. At Charlton Comics, he helped to create characters like Captain Atom, the Question, and Blue Beetle. His most enduring work came with Marvel, where he co-created Spider-Man and Doctor Strange with Lee. His time at Marvel ended under unknown circumstances, and Ditko refused giving interviews for the remainder of his very long life.

WILL EISNER

One of the most respected and literary-minded comics creators, particularly of the Golden and Silver Ages, is Will Eisner. Born and raised in Brooklyn, New York, he was a successful cartoonist prior to getting into comics, and was one of the first to make the leap to the budding new medium in the 1940s. His world-famous character, the Spirit, appeared for years in its own illustrated newspaper supplement, elevating the superhero genre and exposing it to more of an adult audience than most comic books had in those days. He took a deep interest in the art and study of the comic book form, which is reflected in the Eisner Awards, the industry's highest honors, which were named for him in 1988.

BILL FINGER

The story of Milton "Bill" Finger is a sad one, as he contributed equally to the creation of Batman with Bob Kane, the man who had for decades solely been credited with the Dark Knight's creation. Finger came in the 1930s from Denver, Colorado, to New York, where he got his start in comic strips. His official role working with Kane was as a subcontractor and he was relegated to ghost writer status for his contributions not only to Batman, but also to the original Green Lantern, Alan Scott. It wasn't until after his death that his biographer, Marc Tyler Nobleman, located Finger's heirs and helped them fight for DC to officially acknowledge Finger as Batman's co-creator, which they did in 2015.

GARDNER FOX

A brilliant polymath and aspiring lawyer, Brooklyn, New York's own Gardner Francis Fox abandoned his legal ambitions during the Great Depression, seeking to earn quick money as a writer instead. Working as both a science fiction novelist and an early scripter for DC Comics, he was directly involved in the creation of the original Flash, Hawkman, Dr. Fate, Zatanna, the Sandman, and Barbara Gordon. He also co-created the Justice Society of America in the 1940s and re-created them as the Justice League of America a decade later. He also conceptualized the multiverse of alternate realities for DC beginning in 1961. The concept would later be copied by Marvel Comics.

BOB KANE

Kane's legacy is complicated. Although for decades credited as Batman's sole creator, his stifling of fair recognition for co-creator Bill Finger is certainly a blemish on his important work. Born Robert Kahn in New York City in 1915, the son of Eastern European Jewish immigrants, he befriended fellow future comics legend Will Eisner in high school. Prior to working for DC, he spent time as an animator for Fleischer Studios in the 1930s. Following his career in comics, he focused on fine art during the 1960s and enjoyed minor celebrity late in life, even acting as a consultant on the 1980s/1990s *Batman* film franchise.

JACK KIRBY

There's a reason they call Kirby the "King." New York's Jacob Kurtzberg is arguably the single most influential and revered comic book artist in history, known for his bold, dynamic, action-oriented style and the brilliant and fertile mind that led to so many indelible character designs, especially during Marvel/Timely's Golden and Silver Ages. First co-creating Captain America with Joe Simon in the 1940s, he later formed a legendary team with Stan Lee in the 1960s that gave rise to the overwhelming majority of the iconic Marvel characters still with us to this day. In the 1970s he even made a surprising jump to DC, where he created Darkseid and the "New Gods" mythos.

JOE KUBERT

The son of a kosher butcher from East New York, Kubert had immigrated to the United States from Poland as an infant. He got his first inking assignment on a comic book at age twelve. His early initial success in the Golden Age came on Fox Comics' *Blue Beetle*, and even more so on *Hawkman* for DC. His Silver Age DC work was highlighted by his iconic art for the classic war comic *Sgt. Rock*, which was a perfect fit for his gritty, realistic style—as was his work on DC's *Tarzan* line in the mid-1970s. Kubert also spent years in an office role for DC, and later opened his own celebrated comics illustration school.

STAN LEE

The godfather of Marvel Comics, Stanley Martin Lieber was the public face of the company and its pantheon of heroes for nearly sixty years. His tenure at the company, once known as Timely Comics, began in the 1940s when he was hired as an office assistant thanks in part to being the cousin of the wife of Timely publisher Martin Goodman. Lee quickly ascended to the role of editor in chief and spearheaded the birth of the Marvel Era in the Silver Age, generating new superheroes like Spider-Man, the Hulk, the X-Men, Iron Man, Daredevil, Fantastic Four, Thor, and countless others. His contributions to Marvel were acknowledged in his many unforgettable cameos in Marvel films toward the end of his life.

TODD McFARLANE

His exaggerated, almost surreal illustrating style made him an instant darling of comics fans in the mid- to late 1980s, thanks especially to his innovative work drawing Spider-Man, which also led to the creation of the unique villain Venom. The Calgary, Alberta, native had such a large following by the early 1990s that he used it to break away from Marvel Comics and launch his own company, Image Comics, along with other talented friends who sought to own their own superhero creations. His greatest of those original creations would be Spawn, one of the biggest superheroes to emerge from an independent (non-Marvel/DC) publisher. He currently operates McFarlane Toys and the movie/animation studio McFarlane Entertainment.

FRANK MILLER

Born in Maryland and raised in Vermont, Miller wound up having more impact on the narrative style and philosophy of modern comics than almost any other creator. First gaining attention through his revitalization of *Daredevil* in the early 1980s, he later assured his immortality by re-creating Batman with an even darker and more dysfunctional sensibility than ever before through work such as *The Dark Night Returns* and *Batman: Year One*. Although he built on the work of Adams, O'Neil, and others, it's Miller's take that has most influenced all Batman creators after him. Beyond the world of superheroes, he is also known for his stunning work on *Sin City* and *300*.

ALAN MOORE

A gifted writer with a unique take on the medium, the unorthodox and reclusive Englishman grew up a fan of Silver Age superhero comics, and his body of work is informed by that. Most known for the seminal *Watchmen*, which so perfectly deconstructed the classic superhero archetypes, he also had a remarkable run with *Swamp Thing* for DC, and penned the last pre-Crisis Superman story, "Whatever Happened to the Man of Tomorrow?" His other groundbreaking work includes *Batman: The Killing Joke*, which tells the origin of the Joker, as well as the Victorian superteam series

The League of Extraordinary Gentlemen, the dystopian graphic novel *V for Vendetta*, and the chilling Jack the Ripper series *From Hell*.

GRANT MORRISON

A leading member of the so-called British Invasion of American comics that occurred over the course of the 1980s, the Scottish-born Morrison made a big splash at DC in the late 1980s, revamping the rather obscure character Animal Man, and writing the groundbreaking Batman graphic novel *Arkham Asylum*. With a remarkably nontraditional and fresh approach to comic book storytelling, Morrison gained a reputation for specializing in revamps, also spearheading the acclaimed *New X-Men* series of the 2000s, as well as writing the Eisner-winning *All-Star Superman* with artist Frank Quitely. DC's *Final Crisis* was another Morrison brainchild, and helped reboot the entire DC Universe, as did the year-long *52* series of 2006 and 2007.

DENNY O'NEIL

Getting his start at Marvel in the 1960s, the St. Louis-born O'Neil next spent time at Charlton Comics. At the end of the 1960s, he jumped to DC with Dick Giordano. There he'd do the work that would most define his career, as writer on the innovative *Green Lantern/Green Arrow* series with Neal Adams, and even more importantly collaborating with Adams on the Batman family of titles. O'Neil was largely responsible for the dramatic new direction of Batman in the 1970s. He went back to Marvel for a time in the 1980s, but after returning to DC in 1986, he took on the role of editor for all Batman comics, which he held until retirement in 2000.

JOHN ROMITA SR.

Known for his clean line work and timeless style, John Romita was an institution at Marvel in the 1960s and 1970s. Even though he didn't create Spider-Man, his work in those early years came to define the classic look of the character. Among the characters he did have a hand in creating were Wolverine and the Punisher, and his work at the company stretched back to the 1950s when it was still known as Atlas Comics. Romita also worked on romance comics for DC in the 1950s. He is the father of John Romita Jr., another longtime Marvel artist, and his wife Virginia was a managing editor at Marvel for years.

JOE SHUSTER

The cocreator of Superman, Shuster was the first artist to draw the Man of Steel. Born in Toronto, Canada, and raised in Cleveland, Ohio, by his Jewish immigrant parents, he befriended Jerome Siegel in high school, and the two would go on to become a writer/artist team. They broke into comics working for National Allied Publications, the future DC Comics, in the late 1930s. It was there that they pitched the character that would change the course of comic book history and become an institution. Shuster struggled in his career post-Superman, however, and famously fought legal battles with DC over ownership of the character. He was forced to retire in the 1970s due to partial blindness.

JERRY SIEGEL

Siegel's parents fled anti-Semitism in Lithuania, coming to America at the turn of the twentieth century to raise their son in Cleveland, Ohio. A lover of science fiction and adventure stories, he met a kindred spirit in Joe Shuster. The two put their heads together, pairing his words with Joe's illustrations. He and Shuster fought DC for the rights to their Superman character, but even though they lost, Siegel returned to DC later in his career, writing Superman stories in the 1950s and early 1960s. In failing health at the time of the blockbuster *Superman* film in 1978, Siegel, along with Shuster, was offered a $20,000-a-year stipend by DC for the rest of his life.

JIM STARLIN

One of the most important comic book writers of the Bronze Age and beyond, Starlin got his start submitting comic stories while working as a navy photographer during the Vietnam War. His contributions to Marvel were crucial in the company's second wave of the 1970s, and he specialized in "cosmic" stories, giving the world characters like Thanos, Drax and Gamora, and revamping Captain Marvel and Adam Warlock. He was the man behind the Infinity Gauntlet story line of the early 1990s that later became the basis of the MCU's greatest story arc. While at DC, he also scripted the demise of Jason Todd in Batman's "Death in the Family" story.

EVEN MORE COMIC BOOK LEGENDS

Brian Michael Bendis

One of the twenty-first century's most important Marvel writers, Bendis is best known as the architect of the Ultimate Marvel Universe, as well as for relaunching the World's Mightiest Heroes with *New Avengers* in 2004. "Secret War," "House of M," and "Age of Ultron" are among his most celebrated story lines.

Brian Bolland

He will forever be known as the meticulous and striking artist for Alan Moore's *Batman: The Killing Joke*, but Bolland is even better known in his native UK as the most iconic *Judge Dredd* illustrator. He has also done memorable work as a regular cover artist for DC in more recent years.

Ed Brubaker

A crime writer at heart, Brubaker spent years in that genre as both a writer and artist before achieving great acclaim in the superhero world at DC. His work on *Batman*, *Catwoman*, and *The Authority* gained him fame in the 2000s, and he later contributed to *Captain America*, *Uncanny X-Men*, and *Daredevil* at Marvel.

Kurt Busiek

A deconstructionist writer in the Alan Moore mold, Busiek burst on the scene in the 1990s with the acclaimed *Marvels* miniseries illustrated by Alex Ross. He also collaborated with Ross on his independently owned *Astro City* title and enjoyed a four-year run as writer on *Avengers*. In 2004, he launched a *Conan* series for Dark Horse.

Peter David

Arguably the most revered of all *Incredible Hulk* writers, David took the Green Goliath through his most dynamic and dramatic changes in the 1990s, including the unforgettable "Joe Fixit" story arc, and exploring

Bruce Banner's tortured psyche. He has also done great work on *Supergirl*, as well as an Aquaman miniseries that brought new respect to that character.

Warren Ellis

A British writer who has never shied away from social and political commentary in his work, Ellis is the creator of the edgy Authority superteam and wrote Iron Man's "Extremis" 2005–2006 story line, which was adapted into the movie *Iron Man 3*. He's also worked extensively on Marvel's *Moon Knight*, *Thunderbolts*, and *Astonishing X-Men*.

Dave Gibbons

Best known as the illustrator of Alan Moore's *Watchmen*, Gibbons and his grounded style helped get across Moore's often esoteric and challenging themes. Gibbons also worked with Moore on the 1985 Superman story "For the Man Who Has Everything" and was a regular contributor to the UK comics magazine *2000 AD*.

Don Heck

Part of the dawn of the Marvel Era in the 1960s alongside the likes of Stan Lee, Steve Ditko, and Jack Kirby, Heck was a co-creator of such major characters as Iron Man, Black Widow, Hawkeye, and the Wasp, and served as the penciler on *Avengers* for much of its early run.

Geoff Johns

The cofounder of DC Films, Johns was a top executive at DC through the 2010s and played a major role in developing many DC movie properties. As a comics writer, he is responsible for the influential "Flashpoint" story line, as well as *Infinite Crisis, 52*, and Green Lantern's *Blackest Night*.

Gil Kane

Born Eli Katz in Latvia, Kane was a major innovator in the Silver and Bronze Ages, creating the modern Green Lantern and Atom for DC, as well as Adam Warlock and Iron Fist for Marvel. He was the artist on the groundbreaking series of 1971 *Amazing Spider-Man* issues which boldly depict drug abuse.

Jim Lee

An astonishingly gifted artist who first rose to fame at Marvel in the early 1990s thanks to his work on *X-Men, Alpha Flight*, and other titles, Lee started his own WildStorm imprint in 1992. He eventually sold it to DC and remained there, ascending to the role of publisher and chief creative officer.

Mark Millar

An incredibly important writer of recent years, Millar is responsible for Marvel's *The Ultimates*, as well as *Civil War* and the "Old Man Logan" story line. He is the co-creator of *Kick-Ass* and *The Authority*, and while at DC wrote the popular *Superman: Red Son*. For years he was a consultant to Fox on the studio's Marvel films.

George Perez

One of the most beloved of comics pencilers, Perez was known for his naturalistic, highly detailed style, which is on prominent display on *Avengers*, a series he first worked on in the 1970s, then later in the 1990s. His work on *Crisis on Infinite Earths* is distinguished, as well as *The New Teen Titans*, which he launched with Marv Wolfman.

Jerry Robinson

A young staff artist at National Comics (aka DC) in the 1940s, Robinson, a New Jersey native, worked regularly on *Detective Comics* and *Batman* and is best known as the cocreator of Batman's sidekick Robin and his arch-foe the Joker. Robinson was also an early champion of the rights of comic creators.

John Romita Jr.

A prolific second-generation artist, John followed in his father's footsteps at Marvel, with a career that began back in the late 1970s and continues to this day. Like his father, he distinguished himself on *Amazing Spider-Man*, but is also known for his work on *Invincible Iron Man*, *Uncanny X-Men*, and many other titles.

Jim Shooter

At fourteen years old, Jim Shooter began his career writing for DC Comics. He rose to great success and was editor in chief of Marvel Comics from 1978 to 1987. While in that role, Shooter oversaw many of the company's most legendary runs, including Walt Simonson on *Thor*, Claremont and Byrne on *Uncanny X-Men*, and Frank Miller on *Daredevil*. He was also the force behind the blockbuster *Secret Wars* miniseries.

Joe Simon

A major pioneer of the Golden Age, Simon was the first editor of Marvel Comics, back in the 1940s when it was known as Timely. With Jack Kirby he created Captain America and later invented the romance comics genre and helped popularize the horror comics genre. Leaving the industry in the 1950s, he went on to work in advertising.

Gail Simone

The longest-running writer of Wonder Woman comics, the Oregon-born Simone is also known at DC for her work on *Batgirl* and *Birds of Prey*. Known for her sense of humor, she has also contributed to Marvel's sardonic *Deadpool* comics. Outside of superheroes, she also enjoyed a lengthy run on *The Simpsons* comics.

Louise Simonson

Arguably the most accomplished and celebrated female comic book writer, Simonson is the co-creator of such characters as Cable, Apocalypse and Power Pack for Marvel, and Steel and Doomsday for DC. The wife of fellow comics writer Walt Simonson, she also did fine work on *Superman: Man of Steel*, *X-Factor*, and *New Mutants*.

Walt Simonson

A writer and artist with an unmistakably audacious penciling style, he is best known for his historic run on *The Mighty Thor* from 1983 to 1987, which included the creation of Beta Ray Bill. He's worked on *Fantastic Four* and *Detective Comics* and collaborated with his wife, Louise, on *X-Factor*. Todd McFarlane was among the artists greatly influenced by him.

Roy Thomas

Succeeding Stan Lee as editor in chief of Marvel Comics when Lee became publisher, Thomas co-created dozens of characters, including Wolverine, Vision, Luke Cage, and Ghost Rider. He wrote extensively for *Avengers*, as well as *All-Star Squadron* after jumping to DC in the 1980s. He is the author of the essential early history of comics, *All in Color for a Dime*.

Mark Waid

Best known as the writer of the Alex Ross illustrated DC graphic novel *Kingdom Come*, which deconstructed superheroes in the same way Alan Moore's *Watchmen* had, Waid also worked for DC on *The Flash* and the 2000s Superman reboot *Birthright*. He also wrote *Daredevil*, *Fantastic Four*, and *Captain America* for Marvel.

Len Wein

New York City native Wein took part in reinventing *The Uncanny X-Men* in the early 1970s, helping to create characters like Nightcrawler, Colossus, Storm, and Wolverine. At DC he was the co-creator of another wildly popular and unusual character, Swamp Thing. He also served as editor on the *Watchmen* comic miniseries.

Barry Windsor-Smith

A British illustrator best known for adapting Robert E. Howard's Conan the Barbarian to comics for the first time at Marvel in the early 1970s, Windsor-Smith also tackled Wolverine in the 1991 "Weapon X" story line. Much of his later work was for independent comics publishers like Image, Darkhorse, Malibu, and Valiant, where he also was creative director.

Marv Wolfman

Creator of characters like Cyborg, Deathstroke, and Bullseye, Wolfman worked prolifically for DC and Marvel. At DC he reinvented the Teen Titans in the early 1980s with George Perez. He worked again with Perez a few years later on *Crisis on Infinite Earths*. Today, he is best known as co-creator of Blade, from his days writing Marvel's *Tomb of Dracula*.

ICONS #14

Wakanda Forever

Creators: Stan Lee and Jack Kirby

First Appearance: *Fantastic Four* #52, July 1966

Alter Ego: T'Challa

Powers: superhuman strength, speed, agility, and stamina; genius intelligence; ability to draw on knowledge and experiences of past Black Panthers; vibranium suit; expert martial artist

Archenemies: Killmonger, Kraven the Hunter, M'Baku, Klaw, Namor the Sub-Mariner, Doctor Doom, Baron Zemo, White Wolf, Achebe, Tetu

Long a supporting character in the Marvel Universe dating back to the Silver Age and the heyday of Lee and Kirby, **BLACK PANTHER** has risen in popularity and cultural exposure quite dramatically over the past decade. This is in part due to a greater dedication to developing this important character on the part of Marvel creators, as well as the smash success of his portrayal in the Marvel Cinematic Universe by the late beloved actor Chadwick Boseman. A major member of the Avengers throughout much of that team's existence, not to mention the ruler of the technologically advanced

African kingdom of Wakanda, King T'Challa has been a groundbreaking figure in comic books and beyond.

THE ORIGIN

The inheritor of an ancient kingship that gives him ruling power over the secret nation of Wakanda, T'Challa is the son of T'Chaka. T'Challa ascends to the throne after the murder of his father, who was killed by the poacher Ulysses Klaw. Klaw was after Wakanda's supply of the powerful metal vibranium, which long ago led Wakanda's rulers to hide the nation's existence from the world. After going through the rite of passage that includes defeating elite fighters from several Wakandan tribes, as well as consuming the heart-shaped herb poisonous to all but the Wakandan royal line, T'Challa gains the abilities and insights of all Black Panthers before him, as well as the enhanced abilities needed to rule and protect his people.

THE CREATION

Realizing that not only did Marvel have no Black superheroes, but no comic book company had ever created any significant Black heroes, Lee and Kirby both felt it was well past time to correct that gross oversight. The debut of Black Panther in the pages of *Fantastic Four #52*, in which he first battles the superteam and then joins forces with them, predated the naming of the Black Panther political party by a few months. Lee stated that his inspiration for the name came instead from an old pulp adventure character who had a black panther, and some also speculate that the segregated Black Panther tank battalion of World War II may have been part inspiration as well.

THE FIRST BLACK SUPERHERO

Despite not getting his own self-titled comic book for over a decade after his creation, Black Panther was the first superpowered hero of African descent to ever be featured in an American comic book, predating other early examples like the Falcon, Power Man/Luke Cage, Blade, and the Jon Stewart Green Lantern. In the 1950s, Marvel (then known as Atlas) had introduced a nonpowered African hero named Waku, Prince of the Bantu. Marvel's *Sgt. Fury and His Howling Commandos* boasted Pvt. Gabriel Jones, a member of Fury's outfit. Dell Comics had the cowboy star Lobo—the first Black character to star in his own comic. But T'Challa was the first true Black superhero, complete with powers, to grace the pages of a comic book.

OTHERS ON THE THRONE

As a member of a long line of Black Panthers, T'Challa is only one of many who held the mantle bestowed by the mystical panther god, Bast. In a story from 2000, he was overthrown by archrival Erik Killmonger (N'Jadaka), whose time at the top is ended abruptly when he is poisoned by the heart-shaped herb. Shuri, half-sister to T'Challa, also ascended to the throne and became Queen of Wakanda for a time. New York City police officer Kasper Cole became a pretender to the Black Panther role for a time during the early 2000s, but later took on the title of White Tiger after T'Challa was restored to his rightful position.

STORYTELLING INNOVATIONS

After his FF debut, Panther appeared as a supporting character in several comic books, including *Tales of Suspense, Daredevil,* and *Astonishing Tales.*

After appearing for years with the Avengers, he got his own starring feature in *Jungle Action*, including the historic story line "Panther's Rage" in 1973 and 1974, seen by many as comics' first self-contained ongoing story, and a precursor to the graphic novel. He would later face the Ku Klux Klan in a controversial and bold story. There have been several *Black Panther* series, most of which have failed to survive more than a couple years, until the most recent relaunch in 2016 with acclaimed writer Ta-Nehisi Coates, which has been running ever since.

THE LEGACY OF CHADWICK BOSEMAN

The recent popularity of Black Panther has to do with how Oscar-nominated actor Chadwick Boseman brought him to life on screen, first in *Captain America: Civil War* (2016), followed by his own starring turn in *Black Panther* (2018), the first superhero film to be nominated for Best Picture. Boseman reprised the part in *Avengers: Infinity War* (2018) and *Avengers: Endgame* (2019), before his untimely passing in 2020 from colon cancer. The 2022 *Black Panther* sequel, *Wakanda Forever*, notably did not feature a recasting of T'Challa. Prior to the MCU, the character had starred in an animated series on BET in 2010, with Djimon Hounsou in the role of Black Panther.

APPRENTICE OF THE PANTHER GOD

Perhaps the most fascinating thing about Black Panther is the way the character has been thoroughly embraced in Black culture. He has provided a role model and inspiration for fans. Despite being a fictional creation, Black Panther is treated with the respect and love reserved for actual living icons of the Black community, which is a testament to the durability and malle-ability of a character originally created sixty years ago by two white sons of Jewish immigrants. It would not be a stretch to call Black Panther one of the most beloved Black characters in all of fiction, and thanks to his height-ened visibility, he has gone on to become one of the world's most popular superheroes, of any color.

15

THE WEIRD AND THE WONDERFUL

From Condorman to Powdered-Toast Man, and Everything in Between

Most of us know the big ones: Superman, Spider-Man, Batman, Iron Man, Wonder Woman, Captain America. Many of us dive deeper into the genre and have a long and abiding love for characters like Spawn, The Shadow, Plastic Man, Ghost Rider, Zorro, or Hellboy. Then there are the characters that are so far off the beaten path that most aren't aware of them, and for those that are, these superheroes remain odd curiosities, and sometimes sources of fascination. Superheroes are cultural archetypes, but not all soar to the heights of our favorite icons, and some are just so damn bizarre that they were clearly never meant to reach those heights. For every Captain Marvel, Silver Surfer, or Green Lantern, there's one wonderful oddball, proving that the umbrella of superhero fiction is wide and strong enough to cover a broad array of figures, including the obscure and/or utterly strange. Here are just a few.

THE AMBIGUOUSLY GAY DUO

The tightly clad Ace and Gary were created by comedian/writer Robert Smigel and director J. J. Sedelmayer. Intended as a takeoff on pairings such as Batman and Robin, which had long been poked fun at for their perceived homosexual undertones, the Duo (voiced by Steve Carell and Stephen Colbert) debuted in 1996 as an animated segment on *The Dana Carvey Show*. Later, it was moved to its permanent home on *Saturday Night Live* (SNL), where each week as part of the animated "Must-See TV Funhouse" sketch, the Duo's various foes and allies would attempt to figure out their sexual orientation and the nature of their relationship. Also of note from this SNL era was the mutant team of the X-Presidents, also animated by Smigel and Sedelmayer.

AMBUSH BUG

Perhaps the weirdest of all DC characters, Ambush Bug derived from the mind of artist Keith Giffen. He first appeared in 1982 in a debut story written by Paul Kupperberg in *DC Comics Presents* #52. His origins are disputed, as his delusional perception of reality makes it nearly impossible to know much about him. He appears to be an alien, complete with antennae and a green skin-tight suit grafted to his body. It's believed the suit gives him the ability to teleport anywhere in the multiverse. His stories are often quite meta, with the character sometimes breaking the fourth wall. He is a thorn in the side of the more "serious" superheroes, most notably Superman, whom he believes to be his best friend.

BIG BERTHA

Bertha Crawford is a svelte fashion model with the unorthodox mutant ability to swell her body to an extraordinary and unnaturally obese size, thus giving herself greatly increased strength and invulnerability (similar in some respects to the evil mutant known as the Blob). She can also enlarge specific parts of her body individually and can leap great distances like the Hulk. Created by writer/artist John Byrne and first appearing in 1989 in *West Coast Avengers* #46, Bertha is mentored by Hawkeye and Mockingbird. After initially using her powers to aid the West Coast Avengers team, she becomes a charter member of the new Avengers offshoot group known as the Great Lakes Avengers.

BLANKMAN

Considered by many as the star of one of the worst superhero movies ever made, Blankman was really Darryl Walker, played in the 1994 film of the same name by comedian Damon Wayans. A nerdy repairman who idolizes Adam West's classic 1960s Batman, in the wake of the murder of his grandmother, Walker becomes an inept but well-meaning vigilante, using his technical know-how to create an array of clumsy gadgets and weapons, including his robot assistant J-5. While Darryl's exasperated TV cameraman brother Kevin (David Alan Grier) initially tries to get him psychoanalyzed, he eventually joins Blankman's crusade as the sidekick Other Guy. Not surprisingly, the movie was a major critical and box office flop, ensuring there would be no further adventures of Blankman.

CAPTAIN CARROT AND THE AMAZING ZOO CREW

The last gasp in the storied tradition of "funny animals" in comics, the anthropomorphic rabbit Captain Carrot and his team of superpowered animals first appeared in 1982 in DC's *New Teen Titans* #16 and starred in their own short-lived series that followed. Hailing from the alternate Earth known as Earth-C, a world of humanoid animals (later Earth 26 in post-*Crisis* continuity), the team also included the likes of Pig-Iron, Alley-Kat-Abra, Fastback, Rubber Duck, Yankee Poodle, Little Cheese, and the American Eagle. The fanciful creations of writer Roy Thomas and artist Scott Shaw, they are fondly remembered by comic book readers of the era and have occasionally popped up in various DC comics as recently as 2015.

CAPTAIN CAVEMAN

Captain Caveman, a prehistoric superhero with a giant club that gave him the ability to fly, is one of the most recognizable characters of television animation giant Hanna-Barbera's classic Saturday morning lineups of the 1970s and 1980s. He also possessed superstrength and hid weapons and tools in the thick brown hair that camouflaged his body. Voiced by cartoon legend Mel Blanc, he originally appeared alongside the "Teen Angels" detective team in a series of short segments that aired on various Hanna-Barbera platforms starting in 1977. The Captain has appeared in many Hanna-Barbera shows since, uttering his trademark yell of "CAPTAIN CAAAAVEMAAAANNN!!!" In recent years, he's appeared in shows like *Jellystone!* and *Yabba-Dabba Dinosaurs* and is sometimes seen with The Flintstones.

CAPTAIN UNDERPANTS

From the pages of Dav Pilkey's acclaimed series of children's novels comes the underwear-and-tablecloth-clad hero dreamed up by elementary schoolkids George Beard and Harold Hutchins. Their comic book creation comes to life when the two boys succeed in hypnotizing their school principal, Mr. Krupp, who then believes that he is indeed Captain Underpants. Although originally powerless, Captain Underpants did gain superpowers in later installments of the series. With thirteen books and many other spinoffs, and more than eighty million copies sold, Captain Underpants is beloved by kids worldwide, has been adapted into an animated film in 2017, and even appeared as a giant balloon in New York City's Macy's Thanksgiving Day Parade.

CONDORMAN

In one of the most obscure efforts of Walt Disney Productions' "forgotten period" of the 1970s and 1980s, loosely based on Robert Sheckley's 1965 novel *The Game of X*, future *Phantom of the Opera* star Michael Crawford plays comic book artist Woody Wilkins, who creates his own flying suit to mimic that of his comics creation, Condorman. When he is recruited to assist a beautiful KGB agent defecting to the United States, Wilkins has the CIA construct him an array of advanced accessories, including an improved Condorman suit and Condorboat. A 1981 flop that disappeared into Disney oblivion, *Condorman* also starred Oliver Reed as the villainous KGB director Krokov and Barbara Carrera as sultry defector Natalia Rambova.

DETECTIVE CHIMP

One of the last characters created during the Golden Age of DC Comics, Detective Chimp was the wacky brainchild of Carmine Infantino and John Broome. He first appeared in *Adventures of Rex the Wonder Dog* #4 in 1952. A super-intelligent chimpanzee who solves crimes while dressed like Sherlock Holmes, he appeared as a regular backup feature in the *Rex the Wonder Dog* comic throughout the 1950s but wasn't seen much again until a brief cameo in 1985's *Crisis on Infinite Earths*. Modern DC creators enjoyed using the odd character now and then. In recent years he's become quite popular, first in 2005's *Day of Vengeance* limited series and as of 2018, as a central member of *Justice League Dark*.

FLAMING CARROT

A subversive superhero parody/satire created by the iconoclastic Bob Burden, the Flaming Carrot has appeared for comics companies as varied as Image, Dark Horse, Fantagraphics, Mirage Studios, and his original regular publisher, independent group Aardvark-Vanaheim. First appearing in 1979 in the comics magazine *Visions* #1, he later got his own title, which featured him as a nonsensical, working-class hero in a giant carrot mask and flippers, battling criminals with a fairly useless array of tools and weapons stored in his utility belt. Known for his trademark exclamation "Ut!," he is a hard-drinking, womanizing ne'er-do-well also known for associating with the Mystery Men, an eccentric team that got its own movie in 1999. Flaming Carrot was at the cutting edge of the so-called new wave indie comics movement of the late 1970s/early 1980s.

GROOT AND ROCKET RACCOON

Two very bizarre Marvel characters that were once considered obscure curiosities, Groot and Rocket Raccoon have gained great notoriety since becoming members of the relaunched *Guardians of the Galaxy* comic book in the 2000s, leading to their celebrated team up in the MCU films of the same name. However, their histories stretch back much further. The sentient alien tree Groot was a Stan Lee/Jack Kirby creation from Marvel's horror comics days, first appearing in *Tales to Astonish* #13 in 1960, while Rocket, an intelligent racoon and starship captain, took his first bow in 1976 in *Marvel Preview* #7, a creation of writer Bill Mantlo and artist Keith Giffen (creator of the equally odd Ambush Bug for DC).

MA HUNKEL

An anomaly of the Golden Age, Ma Hunkel was a matronly woman who adopts the vigilante persona of the Red Tornado, donning long johns, slippers, a cape, and a soup-pot helmet, fighting crime in her New York City neighborhood. The creation of Sheldon Mayer, she was intended as a superhero parody, in response to the emerging popularity of characters like Superman, Batman, and Green Lantern at the start of the 1940s. She first appeared in 1939 in the pages of *All-American Comics* #3 (All-American was later folded into DC Comics) but didn't adopt the Tornado persona until the following year. A Silver Age version of the Red Tornado introduced by DC in the 1960s was unrelated and was instead an android along the lines of Marvel's Vision.

MATTER-EATER LAD

A member of the thirtieth-century superteam known as the Legion of Super-heroes, Matter-Eater Lad was Tenzil Kem, a resident of the planet Bismoll with the ability to devour any form of matter, no matter how indigestible. A whimsical creation of Superman co-creator Jerry Siegel and artist John Forte, he first appeared in 1962 in *Adventure Comics* #303, and although he became a member of the team in good standing, he rarely appeared in action, as it became difficult to find ways to incorporate his rather strange "power" into any story. He's continued to appear now and then and was recently referenced by John Cena's Peacemaker on the hit HBO Max series of the same name.

MERMAID MAN AND BARNACLE BOY

Hailing from the underwater town of Bikini Bottom, Mermaid Man—a takeoff on Aquaman—and his trusty sidekick Barnacle Boy were elderly, retired superheroes who also happened to be the stars of the favorite TV show of SpongeBob SquarePants and his best pal Patrick. Idolized by SpongeBob and Patrick, they would periodically show up to relive their former glory days, hampered by advanced age and senility. Voiced by veteran actors Ernest Borgnine and Tim Conway—a callback to their appearances together on the 1960s sitcom *McHale's Navy*—they appeared on the early seasons of the animated Nickelodeon juggernaut *SpongeBob SquarePants* from 1999 until Borgnine's death in 2012 at age ninety-five.

MIGHTY MOUSE

"Here I come to save the day!" So went the classic theme song for Mighty Mouse, the Superman-style animated rodent that starred in scores of cartoon shorts for the Terrytoons cartoon studio from the 1940s through the 1960s. Mighty Mouse was the creation of studio head Paul Terry. Clad in yellow with a bright red cape, trunks, and boots, Mighty Mouse debuted in theatrical shorts but had an even greater life on television, where his colorful and melodramatic adventures, usually saving helpless animals from hungry predators, were featured in old and new cartoons even into the 1980s, when he was revived by the Filmation and Ralph Bakshi studios. A proposed feature film for the Mouse of Steel has been in the works since 2019.

POWDERED-TOAST MAN

From the twisted mind of animator John Kricfalusi came this superhero made of powdered toast in human form, a recurring character on Nickelodeon's *Ren and Stimpy Show* of the early 1990s. Whenever danger calls, Pastor Toastman, cool youth deacon, transforms into Powdered-Toast Man, launching himself from a giant toaster and usually succeeding in doing nothing but making things much worse. His unnecessary powers include the ability to scrape powdered toast from his toast-shaped head, as well as raisin breath, croutons fired from his armpits, and lots of talents related to extreme flatulence. He was bombastically voiced by Gary Owens, who also provided the voice for 1960s Hanna-Barbera cartoon superheroes such as Birdman and Space Ghost.

SPIDER-HAM

Created by Marvel editor Larry Hama, along with writer Tom DeFalco and artist Mark Armstrong, the spectacular Spider-Ham (secret identity: Peter Porker) first appeared in 1983 and got a regular series as part of Star

Comics, Marvel's juvenile comics line, where he quickly gained a dedicated cult following of fans of all ages. An anthropomorphic pig with all the powers of Spider-Man, he exists in a world populated by other anthropomorphic animals, including ones based on other popular Marvel characters. Voiced by comedian John Mulaney, Spider-Ham made his screen debut in 2018 in the Oscar-winning animated film *Spider-Man: Into the Spider-Verse*, in which various versions of Spider-Man from multiple alternate realities encountered one another.

THE TICK

Originally created by cartoonist Ben Edlund in 1986 as a mascot for New England Comics, a Massachusetts-based chain of comic book stores, the character got his own independent comic book just two years later and quickly became an underground favorite, with readers responding to its smart and ironic sendup of classic superheroes. With no memory of his life before becoming the Tick, the character is an escapee from a mental institution who sets himself up as a delusional vigilante along with his hapless, pudgy accountant sidekick known simply as Arthur. Possessing unexplained powers of superstrength and invulnerability, he is a good-natured and well-meaning hero who spends his days working for the *Weekly World Planet* newspaper.

TOO MUCH COFFEE MAN

Originally created as a fictional device through which to discuss political and social issues in a humorous way, cartoonist Shannon Wheeler introduced this caffeine- and nicotine-fueled paranoiac in 1991 as a one-page comic strip in the *Daily Texan* newspaper. The character was soon syndi-cated to other underground newspapers, and has since appeared in com-mercials, made several appearances in mainstream comics from Dark Horse and other companies, and even starred in his own opera. Wearing long underwear and a giant coffee mug atop his head, he possesses the ability to pummel opponents in a "manic paranoid frenzy" but usually spends much of his time locked in existential debates with other denizens of the coffee shop below his apartment.

UNDERDOG

One of the very first Saturday morning TV cartoon series, *Underdog* started out as a kids' show, along with a handful of other shows devised by a New York advertising agency, designed to sell General Mills cereal. The show became such a hit that it took on a life of its own, and advertising execs W. Watts Biggers and Chet Stover, along with artist Joe Harris, spun off their creation and built their own production company around it. Running through the mid-1960s, the show featured the adventures of Shoeshine Boy, a downtrodden canine who transforms into the superpowered Underdog and fights the threats of villains like Riff Raff and Bar Sinister, usually com-ing to the aid of his girlfriend, Sweet Polly Purebred.

ICONS #15

Heroes on a Half Shell

Creators: Kevin Eastman and Peter Laird

First Appearance: *Teenage Mutant Ninja Turtles* #1, March 1984

Names: Leonardo, Michelangelo, Donatello, Raphael

Powers: humanoid shape, human strength, size, and intelligence (roughly); masters of all forms of Eastern martial arts, experts with hand-to-hand weapons (Leonardo—katana swords, Michelangelo—nunchucks, Donatello—bo-staff, Raphael—sai daggers)

Archenemies: Shredder, the Foot, Be-Bop, Rocksteady, Krang, the Rat King, Baxter Stockman, the Triceratons, Karai, Leatherhead

There is no doubt that the comic book superhero landscape has been dominated by Marvel and DC for much of the history of the medium. But it can be reasonably argued that outside of those two major publishers, the one superhero property that has proven the most iconic, marketable, and long-lasting consists of four mutated adolescent amphibian humanoids with a penchant for pizza and ninjitsu fighting skills. The **TEENAGE MUTANT NINJA TURTLES** (TMNT) started as an underground cult comic in the mid-1980s, and by the end of the decade had become a mainstream juggernaut known to every kid in America and beyond. They are comics' greatest independent success story.

THE ORIGIN

As originally envisioned by Eastman and Laird, the amphibious foursome began life as a bunch of regular baby turtles. Discarded by their owner, they wind up in the sewer, where they are exposed to radioactive slime (in the original version it is slyly hinted that this is the same substance that also blinded Marvel's Matt Murdock and gave him his Daredevil powers). The irradiated turtles grow to human size and come under the tutelage of Splinter, a mutated rat who also happens to be a master of ninjitsu (in some versions he was always a rat, while in others he was originally human). Taking the names of Italian Renaissance artists, they each become masters of a different ninja weapon.

THE CREATION

Eastman and Laird came up with the unusual concept while living together. Seeking to parody successful comics of the time such as *Daredevil*, *Uncanny X-Men*, and *The New Teen Titans*, they added in the "funny animal" trope and came up with something that lampooned teenage heroes, mutants, and ninjas, all rolled into one subversive package. They pooled their resources and established their own small comic book company, Mirage Studios, cranking out the first issue of *Teenage Mutant Ninja Turtles* right from their home. Through clever advertising, they caught the attention of comics distributors who picked up on the uniqueness of the idea, and before long the issues were selling by the thousands.

FROM UNDERGROUND TO KID FAVORITE

Most Turtles fans didn't discover them during their earliest Mirage phase. By the late 1980s, Eastman and Laird licensed the characters to ToyMates, which made a line of action figures that led to a long-running kids' animated TV series. This series would explode TMNT into the mainstream while moving it in a more child-friendly direction. The violence, language, and other grownup elements were toned down. Color-coding was added to their masks to make it easier for kids to tell them apart, and their trademark affinity for pizza was added. Things were decidedly lighter, but it resulted in a bona fide pop culture phenomenon that had reached epic proportions by the start of the 1990s.

FRIENDS AND FOES

In addition to Master Splinter, the Turtles are aided by the beautiful April O'Neil, usually depicted as a news reporter, but sometimes a lab assistant or computer programmer. There's also the hockey-masked vigilante Casey Jones, sometimes April's romantic interest. On the flipside is the devious Shredder, leader of the organized crime outfit known as the Foot. In some versions, his true identity is that of the dreaded ninja Oroku Saki. Shredder has many allies and minions, but perhaps the best known arose not from the comics but from the classic animated series: the mutant rhino and warthog respectively called Be-Bop and Rocksteady.

TURTLES ON THE TUBE

The original animated series of 1987–1996 was a massive hit and even spawned a separate comics adaption from Archie Comics, but the Turtles would return to television in animated form other times as well. A new series, darker in tone and closer to the original comics, aired on Fox from 2003 to 2009. After Nickelodeon acquired the rights, a third series, this time done with CGI, ran from 2012 to 2017 and returned to the juvenile tone of the original TV series. Finally, a fourth series that aired from 2018 to 2020 on Nickelodeon was done in 2-D animated style, with design and humor similar to the fan favorite Cartoon Network *Teen Titans Go!* series.

BRINGING THE TURTLES TO LIFE

There's no greater benchmark for how successful and long running the TMNT franchise has been than to look at its extensive track record on the motion picture screen. Few superhero franchises can boast as many cinematic outings, beginning with the original 1990 blockbuster, which was quickly followed the following year by *Teenage Mutant Ninja Turtles II: The Secret of the Ooze*. Then the Turtles traveled back to medieval Japan for *Teenage Mutant Ninja Turtles III* in 1993. A generation later, they returned in an all-CGI feature film entitled simply *TMNT* (2007), which plugged into a lot of Turtles nostalgia. A reboot, combining live action and animation, was released in 2014 and followed with its own sequel, *Teenage Mutant Ninja Turtles: Out of the Shadows*, in 2016.

TURTLE POWER

From comic books, TV shows, and movies to toys, video games, amusement rides, concerts, food products, and even appearances at Disney's MGM Studios theme park in Orlando, Florida, the Teenage Mutant Ninja Turtles have become a cultural institution, running strong for nearly forty years. Multiple generations have grown up with the exploits of Leonardo, Michelangelo, Donatello, and Raphael, earning them a place alongside the most popular and beloved creations from Marvel and DC. What started as a quirky idea, developed in Kevin Eastman and Peter Laird's apartment, turned into a powerhouse franchise that also pushed the boundaries of what superhero fiction can be.

16

A GLOBAL PHENOMENON

Superheroes from Around the World

A true test of a pop culture phenomenon is its ability to go beyond its place of origin—to transcend boundaries of nation and culture and be adapted into a multitude of forms. By that measure, superheroes have passed the test with flying colors, spreading to all corners of the globe, resulting in a rich tapestry of superhero fiction and lore worldwide. The concept of the costumed comic book superhero may have originated in the United States in the late 1930s, but it only took a few years before it was embraced by cultures far and wide, often creating comic book heroes of their own, as well as similar characters in other forms of media.

It's important to remember that the underpinning concepts behind the rise of the superhero date back much further than the invention of comic books. Early mythologies and folklores that first introduced the notion of superpowered saviors go back to the earliest days of civilization, ensuring that the idea would be planted inside the minds of all people. As the centuries wore on, fictional figures from Robin Hood and the Scarlet Pimpernel to Superman and Batman would emerge. These creative forces that eventually gave rise to the American comic book superhero could also be said to have played a part in developing the concept worldwide.

The superhero is truly a global figure. When comic book heroes like Superman, Batman, Captain America, Spider-Man, and others were created, they only further accentuated and influenced what was already there, helping us understand why this genre has been so persistent in many different places, each putting their own unique stamp on it. An entire book could reasonably be devoted to the international scope and presence of superheroes, but what follows in this chapter is just a sampling of some of the most well-known and iconic forms they have taken worldwide.

LOS LUCHADORES

It's not hard to understand the connection between superheroes and professional wrestling, as the latter has been populated by over-the-top heroes and villains throughout much of its history, many of them in colorful costumes. In Mexico, this connection has long been stronger than anywhere else in the world, thanks to the Mexican brand of pro wrestling known as *lucha libre* and the masked *luchadores* that have appeared in Mexican wrestling rings going back to the 1930s. In a way, luchadores are real-life superheroes, blurring the boundaries between fiction and reality, battling in the ring in a pseudosport setting, while also portraying fictionalized characters, many of whom have made the transition from the ring into comic book, radio, and motion picture forms.

Chief among these would be the man in the silver mask, El Santo (born Rodolfo Guzman Huerta), who became a major cultural icon in Mexico and starred in a legendary series of more than fifty movies from the 1950s–1970s. Huracan Ramirez (Daniel Garcia Arteaga), another popular luchadore of the era, starred in the very first lucha libre movie, which was released in 1952. But it would be El Santo who would most come to define the often-bizarre genre in which luchadores would be portrayed not just as wrestlers but as intrepid crimefighters, traveling the world and hiding their identities with masks like superheroes, mixing it up with bad guys in stories that blended elements of science fiction, supernatural horror, international espionage, and pulp-style adventure. El Santo would often be accompanied in these films by his frequent partner Blue Demon (Alejandro Munoz Moreno), with the two forming a dynamic duo not unlike that of Batman and Robin. Later came Mil Mascaras (Aaron Rodriguez Arellano), a luchadore character whose fame from motion pictures helped turn him into the first masked Mexican grappler to successfully cross over into major stardom in American pro wrestling.

Other luchadores who parlayed their ring careers into film careers during the lucha libre movie boom included Neutron (Wolf Ruvinskis) and Tinieblas (Manuel Leal). There was also Italian actress Maura Monti who, although not a wrestler, donned a mask (and little else) to play La Mujer Mercielago (The Batwoman) in the 1968 Mexican film of the same name, inspired by the American *Batman* TV series running at the time. And just like in the United States, the Mexican masked superhero craze included a strong presence in the comic book medium, as well. In fact, El Santo appeared first in comic books for many successful years in Mexico before he made the jump to movies. In Mexico, El Santo comics were rivalled in the 1960s only by the Mandrake-like magician superhero Kaliman, who had originated in a popular radio serial drama some years earlier. And although the lucha libre movie craze died out by the mid-1970s, the phenomenon of masked luchadores continues in Mexican pro wrestling to this day, providing fans with "real-life" superheroes they can see live and whose in-ring exploits they can continue to cheer on.

THE SUPERHERO HEADS EAST

Fantastic cinema, and fantasy entertainment in general, has a long tradition in Asia, particularly in Japan. In fact, an entire subgenre known as *tokusatsu* emerged there in the 1950s, focusing on special-effects adventure, science fiction, and monster movies. Perhaps the most well-known films feature Toho's Godzilla and other giant *kaiju*, but developing right alongside them were science fiction-based adventure stories featuring costumed heroes, typically with strong cosmic elements. The first was *Ultraman*, a TV series produced by Toho special effects legend Eiji Tsuburaya, which told the story of a human who can transform into an alien superhero capable of growing to enormous size. Debuting in 1966, *Ultraman* spawned an ongoing franchise of TV series and movies that continues to this day.

The Ultraman phenomenon led to many other tokusatsu movies, shows, and manga comics depicting similar costumed superheroes battling alien forces. *Kamen Rider*, created by manga artist Shotari Ishinomori, chronicles the adventures of college student Takeshi Hongo as he dons his insectoid costume to clash with terroristic forces bent on world domination. Kicking off in 1971, it started a second wave of tokusatsu programming on Japanese TV. Several years later, the Toei studio introduced its *Super Sentai* franchise. Incorporating aspects of the *mecha* subgenre of giant fighting robots, it continued for many years in Japan before making it to American shores in the early 1990s, where it was tweaked to become *Mighty Morphin Power Rangers*, one of the most popular international science fiction franchises of all time.

Prior to the tokusatsu craze, in 1952 Japan produced what can arguably be called its first recognizable modern superhero, with the creation of Astro Boy by writer/illustrator Osamu Tezuka. The manga, featuring an android in the form of a young boy, was adapted into an animated series in the early 1960s, providing the first example of the style that would later come to be known as anime. Since then, Astro Boy has been adapted into many other forms, including a CGI-animated movie in 2009. Another successful manga-to-anime character would be the magical schoolgirl known as Sailor Moon, whose acclaimed 1990s TV series produced by Toei Animation achieved a worldwide cult following. And of course, the post-apocalyptic *Akira* (1988), a full-scale anime motion picture based on the manga of the same name, gave us psychokinetic mutants on an epic scale, in a film often hailed as the finest example of Japanese animation ever created.

SPAGHETTI SUPERHEROES

Of all European nations, it's possible that Italy has had the most colorful, multifaceted, and robust representation in the superhero genre. Or, to put it more accurately, anti-superheroes. Italian output can be much more morally ambiguous than what was found in the United States, with characters that straddle the fence between good and evil, as can also be seen in other Italian subgenres like the western and *giallo* thrillers. In particular, crime-fighters and supervillains came to an Italian audience through the medium of the *fumetti*—the exciting and often lurid Italian comic books that first appeared near the turn of the twentieth century but really hit their stride after World War II. Perhaps chief among these, and a classic example of the *fumetti neri* subgenre, was Diabolik, the violent masked thief with a host of weapons and gadgets at his disposal. Created by Angela and Luciana Giussani, and first appearing in 1962, Diabolik has continued in comics form for sixty years, and has even been adapted into movie form, most notably in the 1968 cult classic *Danger: Diabolik* from acclaimed director Mario Bava.

But Diabolik was only the most well-known and longest lasting of a whole cycle of Italian comics/movies featuring mysterious masked vigilantes/master criminals. Just two years after Diabolik's debut, Max Bunker and Roberto "Magnus" Raviola brought forth the even more ambiguous and frightening Kriminal, a British thief who dons a yellow bodysuit and skull mask. Kriminal ran in fumetti form for ten years and in the late 1960s inspired two motion pictures. Simultaneously, Bunker and Magnus produced *Satanik*, which tells the story of a scarred female chemist who develops a drug that transforms her temporarily into a beautiful seductress, but also turns her into a murderous criminal. Replete with supernatural overtones, the series was also turned into a movie in 1968.

Most directly inspired by Kriminal was Killing, perhaps the most brutal and vicious of them all. Wearing a skeletal suit and possessing the ability to transform his face into that of his victims, Killing is a remorseless torturer and murderer, although his targets are usually other evildoers. Originating in Italian "photo comics," which utilized actual live-action scenes photographed to tell the story, the series became popular worldwide, where the character would be known under several names such as Sadistik, Satanik, and Kiling, or Kilink, as he was known in Turkey, where a series of unauthorized film adaptations were made in the 1960s and 1970s.

COMMONWEALTH CRIMEFIGHTERS

With its direct historical link to the United States, it's no wonder that the heroic fiction of Britain and the greater British Empire would have such a strong influence on the development of superheroes in America. In addition to the medieval legend of Robin Hood, there was also Sir Walter Scott's 1819 novel *Ivanhoe*, credited with igniting the modern fascination with the British medieval period, with its depiction of the rogue knight Wilfred of Ivanhoe and his brave exploits. H. Rider Haggard's intrepid adventurer Allan Quatermain, first appearing in the 1885 novel *King Solomon's Mines* and in a string of stories that followed, had a strong impact on the later creation of similar pulp adventurers and keen-minded men of action. And when it came to adventuring, J. M. Barrie's beloved Peter Pan, first appearing in the 1902 novel *The Little White Bird*, provided a very different but equally influential escapist adventurer, complete with sidekicks, fantastical powers, and a colorful archnemesis in Captain Hook.

Originating in book form from author Ian Fleming, but achieving immortality on the big screen, was the ultimate secret agent himself, James Bond. And although 007 may be more of a garden variety spy than a superhero, the character also inspired a plethora of parodies and rip-offs, many of which, like the 1980s animated TV series *Danger Mouse*, incorporated more overtly superhero and comic book elements. But when it comes to superhuman heroes on British television, as unorthodox as he may be, none hold a candle to the extraterrestrial, interdimensional Time Lord known simply as "The Doctor," as featured on the long-running BBC series *Doctor Who*. Running in various forms since the 1960s to the present, The Doctor is constantly morphing into different physical forms, and has been played by many different actors, always retaining the same wry wit, unique insights, and unflappable ability to escape any situation with the help of the time-and-space-jumping Tardis.

Concurrent with what was happening in the United States, the United Kingdom has had its own comic book explosion, featuring signature superheroes closely associated with the British Isles. After the discontinuation of Fawcett Comics' Captain Marvel due to legal troubles with DC, British publisher L. Miller & Sons turned to writer/artist Mick Anglo to create the

Fawcett-inspired Marvelman in 1954. The book ran for nearly a decade and was later revived in the 1980s by visionary British creators Alan Moore and later Neil Gaiman—during which time the character was renamed Miracleman to avoid trouble from Marvel Comics. Meanwhile, Marvel itself, making inroads into the British market, introduced what was originally a character exclusive to that market—Captain Britain, the 1976 creation of Chris Claremont and Herb Trimpe.

The following year, popular weekly anthology comic *2000 AD* introduced the adult-oriented character Judge Dredd, an edgy law enforcement officer patrolling the streets of dystopian Mega-City One. About a decade later, comics magazine *Deadline* gave British readers Tank Girl, the difficult-to-categorize creation of Alan Martin and Jamie Hewlitt. Drawing heavily on punk culture, it tells the story of renegade drug abuser and libertine Rebecca Buck, who travels a futuristic Australian landscape in her tank alongside her love interest, the mutant kangaroo Booga. The unlikely property was even turned into a 1995 movie starring Lori Petty as Buck.

OTHER EUROPEAN CHARACTERS OF NOTE

Although Italy and the United Kingdom led the pack with homegrown superpowered adventurers, several other European nations produced their own interesting takes on the trope. The likeable investigative reporter known as Tintin first appeared in 1929 in the Belgian newspaper *Le Vingtieme Siecle*, the creation of cartoonist Herge. And although lacking powers, he is a master of machinery, a fearless fighter, and excellent at just about anything he puts his mind to. Belgium also gave rise to the parodic cowboy known as Lucky Luke, introduced by Maurice "Morris" De Bevere in comic book form in 1946. Combining the real American West with various fantastical elements, including the intelligent horse Jolly Jumper, Lucky Luke comics continue to be popular and have been adapted into various animated, toy, and video game forms.

In France, the sly and sophisticated costumed thief known as Fantomas was an early seminal character that would later inspire several of the Italian fumetti creations like Diabolik. A staple of French crime fiction, Fantomas first appeared in 1911 in the novel of the same name by Marcel Allain and Pierre Souvestre, which inspired a whole subgenre of debonair, upper-class jewel thieves (think "The Phantom" from *The Pink Panther*). In the swinging 1960s, Fantomas was reinvented on screen as a blue-masked Bond villain-type in a series of irreverent comedies. And in an even more outside-the-box take on the superpowered, the French comic *Asterix*, begun in 1976 by writer Rene Goscinny and artist Albert Uderzo, follows the exploits of an ancient fictional village of Gallic warriors fending off Roman invasion through the use of a magical potion that makes them invincible.

Dating back to eighteenth-century Germany, the fanciful Baron Munchausen was based on a real-life figure, but was turned into so much more by the eccentric writer and scientist Rudolf Erich Raspe in his 1785 book *Baron Munchausen's Narratives of His Marvellous Travels and Campaigns in Russia*. Characterized as a shameless liar and exaggerator, the baron recounts outlandish tales of superhuman exploits and deeds, like riding cannonballs and visiting the moon. Even though his adventures are portrayed as occurring largely in his own mind, they created a template for fantastical adventure and a larger-than-life personality that would be well-remembered by creators of later generations. And the powerful and calculating telepath and master of disguise known as Dr. Mabuse, who first appeared in the 1921 German novel by Norbert Jacques, provided an influential template for the supervillain. Several film adaptations, including silent movie *Dr. Mabuse, the Gambler* (1922) from director Fritz Lang, and Jess Franco's *The Vengeance of Dr. Mabuse* (1971) helped further popularize the character.

When it comes to superheroes on an international scale, this is just the tip of the iceberg. Canada's Cerberus, Sweden's Pippi Longstocking, India's bizarre take on Superman, and many others demonstrate how the concept that captivated American readers and viewers held the same power over people from nations far and wide. The idea of superpowered beings, heroic or villainous, has been a part of every culture that has ever imagined, and in the modern world of commercial entertainment, they have long provided a diversion sought out by many people worldwide.

ICONS #16

The Hellspawn

Creator: Todd McFarlane

First Appearance: *Spawn* #1, May 1992

Alter Ego: Al Simmons

Powers: Superhuman strength, speed, and stamina; physical regeneration; healing of others; ability to absorb and manipulate energy and hellfire; generating hallucinations; teleportation; time control; telepathy/empathy; invisibility/phasing through matter; manipulation of spiritual forces; shapeshifting; transmutation; telekinesis; precognition

Archenemies: Malebolgia, Violator/Clown, Jason Wynn, Cogliostro, the Freak, the Redeemer, Mammon, Katie Fitzgerald (Satan), Billy Kincaid, Simon Pure

The focal point of one of the most important seismic shifts in the history of comic books, Todd McFarlane's demonic creation **SPAWN** is a unique figure in the history of superheroes. Birthed in an era when comic book collecting was at its absolute zenith, the character represented something of a creative renaissance in the business, and his debut is a moment in time for comic collectors and readers of the era. Over time, his relevance and popularity may have slumped in comparison to those halcyon days of the 1990s, but nevertheless, *Spawn* the book is often cited as the most successful independent comic of all time, and Spawn the character is easily the most iconic independent superhero created in the 1990s.

THE ORIGIN

Al Simmons, highly placed CIA operative, tries to operate with a code of ethics despite a job that requires him to do terrible things. When his unscrupulous superior loses patience with Simmons's morals, he has him bumped off while on a mission. Burned to death, Simmons's soul is damned. The Devil (aka Malebolgia) offers a tantalizing deal: Return to Earth as an instrument of evil in exchange for seeing his wife one more time. Simmons accepts, but the deal isn't all it's cracked up to be. He returns to Earth as Spawn, minion of hell, five years later, with no memory of his former life. Struggling to use his hell-born powers for good, Simmons also works to figure out who he was.

THE CREATION

The idea of Spawn fascinated Todd McFarlane since childhood. At sixteen years old he was already creating sketches of the character. Following McFarlane's breakout success as Spider-Man writer/artist in the late 1980s, he broke away from Marvel in 1992, creating a sea change in the industry by founding Image Comics, an independent company where creators like himself as well as other recruits like Erik Larsen, Jim Valentino, Jim Lee,

Rob Liefeld, Marc Silvestri, and Whilce Portacio could have total ownership of the characters they developed. Leading that pack was McFarlane's own Spawn, with sales of the *Spawn* comic book topping the charts and becoming the talk of the industry from the first issue and for years thereafter.

A CHARACTER IN FLUX

For more than thirty years, the *Spawn* comic book has been published, with well over three hundred issues released and still counting. Along the way, with such a rich and ongoing narrative, the character and his world have undergone great changes. The terrifying Violator, once a mentor to the demonic Spawn, soon became an adversary when Simmons chose light over the darkness. Spawn's new mentor becomes Cogliostro, as he takes residence in Detroit's inner city and uses his powers to fight street crime. This becomes especially important as he discovers he must conserve his powers, as the more he uses them the closer he comes to returning to hell for good. Over the years, McFarlane and other writers have worked hard to try and keep the character fresh and interesting.

TWENTY-FIRST-CENTURY DECLINE

Despite these efforts, the popularity of Spawn, and his status as a cutting-edge character in comics, has certainly dipped significantly from where it was during the 1990s and 2000s. Once the top-selling comic book in the industry, in recent years it has often failed to crack the top 100. Many point to the launch of the 1997 *Spawn* movie as an early warning sign, as despite great hype, it failed to connect with a large audience and didn't warrant a film franchise. Nevertheless, every now and then, a special issue, like the recent #300, will garner impressive numbers, reminding everyone of the place Spawn still holds in the hearts of superhero fans of a certain age.

McFARLANE FIGURES

Superhero action figures have been popular almost as long as there have been superheroes, but the toy line spearheaded by Todd McFarlane, with Spawn and his supporting cast at the vanguard, is truly something special. It has long been applauded by collectors due to its meticulous level of artistic detail and general dedication to quality and accuracy. McFarlane Toys was formed in 1994, and from the company's start, Spawn figures played a major part in its lineup. The initial line of figures is among the most revered and sought-after superhero toys to this day. Over the years, the company has issued new lines to correspond with the evolution of the characters in the comic book itself.

SPAWN ON SCREEN

The 1997 *Spawn* movie featuring Michael Jai White as Al Simmons marked the first time a Black comic book superhero was given a standalone movie (although it's worth noting that the second instance, *Steel*, starring Shaquille O'Neal, was released just two weeks later). The film wasn't a major smash, but was a minor success, leading HBO to greenlight an animated series, which ran in 1998 and 1999, that featured Keith David as the voice of Spawn. In 2015, Todd McFarlane announced a *Spawn* movie reboot was in the works. The project has stalled several times, most notably during the COVID-19 pandemic. As of this writing, it's still believed to be in development, although a release date has not yet been announced.

FROM HELL HE CAME

Something of a poster boy for the excesses of the 1990s comic book market and superhero culture of that era in general, Spawn is an interesting case study. A major breakthrough as far as independently created comic book characters, Spawn also demonstrated in the long run just how much of a chokehold the Marvel and DC marketing machines have on the public's imagination when it comes to superheroes. The character never quite broke through to the same degree as that other major independent creation, Teenage Mutant Ninja Turtles, but there's no denying that Spawn was one of the most important characters of his era and showed the way for many other would-be independent creators.

17

EXCELSIOR!

The Superhero's Place in a Changing World

More than radioactive spiders, red suns, childhood tragedies, or cosmic rays, superheroes owe their origins and their strengths to humanity's seemingly unquenchable need to believe in something greater than itself. Now, more than ever, superheroes are an integral part of our society—inspiring us, entertaining us, providing both escape and relief. They help us make sense of a world that doesn't always make sense. And certainly, what they represent speaks to something within us that's as old as our species. That's just as true now as it was in the time of the ancient Greeks, and in the heady Golden Age era when Superman, Batman, Wonder Woman, Captain America, and others first burst forth from those cheap, four-colored pages.

But never before have they been so ubiquitous, so intrinsic to our culture. The superhero, that specific pop culture invention of Depression-era America, has gone from the frivolous passion pursued by preteen boys, from a fringe entertainment form often scoffed at by mainstream culture, to an overarching modern mythology that is widely known, even to those who have never picked up a comic book in their lives. Thanks especially to the power of television and the movies, the past generation in particular has seen superheroes take over. And more than ever, their deeper meaning and value is clear, as is the important role that they play.

And yet, the world is a very different place today than it was in 1938. How has the superhero managed to stay relevant—that is, beyond the efforts of the relentless Hollywood marketing machine? What do these characters still have to tell us about ourselves, and why are we still listening? The easy answer is that the themes they have addressed from the very beginning are still relevant, perhaps now more than ever. Let's never forget that Superman's first enemies were not aliens, mad scientists, and robots, but rather slumlords, corrupt government, abusive husbands, and other highly relatable adversaries. Superheroes resonate with us because at their very foundation, they plug into our deepest, real-world concerns. "These themes are not new to the superhero genre, but they have become far more prominent in recent years," remarked noted social critic and social justice advocate Alan Jenkins in a 2019 article for *The Hollywood Reporter*. "As creators—including directors like Ryan Coogler [*Black Panther*] and Patty Jenkins [*Wonder Woman*], and writers like Eve Ewing [*Iron Heart*] and G. Willow Wilson [*Ms. Marvel*]— have become more diverse, story lines about racial profiling, sexual harassment, queer equality and the humanity of immigrants have become more common in comic book, film and TV superhero tales."

Indeed, those surprised by the social justice bent of much of modern superhero fiction would be less surprised the more familiar they became with the origins of the genre in the minds of poor, working-class, immigrant creators, crafting stories that spoke to their own experiences, and were very often directed at readers who resembled them in many ways. This is not a new development in the genre, although as Jenkins and others have noted, the voices have grown more diverse over time. As Jenkins goes on to write, superheroes are "the dominant cinematic and cultural force of the moment," and as such, "have a critical role to play in elevating our shared values of human rights, universal dignity and opportunity for all, even as they entertain millions and rake in billions around the world."

We seem to be living in a time that makes us more predisposed to welcome superheroes into our imaginations. But beyond specific social concerns, superheroes continue to tap into something universal, something not very different from what has long caused human beings to seek a higher power and the greater forces outside ourselves. They give us something to believe in not only about the world, but also about ourselves. "This is the mythos of modern superheroes: they are fundamentally good, powerful, and immortal," write University of Alberta psychology professors Andy Scott and Jeff Schimel in a March 2021 paper on the subject. "Is this also the allure of superheroes? Do they allow us to fantasize that perhaps we too can be good, powerful, and immortal? Or, at minimum, that there are all-powerful beings watching over us and protecting us; that our world is at its core orderly rather than chaotic, good rather than bad."

If all that sounds familiar, it should. Many have pointed out how much the superhero phenomenon and the attitudes that support it bear striking similarity to some of the underpinning ideologies of the world's great religions. Cultural anthropologist and existential psychologist Ernest Becker, in his landmark 1971 book *The Birth and Death of Meaning*, expressed the notion that one of the primary forces that drive religious belief is the comfort derived from its establishment of a supernatural order to life and the universe. Religion structures existence into the duality of good and evil and provides instruction to believers on how to achieve the good. It should come as no surprise then, that in a time in which traditional religious belief is being abandoned to a degree never before seen in human history, that we should flock to concepts like superheroes with such fervency.

The fact is, although we may believe ourselves evolved and moving beyond archaic dogmas, we are in many ways still the same at heart as we always were. We need something to believe in. We need something outside ourselves. At some root level, the human intellect has difficulty operating in a world without meaning, without higher cause. And so, we look for it wherever we can, even if we have to invent it. And to be sure, the fact that superheroes are fictional creations does not negate the power and attraction they hold over the human psyche. Because whether actual or simply based on symbols and principles, what the superhero represents is extremely real, and belief in those principles is not only important, but many would argue is necessary to the preservation of a healthy and functioning society. So, wherever they are coming from, the ideals are essential. And if they come from men and women in capes and shiny boots, then so be it.

We see it in the way that so many people have taken these characters to heart. And perhaps nowhere today is this dedication so visibly apparent than in the phenomenon known as cosplay, which has exploded alongside superhero culture over the past several decades. The term "cosplay" originated in 1984 from the Japanese portmanteau *kosupure*, combining the words "costume" and "play," and refers to the practice of dressing up like specific fictional characters, which naturally lends itself to superheroes and comic book characters in general. In the modern sense, the beginning of the practice is often cited as the 1939 World Science Fiction Convention in New York City, where legendary sci-fi and fantasy superfans Forrest J. Ackerman and Myrtle "Morojo" Douglas dressed in futuristic costumes ("futuristicostumes") based partly on the film *Things to Come* (1936) and partly on the science fiction pulp novel art of Frank R. Paul.

Cosplay as we know it today took off in Japan in the 1980s and exploded in popularity beyond Japanese borders, particularly in the United States, in the 1990s. Science fiction and other kinds of pop culture conventions, but especially comic book conventions, have seen the practice skyrocket in popularity. From its beginnings in the Western world especially, superheroes have been among the chief characters that cosplayers enjoy dressing up as. While other pop culture properties like *Star Wars*, as well as role-playing and video game characters, are commonly found, comic book characters have become especially ubiquitous at conventions. Perhaps this owes to the "meta" aspect of superhero cosplay, as it lets people dress up as fictional characters who already are dressing up in costumes to hide their identity even in the source material.

More than just a fun diversion, cosplaying has evolved almost into a lifestyle, or at the very least a kind of underground community. It allows fans to step into the shoes of their favorite characters, and it's one of the most potent examples of how superheroes have infiltrated the public consciousness in deeper ways than ever before. And it goes without saying that superheroes have proven to be among the most fertile ground for merchandising and other adaptations. Superhero action figures have been with us for as long as there have been superheroes, with the first wooden Superman doll being sold in 1939, mere months after the publication of *Action Comics* #1. Unsurprisingly, the Man of Steel was also the first superhero to get his own video game, manufactured in 1979 for the Atari 2600 game console in the wake of the blockbuster film the previous year. Since then, video games and superheroes have gone hand-in-hand, as the genre grew in popularity right alongside video games themselves.

In addition to action figures and video games, other toys, accessories, games, and tie-ins are virtually limitless in scope, and would require an entire book just to chronicle. All together, they help tell the larger story of how these characters have touched us, how they have become a part of us, perhaps because they were always a part of us to begin with. In a way, they came from us, both in the sense that they were created from the minds of mere mortals, but also because they reflect qualities that represent us—or, at least us at our very best. They give us something to strive for. And that aspect of our character—the need to be more than what we are—is something that really never changes.

In the end, that's what has made superheroes endure. It also demonstrates that maybe our world hasn't changed as much as we think it has. However, through whatever change there has been, we've always needed heroes. They may change in form, appearance, attitude, in almost every way possible, but whether it's Hercules slaying the Nemean Lion, Robin Hood stealing from the rich to give to the poor, The Shadow seeing the evil that lurks in the hearts of men, Superman upholding truth and justice, Spider-Man wielding great power with great responsibility, the Ninja Turtles cracking skulls and eating pizza, Deadpool dispensing violence with a wry joke, or any of the myriad other characters we've grown to love so dearly, they are always there, watching over us, inspiring us, entertaining us.

In the original, and perhaps greatest classic superhero film of them all, *Superman: The Movie* (1978), Jor-El says as he readies his mighty son for his life's mission: "They can be a great people, Kal-El; they wish to be. They only lack the light to show the way. For this reason above all, their capacity for good, I have sent them you . . . my only son." This line perfectly sums up the superhero's very reason for being. The Christ-like allusion is clear, and it makes quite obvious the parallels between Superman (and by extension, the superhero in general) and the most potent and iconic savior figures of our culture. Now, just as then, superheroes provide the light to show us the way. And for as long we seek out that light, we will continue to look to them.

Index